Approaches to
Teaching Shakespeare's
Romeo and Juliet

Aproaches to Teaching World Literature

Joseph Gibaldi, series editor

For a complete listing of titles,
see the last pages of this book.

Approaches to Teaching Shakespeare's *Romeo and Juliet*

Edited by

Maurice Hunt

The Modern Language Association of America
New York   2000

For information about obtaining permission to reprint material from
MLA book publications, send your request by mail (see address below) or by
e-mail (permissions@mla.org).

Library of Congress Cataloging-in-Publication Data

Approaches to teaching Shakespeare's Romeo and Juliet / edited by Maurice Hunt.
p. cm. — (Approaches to teaching world literature, ISSN 1059-1133 ; 67)
Includes bibliographical references and index.
ISBN 0-87352-757-7 (cloth) — ISBN 0-87352-758-5 (pbk.)
1. Shakespeare, William, 1564–1616. Romeo and Juliet. 2. Shakespeare, William,
1564–1616—Study and teaching. I. Hunt, Maurice, 1942– II. Series.

PR2831 .A89 2000
822'.3'3—dc21   00-056056

Cover illustration for the paperback edition: Still from the 1968 production
of Romeo and Juliet, directed by Franco Zeffirelli and starring
Leonard Whiting and Olivia Hussey.
Photograph: Photofest

Set in Bodoni and New Caledonia. Printed on recycled paper

Published by The Modern Language Association of America
10 Astor Place, New York, New York 10003-6981
www.mla.org

CONTENTS

PREFACE TO THE SERIES

In *The Art of Teaching* Gilbert Highet wrote, "Bad teaching wastes a great deal of effort, and spoils many lives which might have been full of energy and happiness." All too many teachers have failed in their work, Highet argued, simply "because they have not thought about it." We hope that the Approaches to Teaching World Literature series, sponsored by the Modern Language Association's Publications Committee, will not only improve the craft—as well as the art—of teaching but also encourage serious and continuing discussion of the aims and methods of teaching literature.

The principal objective of the series is to collect within each volume different points of view on teaching a specific literary work, a literary tradition, or a writer widely taught at the undergraduate level. The preparation of each volume begins with a wide-ranging survey of instructors, thus enabling us to include in the volume the philosophies and approaches, thoughts and methods of scores of experienced teachers. The result is a sourcebook of material, information, and ideas on teaching the subject of the volume to undergraduates.

The series is intended to serve nonspecialists as well as specialists, inexperienced as well as experienced teachers, graduate students who wish to learn effective ways of teaching as well as senior professors who wish to compare their own approaches with the approaches of colleagues in other schools. Of course, no volume in the series can ever substitute for erudition, intelligence, creativity, and sensitivity in teaching. We hope merely that each book will point readers in useful directions; at most each will offer only a first step in the long journey to successful teaching.

Joseph Gibaldi
Series Editor

PREFACE TO THE VOLUME

This volume would not have been possible without the help of the teachers of *Romeo and Juliet* whose names and academic affiliations appear in the list of survey participants at the end of the book. Part 1, "Materials," depends heavily on information gleaned from survey participants' completed questionnaires. The twenty teachers whose essays make up part 2 were chosen from this group of instructors and invited to describe a distinctive approach to teaching Shakespeare's *Romeo and Juliet*. The nature and distribution of the approaches reflect the interests and opinions of the larger pool of respondents.

My duties as chair of the English department at Baylor University necessitated several major interruptions in the preparation of this book. I want to thank both the contributors and my Baylor colleagues for their patience. I owe special thanks to my research assistant, Sean McLain, for his fine work on this project as well as to Janet Sheets and Phil Jones, Baylor reference librarians, for data that made possible the completion of the section on audiovisual materials. Finally, I am grateful for the support offered by my wife, Pamela, and by Alison, Jeffrey, Andrew, and Thomas. The high schoolers in my family showed an interest in *Romeo and Juliet*, even though it was not "cool" for them to do so.

Part One

MATERIALS

Editions

Complete Editions of Shakespeare

Of those instructors preferring to teach *Romeo and Juliet* out of a complete Shakespeare, most are equally divided between David Bevington's *Complete Works of Shakespeare* (4th ed.) and G. Blakemore Evans's *Riverside Shakespeare* (2nd ed.). Only one respondent said that she planned to move to Stephen Greenblatt's *Norton Shakespeare* (instructors completed the survey shortly after *The Norton Shakespeare* appeared), though three contributors now use this edition. For one respondent, *The Riverside Shakespeare* "includes a good general introduction to the history and practice of editing Shakespeare's plays as well as some excerpts from the quarto 1, quarto 2, and folio text [of *Romeo and Juliet*] not included in the modern text." Other instructors remark that in this volume the "layout of the text is satisfactory, and the comments on editing evoke a surprising amount of interest from students. [. . .] Frank Kermode's introduction [to *Romeo and Juliet*] remains interesting despite the passage of time." Both the old and the new Riverside texts are keyed to Marvin Spevack's *Harvard Concordance to Shakespeare*. New features of the second edition of *The Riverside Shakespeare* include updated bibliographies, an interpretive essay by Heather Dubrow titled "Twentieth-Century Shakespeare Criticism," and an account by William Liston of Shakespeare's plays in performance since 1970. Criticisms of *The Riverside Shakespeare* focus on its bulkiness (difficult to manage for students on their feet in a classroom performance situation); the thinness of its paper (better, though, than that of the first edition or the onionskin of the new *Norton Shakespeare*); its editorial inconsistency in modernizing the spelling of some words while leaving others archaic; and its intrusive use of brackets in the text around variant readings.

Colleagues using the Bevington *Complete Works* generally find it "more student friendly than the Riverside edition"; it is "far more readable and eas[ier] for [. . .] undergraduates to understand than the alternatives." "Textual glosses in boldface amount to an attractive feature," notes one respondent. Bevington glosses much more of Shakespeare's bawdry than does G. Blakemore Evans (who has been accused of sanitizing Shakespeare's texts in this respect). And yet some respondents label Bevington's editing "conservative" and his introductions to plays "old-fashioned." A larger number, however, find the essays in the general introductions "superior" and the "notes and introductions to this anthology excellent." Predicting how widely the new *Norton Shakespeare* will be adopted is impossible at this early date. Its text is the controversial Oxford text, edited by Stanley Wells and Gary Taylor, very slightly amended. The volume does contain an essay on the Shakespearean stage written by Andrew Gurr. Finally, several instructors regret that complete Shakespeares necessarily cannot include partial or whole reprints of sources of plays and "historical documents that would give these editions some highly desirable casebook qualities."

Single Editions

Instructors who teach *Romeo and Juliet* to undergraduates out of a single volume recommend in equal numbers the Signet Classic edition, edited by J. A. Bryant, Jr., and Barbara Mowat and Paul Werstine's New Folger Library Shakespeare edition. Teachers praise the selection of critical essays on *Romeo and Juliet* in the Bryant volume. These include excerpts from Samuel Johnson's *The Plays of William Shakespeare* (1765); Samuel Taylor Coleridge's *The Lectures of 1811–1812*; H. B. Charlton's *Shakespearian Tragedy* (1948); Michael Goldman's *Shakespeare and the Energies of Drama* (1972), titled "Romeo and Juliet: The Meaning of a Theatrical Experience"; Susan Snyder's *The Comic Matrix of Shakespeare's Tragedies* (1979), titled "Beyond Comedy: Romeo and Juliet"; and Marianne Novy's *Love's Argument: Gender Relations in Shakespeare* (1984), titled "Violence, Love, and Gender in *Romeo and Juliet*." Also included is Sylvan Barnet's original essay "*Romeo and Juliet* on Stage and Screen" (1986). Instructors especially like "the Snyder and Barnet pieces [because they are] useful on genre and film issues respectively." Nevertheless, respondents adopting this paperback edition repeatedly say the appended critical essays need updating. "The attention given to early critics is disproportionate to its worth," one instructor complains. Another argues that "some of the older articles could be eliminated in favor of more recent works." Regarding the New Folger Shakespeare *Romeo and Juliet,* instructors appreciate "the much-needed plot summary at the beginning of each scene," the "Modern Perspective" essay at the back of the book, the editors' excellent notes, and the fact that "annotations are [on the] facing page." Several instructors note that "the scene-by-scene plot summaries are helpful for students who have had little or no exposure to Shakespeare" and for those whose reading abilities are not as developed as they might be. Others comment that New Folger Shakespeares are "well priced" and "generous in contextualizing materials."

The single edition of the tragedy most useful for graduate students remains the Arden Shakespeare, second series, text of the play edited by Brian Gibbons. The volume's "extensive notes and the source text at the end are especially valuable for graduate students." (The transcript of Brooke's *Romeus and Juliet* is, however, incomplete). Graduate English faculty members like this edition "for its portability, ease of reading, thorough notes, and good introduction" (although one respondent wishes that the second Arden *Romeo* had "fewer notes on text-editing cruxes and more on points of interpretation," while another criticizes Gibbons's judgments in the introduction as "extremely conservative"). The Arden Shakespeare, third series, text of the play edited by Lynette Hunter and Peter Lichtenfels, is scheduled to appear in 2000; it will include some discussion of the tragedy's performance history.

Less used (but still popular) single editions of *Romeo and Juliet* include David Bevington's Bantam edition, G. Blakemore Evans's New Cambridge text of the play, and John Andrews's Everyman *Romeo*. Although the Bantam edition has "good sections on performance history, date and text [. . .] and further reading," one instructor would like to see more extensive reprinting of Brooke's poem in the book. Other instructors like the New Cambridge edition's "extensive theatrical history" as well as its "emphasis on film history." Evans's edition appends a much more complete text of Brooke's *Romeus* and excellent supplementary notes and analyses of the play's textual situation. Those teachers recommending Andrews's edition find its "original orthography and punctuation very useful" (although one respondent warns that "the Quaint Capitals [in the text], though useful for guiding spoken emphasis, are somewhat suspect"). Nevertheless, the right-page-only format of this compact edition (with useful notes on the facing left page) helps students keep their place when doing in-class acting. Andrews's introduction is praised for its clear description of the play's textual problems. Useful for undergraduates are the Everyman edition's plot summary and its excerpts of criticism on the play arranged as a narrative and titled "Perspectives on *Romeo and Juliet*."

Even less used is John E. Hankins's Pelican text of *Romeo and Juliet*. The few instructors employing it record no virtues or flaws. At least two respondents would like to read and teach the play in the new Bedford Shakespeare series, praised for contextualizing drama by means of contemporary documents. Dympna Callaghan is editing *Romeo and Juliet* for this series, scheduled for publication in 2001. One respondent looks forward to using Gary Taylor's new CD-ROM edition of the play. An instructor concludes, "Perhaps an electronic edition of the play, with all of the textual variants in hypertext form, will help make discussing the question of texts easier."

The Instructor's Library

Reference Works

Samuel Schoenbaum's three volumes on Shakespeare's life distinguish facts from speculations. An earlier collection of material is found in E. K. Chambers, *William Shakespeare: A Study of Facts and Problems*. Chambers's *Elizabethan Stage* (4 vols.) remains a basic resource for subjects such as the revels office, the control of the stage, the acting companies, and staging at court. Marvin Spevack's *Harvard Concordance to Shakespeare* is the definitive reference work of this kind. Other standard reference works include Alexander Schmidt's *Shakespeare-Lexicon* and C. T. Onions's *Shakespeare Glossary*; Morris P. Tilley's *Dictionary of the Proverbs in England in the Sixteenth and Seventeenth Centuries* and R. W. Dent's *Shakespeare's Proverbial Language: An Index*; and *The Geneva Bible: A Facsimile of the 1560 Edition*. Shakespeare's bawdry is clarified by Eric Partridge's *Shakespeare's Bawdy*, E. A. M. Colman's *The Dramatic Use of Bawdy in Shakespeare*, and Frankie Rubenstein's *A Dictionary of Shakespeare's Sexual Puns and Their Significance*.

The standard annotated bibliography of books, articles, and reviews on Shakespeare's plays is issued by the Shakespeare Association of America as an annual number of *Shakespeare Quarterly*, edited by James Harner. For material on *Romeo and Juliet* published before 1958, after which the annual listings in *Shakespeare Quarterly* and the *MLA International Bibliography* suffice, see *A Shakespeare Bibliography* (1931) and the *Supplement for the Years 1930–1935*, both by Walther Ebisch with the assistance of Levin L. Schücking, and Gordon Ross Smith's *Classified Shakespeare Bibliography, 1936–1958*. Especially useful in the classroom are David M. Bergeron and Geraldo de Sousa's *Shakespeare: A Study and Research Guide*, a bibliographical tool that contains a section on writing a research paper on a Shakespearean subject, and Stanley Wells's *Shakespeare: A Bibliographical Guide*. In a chapter in the Wells volume, R. S. White keys the references in his survey of critical commentary on *Romeo and Juliet* to items in a select bibliography.

Critical and Pedagogical Studies

Many of the studies listed in this section could just as easily appear in the section titled "Required and Recommended Student Readings." (In fact, a number of respondents would place them there.) Conversely, certain readings listed there could appear here. My placement of works in each section reflects majority use and opinion.

Strategies for reading *Romeo and Juliet* as a tragedy generally encourage students to decide to what degree, if any, the lovers become the victims of the humanist warning that romantic passion easily overcomes reason and that unregulated emotion is deadly. Are students to judge the lovers morally for making so-called narcissistic or adolescent decisions and for failing to check their emotions (Friar Lawrence's perspective)? A number of critics locate the experience of tragedy in this moral dimension of the drama. Representative studies include Roy Battenhouse's *Shakespearean Tragedy: Its Art and Its Christian Premises,* Douglas Peterson's "*Romeo and Juliet* and the Art of Moral Navigation," Franklin Dickey's *Not Wisely but Too Well: Shakespeare's Love Tragedies,* and Clifford Leech's "The Moral Tragedy of *Romeo and Juliet.*" Also see John W. Draper's "Shakespeare's 'Star-Crossed Lovers'" and Stanley Stewart's "Romeo and Necessity." John Andrews in "Falling in Love: The Tragedy of *Romeo and Juliet*" and Ruth Nevo in "Tragic Form in *Romeo and Juliet*" debate whether the play is Aristotelian in its providential or fateful restoration of relative order.

With assistance, students read the tragedy of *Romeo and Juliet* as a *Liebestod,* a possibility established by Norman Rabkin in *Shakespeare and the Common Understanding.* Almost all critical analyses of the simultaneously positive and negative love-in-death phenomenon depend on the cultural explications of Denis de Rougemont (*Love in the Western World* and *Passion and Society*). Instructors wishing to clarify the mythic status of the play as tragic *Liebestod,* particularly with reference to other deathly love–lovely death stories such as the tales of Tristan and Isolde, Héloïse and Abelard, and Hero and Leander should read Julia Kristeva's "Romeo and Juliet: Love-Hatred in the Couple" in her *Tales of Love* and Roger Stilling's *Love and Death in Renaissance Tragedy.* Another especially useful study is Maya Bijvoet's *Liebestod: The Function and Meaning of the Double Love-Death,* which connects *Romeo and Juliet* not only with the aforementioned *Liebestods* but with Richard Wagner's transformations of the theme as well. Nevertheless, a qualification is necessary here. M. M. Mahood has shown that some wordplay in *Romeo and Juliet* realizes the play's *Liebestod*—but ironically so, with irony charting Shakespeare's deviations from the theme's mythic conventions. Shakespeare's *Liebestod,* Mahood argues, is not pure. For example, adultery does not figure in Romeo and Juliet's love and marriage; the lovers make no suicide pact; their deaths do not give us the satisfaction of a wish fulfillment; and their love (for Mahood at least) transcends (and thus eludes) death rather than finds consummation in it.

Among literary critics who have been responsive to Shakespeare's bold, perhaps experimental, blend of comic and tragic elements in *Romeo and Juliet* are Susan Snyder in *The Comic Matrix of Shakespeare's Tragedies,* Martha Tuck Rozett in "The Comic Structures of Tragic Endings: The Suicide Scenes in *Romeo and Juliet* and *Antony and Cleopatra,*" and Charles Lower in "*Romeo and Juliet,* IV.v: A Stage Direction and Purposeful Comedy." Their approaches are grounded in Marvin Herrick's *Tragicomedy: Its Origin and Development in Italy, France, and England.* Instructors wishing to teach the play psychoanalytically might draw on Katherine Dalsimer's essay "Middle Adolescence: *Romeo and Juliet,*" Otto Kernberg's "Adolescent Sexuality in the Light of Group

Processes," Hyman Muslin's "Romeo and Juliet: The Tragic Self in Adolescence," and M. D. Faber's "The Adolescent Suicides of *Romeo and Juliet.*"
Relevant to teaching the play according to the theories of Melanie Klein and
her disciples is Michael Rustin's essay "Thinking in *Romeo and Juliet.*" Various
models of psychoanalysis have become part of the critical methodologies of
feminism, gender studies, the new historicism, and cultural materialism.
Instructors teaching students how to read *Romeo and Juliet* in the light of one
or more of these methodologies might draw on Edward Snow's "Language and
Sexual Difference in *Romeo and Juliet*" (for the depiction of gender and female
ontology in the play), Jonathan Goldberg's "Romeo and Juliet's *Open Rs*" (for a
representation of polymorphous sexuality in the play), Gail Kern Paster's chapter "Quarreling with the Dug; or, I Am Glad You Did Not Nurse Him" in *The
Body Embarrassed: Drama and the Disciplines of Shame in Early Modern
England* (for an account of female sexuality and childbearing in the play in relation to a patriarchal coding of them), and Catherine Belsey's article "The Name
of the Rose in *Romeo and Juliet*" (for a portrayal of the process by which sexual
desire in the play deconstructs the Cartesian opposition between mind and
body). Belsey is particularly interested in the notion that culture in the play "enables love to make sense [of itself]" (127).

Students need assistance in understanding the conventions of early modern
patriarchy that privilege men in the play (especially Old Capulet and Paris) and
oppress or restrict women (most notably Juliet). Kirby Farrell in a chapter titled
"Love, Death, and Patriarchy in *Romeo and Juliet*" argues that early modern
patriarchy "systematized heroic fantasies of immortality" and thus tragically reinforced in playgoers' minds Romeo's and Juliet's inclination to consummate
love in death (131). Many critics have written about not just the personal but
also the familial and social tragedies resulting from sixteenth-century penalties
entailed in the defiance of patriarchal strictures. Among them are Marianne
Novy in *Love's Argument: Gender Relations in Shakespeare,* Coppélia Kahn in
her seminal essay "Coming of Age in Verona," Diane Dreher in *Domination
and Defiance: Fathers and Daughters in Shakespeare,* and Irene G. Dash in
Wooing, Wedding, and Power: Women in Shakespeare's Plays. These and other
critics describe early modern ideas of gender and sexuality as part of their
analyses of patriarchal systems in *Romeo and Juliet,* an association fully developed by Thomas Moisan in the article " 'O Any Thing, of Nothing First
Create!': Gender and Patriarchy and the Tragedy of *Romeo and Juliet.*"

Essays important for approaching the play through various sixteenth-century
cultural contexts are Joan Ozark Holmer's " 'Draw, If You Be Men': Saviolo's
Significance for *Romeo and Juliet*" and Jill Levenson's " 'Alla Stoccado Carries
It Away': Codes of Violence in *Romeo and Juliet*" (for early modern codes of
blood revenge and dueling), James C. Smith's "Ptolemy and Shakespeare: The
Astrological Influences on *Romeo and Juliet*" (for Elizabethan theories of astrological influence), T. J. Cribb's "The Unity of *Romeo and Juliet*" (for Renaissance Neoplatonism), Philip C. McGuire's "On the Dancing in *Romeo and*

Juliet" (for sixteenth-century theories of dancing), and Paster's aforementioned essay (for the practice of wet-nursing).

The essentially antiromantic characters of the Nurse, Mercutio, and Friar Lawrence in a memorably romantic play usually require the teacher's explanation, especially if students are to grasp the play's ironies and Shakespeare's practice of complementarity (see Norman Rabkin in this last respect). Writings helpful for overcoming this challenge are Stanley Wells's "Juliet's Nurse: The Uses of Inconsequentiality," Barbara Everett's "*Romeo and Juliet*: The Nurse's Story," and Joan Rees's "Juliet's Nurse: Some Branches of a Family Tree" (for the Nurse); Joseph A. Porter's *Shakespeare's Mercutio: His History and Drama*, Norman Holland's "Mercutio, Mine Own Son the Dentist," and Nicholas Brooke's chapter on the play in *Shakespeare's Early Tragedies* (for Mercutio); and Gerry Brenner's "Shakespeare's Politically Ambitious Friar," James C. Bryant's "The Problematic Friar in *Romeo and Juliet*," and Bertrand Evans's "The Brevity of Friar Laurence" (for the Friar). Studies of the characters of Romeo and Juliet tend to be part of larger critical analyses or aims such as those concerned with themes, image patterns, or new historicist or gender issues.

Colleagues interested in the play's remarkable use of several linguistic styles, especially the juxtaposition of Petrarchan and other highly rhetorical poetry with the antirhetorical (or plain) idiom heard clearly at times in the Nurse's and Juliet's utterances, should read Harry Levin's famous article "Form and Formality in *Romeo and Juliet*," James L. Calderwood's "*Romeo and Juliet*: A Formal Dwelling," and Robert O. Evans's *The Osier Cage: Rhetorical Devices in* Romeo and Juliet. Thomas Moisan, in his article "Rhetoric and the Rehearsal of Death: The 'Lamentations' Scene in *Romeo and Juliet*," shows that Petrarchanisms often obscure reality in the play for speaker and auditor alike. Alternatively, Paul Siegel in "Christianity and the Religion of Love in *Romeo and Juliet*" demonstrates the powerful fusion in the drama of Petrarchan conceits with the language of Christianity. Ann Pasternak Slater's "Petrarchanism Come True in *Romeo and Juliet*" clarifies a progression in the tragedy from a satiric use of Petrarchan tropes to their actualization in the staging of the second half of the play. In a different vein, Gayle Whittier charts in the play the decline of Petrarchan conceits from "lyric freedom to tragic fact through a transaction that diminishes the body of the sonnet, and scatters the terms of the *blason du corps*" (27). Her approach underscores the relevance for the play of not simply the motifs but also the techniques of Shakespeare's *Sonnets*. Finally, an instructor focused on the language of *Romeo and Juliet* will not want to overlook the relation between the play's ironic puns and its "conflict of incompatible truths" (Mahood 56).

A large body of criticism exists that can help instructors relate *Romeo and Juliet* to other Shakespeare plays, to Shakespeare poems, and to later early modern English drama. Thomas P. Harrison's "*Romeo and Juliet, A Midsummer Night's Dream*: Companion Plays" and Hugh Richmond's "Peter Quince Directs *Romeo and Juliet*" assist instructors in placing the tragedy in the larger context of the Pyramus and Thisbe story as presented in *A Midsummer Night's Dream*. Most important in this respect, however, is Mark Stavig's *The Forms of Things Unknown: Renaissance Metaphor in* Romeo and Juliet *and* A Midsummer Night's Dream. G. K. Hunter's "Shakespeare's Earliest Tragedies: *Titus Andronicus* and *Romeo and Juliet*" relates elements of the later tragedy to codes of blood revenge and the puns and rhetorical language of *Titus* and of *Julius Caesar*. Maurice Hunt's "Use and Abuse in *Romeo and Juliet*" and a chapter of Ralph Berry's *The Shakespearean Metaphor* explain the importance of certain sonnets for the tragedy. Relevant for teaching *Romeo and Juliet* in the context of the suicidal love tragedies of *Othello* and *Antony and Cleopatra* is Rosalie Colie's essay "*Othello* and the Problematics of Love," published as a chapter in her *Shakespeare's Living Art*. Harriet Hawkins in "Disrupting Tribal Difference: Critical and Artistic Responses to Shakespeare's Radical Romanticism" relates *Romeo and Juliet* to *Troilus and Cressida*, *Othello*, and *Antony and Cleopatra* on the basis of tribal conflict and the problems it poses for inter-tribal love. Ronald Huebert in *John Ford: Baroque English Dramatist* and R. L. Smallwood in "*'Tis Pity She's a Whore* and *Romeo and Juliet*" both establish the transformed presence of Shakespeare's late-Elizabethan tragedy in Ford's late-Stuart masterpiece, a fact that recommends *'Tis Pity* as one of the non-Shakespearean works selected for teaching in conjunction with Shakespeare's play.

Instructors of *Romeo and Juliet* profit from reading selected articles appearing in six recent edited volumes devoted to the play: Romeo and Juliet: *Critical Essays*, edited by John F. Andrews; *Shakespeare's* Romeo and Juliet: *Texts, Contexts, and Interpretation*, edited by Jay Halio; volume 49 of *Shakespeare Survey* (Romeo and Juliet *and Its Afterlife*), edited by Stanley Wells; *Critical Essays on Shakespeare's* Romeo and Juliet, edited by Joseph A. Porter; and volumes 11 and 33 of *Shakespearean Criticism* in this Gale Research series. Volume 11 reprints a generous selection of previously published chapters and essays on *Romeo and Juliet* in addition to "Reviews and Retrospective Accounts of Selected Productions" and papers concerned with staging issues, while volume 33 does the same for the play, giving special attention to sexuality, adolescence, language and imagery, and characterization.

Those interested in current classroom teaching methods for exploring *Romeo and Juliet* should read Joan Ozark Holmer's "'O, What Learning Is!' Some Pedagogical Practices for *Romeo and Juliet*" and Sophie Haroutunian-Gordon's *Turning the Soul: Teaching through Conversation in the High School*, which uses selected aspects of *Romeo and Juliet* to illustrate the author's pedagogy of student-student and student-teacher conversation. Highly recommended is *Shakespeare Set Free: Teaching* Romeo and Juliet, Macbeth, A Midsummer Night's Dream, edited by Peggy O'Brien. The volume contains many suggestive lesson plans, exercises, and assignments for teaching *Romeo and Juliet* in performance in the literature classroom. Of special interest are essays on the tragedy by Russ McDonald and by Jeanne Addison Roberts, the first challenging the concept of a characterological tragic flaw, the second describing various similarities and relations among the three plays forming the book's subtitle. Finally, Bruce McIver and Ruth Stevenson, in their volume *Teaching with Shakespeare: Critics in the Classroom,* have included a transcript of a workshop conducted by Helen Vendler on teaching *Romeo and Juliet* 1.5.93–106 in conjunction with six Shakespeare sonnets.

Background Studies

This section includes historical, cultural and intellectual, and background studies of topics important for teaching *Romeo and Juliet.* The two most cited sociopolitical histories of Shakespeare's age are Keith Wrightson, *English Society, 1580–1680,* and Christopher Hill, *Reformation to Industrial Revolution: A Social and Economic History of Britain, 1530–1780.* Friar Lawrence's characterization, his anxiety, and certain Catholic elements in *Romeo and Juliet* recommend a reading of Arnold Oskar Meyer, *England and the Catholic Church under Queen Elizabeth*; Patrick McGrath, *Papists and Puritans under Elizabeth I*; and J. Allen Morris, *Richard Topcliffe: "A Most Humbell Pursuivant of Her Majestie."* Morris's account focuses on a relatively obscure figure responsible for the protection of Queen Elizabeth from Catholics and for the torture of Papists, including Father John Gerard in 1594. Morris provides details of some of Topcliffe's torture methods. This work represents a lesson on the tense politico-religious climate in Elizabethan England around the time that Shakespeare was writing *Romeo and Juliet,* a play in which tragedy is indirectly brought about by a Catholic priest who fears punishment. After giving a vivid account of the phenomena surrounding bubonic plague (the black death virtually becomes a character in *Romeo and Juliet*), Antonin Artaud in "The Theater and the Plague" explains the plague's theoretical relevance for the genre of drama. Andrew Appleby's *Famine in Tudor and Stuart England* gives instructors of *Romeo and Juliet* an understanding of contemporary problems of hunger essential to grasping the significance of the Apothecary's character and to rationalizing his motives for selling poison.

A sense of what it was like to live day to day in Shakespeare's London is provided in Russell Fraser's imaginative two-volume study *Young Shakespeare* and *Shakespeare: The Later Years.* Of special importance for *Romeo and Juliet* are Lawrence Stone's *Crisis of the Aristocracy, 1558–1641* and *Family, Sex, and Marriage in England, 1500–1800.* Stone's studies have become required reading for Shakespeareans interested in early modern patriarchy, gender relations, the value attached to the nuclear family, the place of women, different attitudes toward sex, and the aristocracy's view of these and other cultural matters. (Nevertheless, David Cressy has demonstrated that Stone's findings sometimes require major qualifications.)

Stone's *Crisis of the Aristocracy* gives readers a cultural appreciation for the different anxieties among members of the Capulet family regarding their inter-actions and their place in the world. His *Family, Sex, and Marriage* contextual-izes Romeo's and Juliet's understanding of these topics but needs to be supplemented by Susan D. Amussen's frequently cited *An Ordered Society: Gender and Class in Early Modern England* and especially by Anthony Fletcher, *Gender, Sex, and Subordination in England, 1500–1800.* Also relevant are sev-eral of the essays in Fletcher and John Stevenson's *Order and Disorder in Early Modern England,* notably D. E. Underdown's "The Taming of the Scold: The Enforcement of Patriarchal Authority in Early Modern England." A fine de-scription of early modern conventions of courtship, betrothal, and wedding appears throughout Ann Jennalie Cook's *Making a Match: Courtship in Shake-speare and His Society.* Those wishing background for a feminist or gender-oriented approach to *Romeo and Juliet* might consult Linda Woodbridge's *Women and the English Renaissance: Literature and the Nature of Womankind, 1540–1620,* Katherine Usher Henderson and Barbara F. McManus's *Half-Humankind: Contexts and Texts of the Controversy about Women in England, 1540–1640,* and Ian Maclean's *Renaissance Notion of Woman.* Finally, Anders Nygren's famous *Agape and Eros* provides a cultural background useful for ap-preciating the play's distinctions between spiritual and romantic love and for recognizing Romeo and Juliet's frequent mixture and occasional separation of the two forces.

At this late date in Shakespeare studies, E. M. W. Tillyard's *Elizabethan World Picture* is useful for teachers either as an example of the analogical rea-soning that was prevalent in the period and that was important for the dramatist or as a presentation of static postulates to be deconstructed by gender-based, new-historicist, or cultural-materialist approaches. The background study rec-ommended for the poetic conceits in the play is Rosemond Tuve's *Elizabethan and Metaphysical Imagery.* More useful for this dimension of *Romeo and Juliet* is Heather Dubrow's *Echoes of Desire: English Petrarchanism and Its Counter-discourses.*

Background material for teaching Romeo and Juliet as sacrificial victims in a community ritual with mythic tragic or regenerative overtones might be assem-bled from René Girard's *Violence and the Sacred,* Victor W. Turner's *The Ritual Process: Structure and Anti-structure,* and Mary Douglas's *Purity and Danger: An Analysis of Concepts of Pollution and Taboo.* Finally, Alan Hager's *Under-standing* Romeo and Juliet, a volume in the Greenwood Press Literature in Context series, supports an interdisciplinary approach to the play by placing it in selected historical and cultural contexts.

Textual and Source Studies

The three primary texts of *Romeo and Juliet* are the 1597 "bad" (memorially re-constructed) quarto (Q1); the 1599 "good" ("Newly corrected, augmented, and amended") quarto (Q2), and that of the 1623 First Folio (F1), which was set directly from the 1609 quarto (Q3), itself derived from Q2. Instructors and students may examine the First Folio text of *Romeo and Juliet* in Charlton Hinman's *The First Folio of Shakespeare: The Norton Facsimile*. Teachers desirous of comparing details of their classroom text or the First Folio text of the play with the 1597 or 1599 quarto can consult Michael J. B. Allen and Kenneth Muir's *Shakespeare's Plays in Quarto: A Facsimile Edition of Copies Primarily from the Henry E. Huntington Library* (117–201). Comprehensive accounts of the problematic relation between quarto and folio texts of the play appear in Brian Gibbons's second Arden edition, in G. Blakemore Evans's New Cambridge edition, and especially in George Walton Williams's The Most Excellent and Lamentable Tragedie of Romeo and Juliet: *A Critical Edition*. In this respect, also see Stanley Wells and Gary Taylor's *William Shakespeare: A Textual Companion*. Wells and Taylor and Williams provide extensive scene and line textual notes and lists of quarto or folio stage directions.

Harry R. Hoppe in *The Bad Quarto of* Romeo and Juliet, Michael Mooney in "Text and Performance: *Romeo and Juliet,* Quartos 1 and 2," and David Farley-Hills in "The 'Bad' Quarto of *Romeo and Juliet*" illustrate the notably vexed relation of Q1 and Q2 of the play. This relation requires teachers of *Romeo and Juliet* to understand that preferring one text's reading of a line or passage over the other's—or on occasion conflating the two—can significantly alter students' appreciation of the work. A graphic illustration of this fact is Charles Lower's textual analysis of act 4, scene 5 (Lower argues for a conflated text in this instance). Jonathan Goldberg in an essay titled " 'What? In a Names That Which We Call a Rose': The Desired Texts of *Romeo and Juliet*" reinforces the importance of editorial choice in textual matters, warning against the desire to privilege categorically the "good" quarto (Q2) over the "bad" quarto (Q1) and implicitly showing that a methodology divorced from the idealist assumptions of the New Bibliography offers opportunities to enrich the tragedy's meaning. This means that Goldberg necessarily increases the importance of Q1 in matters of editorial selection from the two texts. In fact, Hugh Richmond argues that a text based on Q1 makes *Romeo and Juliet* less a "sentimental icon for the literary imagination" than a stageable play engrossing the audience's attention (223). Recently, Jay Halio has stated in "Handy Dandy: Q1/Q2 *Romeo and Juliet*" that Q1 may be not a memorial reconstruction (and thus not such a "bad" text) but rather "a revised and abridged version [. . .] of the play that Shakespeare originally conceived and wrote (as Q2 represents it)" (128). (Farley-Hills makes a similar claim.) Also privileging Q1, especially its theatrical vocabulary, is Alan Dessen in "Q1 *Romeo and Juliet* and Elizabethan Theatrical Vocabulary." Essays by Goldberg, Halio, Dessen, and others include many examples of adjudicated textual matters from which teachers might choose to create their own texts of *Romeo and Juliet* for different kinds of classrooms.

A basic understanding of the text of a Shakespeare play can be got by reading G. Blakemore Evans's essay "Shakespeare's Text," which appears in the first edition of *The Riverside Shakespeare* and has been thoroughly revised with the assistance of J. J. Tobin for the second, as well as Stephen Greenblatt's "The Dream of the Master Text" in *The Norton Shakespeare,* an essay that essentially amounts to a defense of Wells and Taylor's much-debated Oxford texts of the plays appearing in this recent collection. More advanced treatments of the subject of Shakespeare's text appear in W. W. Greg's *The Editorial Problem in Shakespeare: A Survey of the Foundations of the Text* and in Wells and Taylor's *William Shakespeare: A Textual Companion.* Also useful is Charlton Hinman's two-volume *Printing and Proofreading of the First Folio of Shakespeare.*

Performance and Theater Studies

Research has shown that analyses of the performance art of Shakespeare's plays clarify abstract, intellectual motifs traditionally reserved for literary criticism. In treating performance values, many writers have demonstrated that this fact applies especially to *Romeo and Juliet,* a play noteworthy not only for its many special locations (Juliet's window, the Friar's cell, the Capulet tomb, etc.) but also for the dynamics of its vigorous staging, for example, Capulet's dance and the swordplay of act 3, scene 1. Studies in this vein include Harley Granville-Barker's essay on the play in volume 2 of his *Prefaces to Shakespeare*; John Russell Brown's *Shakespeare's Plays in Performance*; Barbara Hodgdon's "Absent Bodies, Present Voices: Performance Work and the Close of Romeo and Juliet's Golden Story"; and Jill Levenson's masterful *Shakespeare in Performance:* Romeo and Juliet, whose chapter titles are "Shakespeare's *Romeo and Juliet*: The Elizabethan Version," "Early Revivals: David Garrick versus Charlotte Cushman," "Recovery, 1935: John Gielgud," "Paraphrase, 1947: Peter Brook," and "Translation, 1960–1968: Franco Zeffirelli."

 The performative potential of the tomb scene is imaginatively described by Alan Dessen in " 'Romeo Opens the Tomb,' " an essay in his *Recovering Shakespeare's Theatrical Vocabulary.* Dessen's study draws on his analysis of the stagings of tomb or monument scenes in more than two dozen early modern English plays, an analysis that highlights the difference between theatrical and fictional stage directions. Dessen's emphasis on what playgoers in the mid-1590s might have seen onstage in *Romeo and Juliet* complements Leslie Thomson's article " 'With Patient Ears Attend': *Romeo and Juliet* on the Elizabethan Stage." Thomson focuses on the contemporary staging of the tragedy, staging that tracks the falling turn of fortune's wheel, which is paradoxically at odds with the play's images of elevation and transcendence. Samuel Crowl's chapter "Watching the Torches Burn Bright: The Diary of a Royal Shakespeare Company Observer," in his *Shakespeare Observed: Studies in Performance on Stage and Screen,* consists of fascinating entries from the author's notebook on his experience of watching Ron Daniels's "work with *Romeo and Juliet* from first rehearsal through opening night" (103). Also relevant is Peter Holding's Romeo and Juliet: *Text and Performance,* which includes fine analyses of productions of *Romeo and Juliet* by Franco Zeffirelli (1961), Terry Hands (1973 and 1989–90), Trevor Nunn and Barry Kyle (1976), and Michael Bogdanov (1986–87).

The background works on Shakespeare's stage for *Romeo and Juliet* are Bernard Beckerman's *Shakespeare at the Globe, 1599–1609* and Herbert Berry's *Shakespeare's Playhouses*, both supplemented by Andrew Gurr's "The Date and Expected Venue of *Romeo and Juliet*." Berry describes the design and use of the Theatre in Shoreditch and includes three chapters on the Globe concerning its documents and ownership, a lawsuit, and reviews of performances after Shakespeare's death. No record of the play's performance at the indoor Blackfriars theater exists. (In fact, no record of any performance exists during the Elizabethan age and the pre-Restoration seventeenth century.) For an overview of contemporary theatrical companies, players, playhouses, staging, and audiences, see Andrew Gurr's *Shakespearean Stage, 1574–1642*. Gurr's *Playgoing in Shakespeare's London* and Ann Jennalie Cook's *The Privileged Playgoers of Shakespeare's London, 1576–1642* remain highly informative on playgoing behavior and the makeup of Shakespeare's audiences. Gurr's *Playgoing*, chapter 4, on the mental composition of playgoers, is especially suggestive. Finally, J. L. Styan's *Shakespeare Revolution: Criticism and Performance in the Twentieth Century* includes accounts of how different generations have performed *Romeo and Juliet*.

Visual Materials and Other Artistic Media

Teachers of *Romeo and Juliet* are fortunate in having available film versions from the 1930s, the 1960s, and the 1990s to show students how different cultural preoccupations inform the moment of production. Six major film versions of the tragedy exist on videocassette, those of George Cukor (1936), starring Leslie Howard, Norma Shearer, and John Barrymore; Renato Castellani (1954), starring Laurence Harvey and Susan Shentall; Franco Zeffirelli (1968), starring Olivia Hussey, Leonard Whiting, and Laurence Olivier; Cedric Messina (1978), starring Rebecca Saire and Patrick Ryecart; Norman Campbell (1993), starring Megan Porter Follows and Antoni Cimolino; and Baz Luhrmann (1996), starring Leonardo DiCaprio and Claire Danes. (Details necessary for obtaining these videocassettes appear at the end of the list of works cited.) The most popular of these are the Zeffirelli and Luhrmann films, which between them counterpoint the rebellious values of the 1960s and the MTV qualities of the 1990s. Though one respondent finds Luhrmann's *Romeo and Juliet* "cartoonish," the film has been widely praised for representing the play's focus on male violence and male bonding and on gender bending. This last facet might be related in the classroom to queer aspects of Mercutio's characterization. One instructor asserts that the ending of Luhrmann's film is not, in sixteenth-century terms, tragic and thus is useful for starting a discussion of the nature of tragedy. Luhrmann does omit the reconciliation between the families that several commentators have claimed is essential to the tragic structure of the play. Some instructors use the Cukor film to get students to talk about how the appearance of forty-year-old lovers affects the poetry that Shakespeare wrote for teenagers and thus to start a discussion of how the original language conditions audiences' ideas about the lovers' maturity or lack thereof. Few respondents have good things to say about the Messina BBC film. In fact, one instructor uses it to show students how much can go wrong with a production.

An award-winning film that was popular during late 1998 and in 1999 is John Madden's *Shakespeare in Love*. With screenplay by Marc Norman and Tom Stoppard and an all-star cast including Gwyneth Paltrow, Joseph Fiennes, Geoffrey Rush, Ben Afleck, and Judi Dench, the movie depicts young Shakespeare (Fiennes) struggling to find authentic tragic and lyrical voices through the painful creation of the play *Romeo and Juliet*. The film is most notable for its amusing, original take on the progression of art imitating life, life imitating art, art imitating life, and so on. (A paperback text, Shakespeare in Love: *A Screenplay*, exists for classroom use.)

Readings that will assist instructors in teaching one or more film versions of the play appear in H. R. Coursen's *Shakespeare in Production: Whose History?*, Roger Manvell's *Shakespeare and the Film*, Jack Jorgens's *Shakespeare on Film*, and Peter Donaldson's *Shakespearean Films / Shakespearean Directors*. Also useful are Paul Jorgensen's "Castellani's *Romeo and Juliet:* Intention and Response," Albert Cirillo's "The Art of Franco Zeffirelli and Shakespeare's *Romeo and Juliet*," and Barbara Hodgdon's "*William Shakespeare's Romeo + Juliet:* Everything's Nice in America?" Several reviews of the 1947 NBC television *Romeo and Juliet* and the 1978 BBC version of the play appear in J. C. Bulman and H. R. Coursen's *Shakespeare on Television: An Anthology of Essays and Reviews*. The videocassette version of Leonard Bernstein's *West Side Story* might also be compared to the play text or to one or more film versions of the play. For this lesson plan, see Norris Houghton's edition *Romeo and Juliet / West Side Story* and Robert Hapgood's essay "*West Side Story* and the Modern Appeal of *Romeo and Juliet*." Gary Schmidgall in a chapter titled "Wherefore Romeo?" in his *Shakespeare and Opera* describes the transformation of Shakespeare's play into this medium, mainly through analysis of Charles-François Gounod's *Roméo et Juliette* (1867). A videocassette of a 1966 film of Sergei Prokofiev's ballet *Romeo and Juliet,* starring Rudolf Nureyev and Margot Fonteyn, is available as well. Also relevant to this approach are Fred D'Aguiar's novel *The Longest Memory* and spin-off films such as Mira Nairs's *Mississippi Masala*, Abel Ferrara's *China Girl*, and Jiri Weiss's *Sweet Light in a Dark Room* (also known as *Romeo, Juliet, and Darkness*).

Required and Recommended Student Readings

Many instructors, especially those of undergraduate Shakespeare courses, do not assign required or recommended readings in conjunction with their teaching of *Romeo and Juliet*. "I would rather have [students] reading deeply in and seeing filmed versions and staged productions of the plays themselves," a respondent writes. "Students have enough to do to read the play and the introduction to the play in the text," another comments. A third concludes, "Because students are experiencing more and more difficulty with Shakespeare's language, I find myself assigning less and less critical reading, particularly since recent critical writing poses such a challenge to readers inexperienced with the postmodernist styles. [. . .] If anything, I want to make time available for students to listen to the audio tapes which I keep on reserve." One group of instructors restricts student readings on *Romeo and Juliet* to the editor's introduction and various materials included in the edition being used. Singled out for special mention in this respect are introductions by Brian Gibbons in the Arden second series edition and by G. Blakemore Evans in the New Cambridge edition. Also commended are a section of Michael Goldman's *Shakespeare and the Energies of Drama* reprinted as "*Romeo and Juliet*: The Meaning of a Theatrical Experience" and a part of Susan Snyder's *The Comic Matrix of Shakespeare's Tragedies* called "Beyond Comedy: *Romeo and Juliet*," both appearing at the end of the Signet Classic edition. Snyder's treatment of *Romeo* in *Comic Matrix* remains the critical reading of the play most frequently recommended or required. (Coppélia Kahn's revised and reprinted essay "Coming of Age in Verona" is a close second). Praised likewise is Gail Kern Paster's essay "*Romeo and Juliet*: A Modern Perspective," in Mowat and Werstine's New Folger Library Shakespeare edition of *Romeo and Juliet*.

Of student reading not specifically focused on the tragedy, teachers most often require or recommend Russ McDonald's *The Bedford Companion to Shakespeare: An Introduction with Documents*. Chapters in *The Bedford Companion* include "Shakespeare, 'Shakespeare,' and the Problem of Authorship," "Performances, Playhouses, and Players," " 'What Is Your Text?'," " 'I Loved My Books': Shakespeare's Reading," "Theater à la Mode: Shakespeare and the Kinds of Drama," " 'To What End Are All These Words?': Shakespeare's Dramatic Language," "Town and Country: Life in Shakespeare's England," "Men and Women: Gender, Family, Society," and "Politics and Religion: Early Modern Ideologies." Appended to these chapters are ninety-one contemporary illustrations and whole or excerpted documents ranging from "Chart of the Relative Proportions of Poetry and Prose in Shakespeare's Plays" to *An Homily of the State of Matrimony* (1563) and selections from John Stow's *Survey of London* (1598). Also recommended in this category are the volumes William Leary's *Shakespeare Plain: The Making and Performing of Shakespeare's Plays* and Maurice Charney's *How to Read Shakespeare*, Leah

Scragg's *Discovering Shakespeare's Meaning*, Kenneth Muir and S. Schoenbaum's *A New Companion to Shakespeare Studies*, and Joseph Papp and Elizabeth Kirkland's *Shakespeare Alive!* Scragg's chapters include "Verse and Prose," "Imagery and Spectacle," "Shakespeare's Expositions," "Parallel Actions," and "The Treatment of Character." Papp and Kirkland's volume, ideal for sophomores and nonmajors, addresses subjects in an easy style with chapters such as "Don't Talk to Strangers: Foreigners and Immigrants in England," "Like a Virgin: Queen Elizabeth and the Status of Women," and "Getting Their Acts Together: Playwright and Audience." A detailed summary of the play with a continuous basic interpretation of words and deeds appears in Victor Cahn's *Shakespeare the Playwright*.

Among the readings often assigned to undergraduates are John Drakakis's *Shakespearean Tragedy* (for an introduction to theories of tragedy and different critical approaches to the genre), Douglas Cole's *Twentieth-Century Interpretations of* Romeo and Juliet, Mark Rose's *Shakespeare's Early Tragedies: A Collection of Critical Essays*, Bertrand Evans's *Shakespeare's Tragic Practice* (for the play as a tragedy of fate), Marjorie Garber's *Coming of Age in Shakespeare* (for problems of maturation in the play) and her *Dream in Shakespeare: From Metaphor to Metamorphosis* (for an especially good analysis of Mercutio's Queen Mab speech), Northrop Frye's *"Romeo and Juliet,"* James Hirsh's *The Structure of Shakespearean Scenes* (for a structuralist reading of nine scenes of the play), and G. Thomas Tanselle's "Time in *Romeo and Juliet.*"

Recommended or required readings for advanced undergraduates and graduates (besides many of those already cited in the section "Critical and Pedagogical Studies") include selections from Naomi Conn Liebler's *Shakespeare's Festive Tragedy*, Shirley Nelson Garner and Madelon Sprengnether's *Shakespearean Tragedy and Gender*, and Lynda Boose's "The Father and the Bride in Shakespeare." Three singled-out articles are Jill Levenson's "The Definition of Love: Shakespeare's Phrasing in *Romeo and Juliet,*" Dympna Callaghan's "The Ideology of Romantic Love: The Case of *Romeo and Juliet,*" and J. Karl Franson's " 'Too Soon Marr'd': Juliet's Age as Symbol in *Romeo and Juliet.*"

NOTE

Except where otherwise noted, citations to *Romeo and Juliet* in this volume are from *The Riverside Shakespeare*, second edition, edited by G. Blakemore Evans.

Part Two

APPROACHES

Introduction

Survey respondents mention *A Midsummer Night's Dream* as the play they are most likely to relate in the classroom to *Romeo and Juliet*. This early comedy was cited three times more often than *Antony and Cleopatra* and five to six times more often than the *Sonnets*, *Much Ado*, and *Richard II*. In the words of one instructor, "some issues that link [*A Midsummer Night's Dream* and *Romeo*] are law and authority, transformation of the individual, discord versus concord, characters in crisis—public roles and private desires, the construction of the lover via gender roles, and father-daughter relationships." Both Hermia and Juliet react rebelliously to the *senex iratus*. Other issues that the two plays share are "monosexual and heterosexual bonding, the conflict between the worlds of 'romance' and 'everyday,' the movement from infatuation ('dotage') to mature love, and the relation between verbal style and emotion." *Romeo and Juliet* can be fruitfully compared with not only *A Midsummer Night's Dream* but also *Richard II* on the basis of characters' lyrical speech.

Furthermore, instructors compare *Romeo and Juliet* and *A Midsummer Night's Dream* to show how the former play "begins with the typical structure of a romantic comedy but veers off" toward tragedy in act 3. To justify this generic shift instructors "quote extensively from Lysander and Hermia's description of the fate of true love in act 1 of *A Midsummer Night's Dream*." Contrasts drawn between *Romeo*'s tomb scene and *A Midsummer Night's Dream*'s playlet "Pyramus and Thisbe" prove illuminating. According to one teacher, "the contrast between Romeo's suddenly mature verse and [the ludicrous style of] 'Pyramus and Thisbe' is very helpful in showing how style conditions content. [The contrast] is also helpful to show that the world of Pyramus and Thisbe, under the silliness of the verse, is as grim and unprovidential as that of Romeo and Juliet." Both plays "are inextricably bound up with eroticized violence." One instructor invites students "to use the dream figure of *A Midsummer Night's Dream* to interpret the poetic reality which Romeo creates for himself (and for Juliet) with language—the reality which the eye salve of *A Midsummer Night's Dream* re-creates for the lovers in the woods. Since both plays draw heavily on the Petrarchan love language and its love ideology, students come to *Romeo and Juliet* already sensitized to Romeo's 'style' as a lover."

The mature romance of *Antony and Cleopatra* invites comparison with the adolescence of Romeo and Juliet. Both tragedies might be joined with *Othello* to ground a discussion of Shakespearean *Liebestod* and *Liebestod* in general and of the cultural assumptions that generate the fatal yet positive associations of romantic love and suicidal death. An instructor of graduate students devotes a major part of a course to a multifaceted comparison of Shakespeare's treatment of gender issues and love in *Romeo and Juliet* and in *Antony and Cleopatra*: "both [plays] feature superficially similar motifs—infatuated lovers who hastily and recklessly fall in love, rather separate male and female 'worlds,' the lure of forbidden passion, a love relationship blocked and complicated by political considerations, a confidante (the Nurse, Enobarbus) who turns against the lovers, suicides that are both idealized and pathetic." Having posed these comparisons, this instructor then emphasizes certain differences: "the ages of the lovers, the ideological constructions of passion and pleasure, the very different specific political landscapes of the plays, the different shapes of the tragic plot, the place and conception of sexuality in each play, and the specific relationships of love and death. [. . .] Such comparisons help students sharpen their understanding of Shakespeare's (re)development of a body of concerns and problems throughout his career."

Both *A Midsummer Night's Dream* and *Romeo and Juliet*, in the words of one instructor, "depict the failing of *Sonnet* ideals (as do the *Sonnets* themselves!)." Another instructor notes, "Students were asked to imagine a play based on Shakespeare's *Sonnets*, and then we examined the poetry of act 1 of *Romeo and Juliet*, asking what it means when characters do or don't 'kiss by the book.' " Romeo and Juliet's Petrarchan dialogue in act 1, scene 5 forms a period sonnet, which can be compared with other stylized (and relatively unstylized) sonnets of Shakespeare. "It's much easier to show Romeo's Petrarchanism," an instructor remarks, "if the class has already learned about conventional tropes of love poetry in the period." The introduction of a plot-enabling Catholic Friar Francis in *Much Ado* begs comparison with Friar Lawrence's similar function in *Romeo*, primarily because the juxtaposition allows students to discover that dramatic genre preconditions the success of Friar Francis and the failure of Friar Lawrence.

By means of Lady Montague's and especially Lady Capulet's roles, *Romeo* can be compared with later motherless tragedies such as *King Lear*, *Othello*, and *Antony and Cleopatra*. One instructor relates *Romeo and Juliet* to *Julius Caesar, Measure for Measure,* and *The Winter's Tale* on the grounds that all four are "hinged" plays that change direction midway. In one respect, the clan feud fracturing Verona resembles the similar feuds stirring the Henry VI plays. One teacher compares the Prince's failure to suppress the feud in *Romeo and Juliet* with King Henry VI's failure to suppress the feud between the York and Lancaster factions in *Henry VI, Part 2* and *Part 3*. This teacher also relates "Juliet's parrying Paris's overtures in stichomythia in 4.1 to Richard of Gloucester's exchanges with Anne and with Elizabeth in *Richard III*" and compares the "Friar's comments to Romeo on banishment (3.3) with Gaunt's comments to Bolingbroke in *Richard II*." Furthermore, "the similarity of Juliet's and the French women's understanding of true love [in *Love's Labor's Lost*] is balanced by the similarity of Romeo's and Navarre's men's confusion of self-love and true love." Instructors can compare the choruses of *Romeo and Juliet* with those of *Pericles* and especially *Henry V*, noting that in the latter plays the choruses determine generic outcome less and playgoers' imaginative enabling of dramatic providence more than they do in *Romeo and Juliet*. The parallel between Imogen and Juliet—each of whom wakes up beside her (supposedly) dead husband—determines a comparison of the tragicomedy *Cymbeline* with *Romeo*, a comparison that distinguishes the prerequisites of tragedy from those of tragicomedy (which *Romeo* initially seems to be).

As the non-Shakespeare works most useful for teaching aspects of *Romeo and Juliet*, survey respondents most often name Renaissance sonnets, especially those of Petrarch, Wyatt, and Sidney; Arthur Brooke's *The Tragicall Historye of Romeus and Juliet*; and the video musical *West Side Story*. Coupled with *West Side Story* is Eric Segal's novel *Love Story* and the film version of it. Brooke, respondents claim, is useful mainly for showing how Shakespeare made his young lovers more sympathetic than their counterparts in the source poem. In addition to Shakespeare's sonnets, those of earlier Renaissance poets "suggest how Petrarchanism shapes Romeo and Juliet's understanding of their passions," permitting students to see how the play "subtly reshapes and resituates Petrarchan conceptions of love." Also useful in this respect are Henry Constable's *Diana* and Bartholomew Griffin's *Fidessa*. One innovative instructor has students read the "Solemnization of the Estate of Holy Matrimony," copied directly from *The Book of Common Prayer* (1559), in order that they understand "the 'public' or 'civic' love ideology" of the sixteenth century, "which rivals the private, class-specific, or cultic Petrarchan love ethos." This Petrarchan love ethos "communicates a complex set of notions" important for Shakespeare's play: "that the lover-poet is a recognizable type; that he draws on a body of received figures to celebrate and create the image of his 'mistress' (a word which must be glossed for students); that a lover-poet may be quite conscious (or not) of the stylized nature of the language he employs to court his beloved; and that, more often than not, the language corresponds little, or not at all, to the person of his love, so that he is in the awkward situation of either lying to and about his love or running the risk of insulting her with the truth of how much her looks deviate from the poetic ideal; and finally that the lover-poet in [Shakespeare's] sonnet 130 *chooses* to celebrate his beloved and his love with the unpoetic truth of her looks." All this is relevant for students' understanding of the private nature of Romeo's constructions of his romantic love for Rosaline and Juliet, an understanding clarified by a familiarity with the period's contrasting ethos of public, married love.

Other early modern non-Shakespearean works mentioned as taught in conjunction with *Romeo and Juliet* are Christopher Marlowe's *Dido and Aeneas*, *Arden of Feversham* (a tawdry version of Romeo and Juliet's romance), and John Ford's *'Tis Pity She's a Whore* (*Romeo and Juliet* transformed by late-Stuart values). Mowat and Werstine, in their edition of *Romeo and Juliet*, assert that Henry Porter's *The Two Mad Women of Abington* (1598–99?) "parallels *Romeo and Juliet* both verbally and in its 'balcony scene.' The family feud between Mistress Barnes and Mistress Goursey had led some critics to regard the play as a gentle spoof of *Romeo and Juliet*. Other critics, however, date the play as early as 1588 and claim that Porter's work was a source for Shakespeare" (269). For one instructor, Ovid's story of Pyramus and Thisbe in the

Metamorphoses provides a better context for appreciating Shakespeare's transformation of it in *Romeo and Juliet* than its representation in *A Midsummer Night's Dream* does. Another instructor uses Chaucer's portrait of the Wife of Bath to illuminate the Nurse's ancestry and contextualizes the tone and substance of Romeo and Juliet's love talk with several passages from *Troilus and Criseyde*. Finally, one enterprising teacher imaginatively compares certain aspects of the feud in *Romeo and Juliet* with the Grangerford episode of *Huckleberry Finn*.

When asked to identify the features of *Romeo and Juliet* that students find most engaging, survey respondents most often name the interfamilial conflict in the play, the love story, Romeo's and especially Juliet's maturation as characters, and the tragedy's poetic language. In the opinion of one instructor, "almost all [students] appreciate the poetry and are impressed by the way Shakespeare weaves together imagery, paradox, foreshadowing" and so on. Another teacher writes, "The repeated oxymorons (1.1.175–83) and the touching pilgrimage sonnet (1.5.93–106) provide [students with] wonderful examples of highly charged dramatic language." Being young, students focus on the lovers' defiance of parental authority for the sake of sexuality and independence, on "the way Romeo and Juliet rebel against their parents and social conventions to pursue their relationship." Students' engagement with the idealistic, romantic elements of the love story sometimes generates intense classroom involvement with the text. A final identified source of attraction for students is the play's representation of several forces—fate, chance, destiny, the stars, and human ignorance—as they work together to produce a catastrophic tragic effect.

Asked to name the features of *Romeo and Juliet* that are most difficult or challenging for students, respondents by a wide majority cite the play's poetic language—a feature specified by some as most engaging. Concerning the play's Petrarchan conceits and density of rhetorical devices, one instructor remarks that students "often see this kind of speech as 'high-falutin' and 'insincere,' and this leads us to discuss the differences in attitude toward the 'high style' between Renaissance England and modern America." Students have difficulty with the unrealism of Romeo's and Juliet's eloquence, the mechanics of blank verse, and the play's embedded sonnets. "Careful definition of Petrarchanism with an emphasis on its narcissism helps students see how Romeo's love for Juliet invites reciprocity, while his earlier love does not." Finally, several instructors assert that the relation between the play's notorious bawdry and its romantic discourses is obscure to many students.

The next most cited obstacles to student understanding of the play involve undergraduates' and even graduate students' unfamiliarity with certain early modern patriarchal arrangements for marriage and students' perception of Juliet and especially Romeo as immature and their faulting of the lovers on this account. Generally unaware of sixteenth-century English issues of "property versus marriage" and practices such as "the relative sequestration of noble women," students puzzle over "Juliet's isolation from her parents," Capulet's apparent authority over Lady Capulet and Juliet, the latter's virtual imprisonment within the family, and the code that effectively hands Juliet over to Paris. The cultural dislocation of students often makes them impatient with the young lovers: Why doesn't Juliet just run away with Romeo? Why don't those who know about the secret marriage tell the authorities sooner? Moreover, many find it "difficult to sympathize with Romeo and Juliet's excessive behavior and language" and balk on encountering the love-at-first-sight premise of the play. Undergraduates especially disbelieve Romeo's movement from boy to man and Juliet's from girl to woman in a span of four days.

Almost as often noted are students' preconceptions about the play, created by countless references to it in popular culture and by students' encounter with it in high school. Perhaps related to this early experience is the tendency of some students to "arrive too quickly at moralistic interpretations, dissecting Romeo's and Juliet's tragic 'flaws' before fully experiencing their romantic attractiveness." Moreover, many students have trouble accepting "the power of Fate in determining the plot." Additionally, of all the speeches in the play "it is Mercutio's 'Queen Mab' speech that gives my students the most problems," one respondent reports. "They cannot easily see its thematic connections with the rest of the play or its place in the developing characterization of Mercutio; I typically spend at least one-half a class period on it, and relate it to Mercutio's misogyny [. . .] and the motives that lie behind that misogyny." Misogynistic and homoerotic, Mercutio proves difficult for students to categorize and thus recognize.

The least-mentioned of student comprehension difficulties include grasping the role of the Chorus in the play, the position of nurses in early modern noble households, and the dramatic functions of Juliet's meditation before she takes the potion. One respondent, in conclusion, laments students' fixation on "the impotence of Justice [in the play] and on the Placing of Blame (i.e., who is most responsible for the tragedy of *Romeo and Juliet* and why do we, as readers, need to place blame?)."

In one way or another, the twenty essays making up part 2 of this volume address each of the challenges described above and offer instructors of *Romeo and Juliet* imaginative approaches for dealing with potential obstacles. Because of students' difficulty in knowing how to read *Romeo and Juliet,* the first four essays address that issue, in a section titled "Reading Strategies." Arthur F. Kinney outlines an imaginative pedagogy for helping students locate in the play the authoritative agent of tragedy (from among such possibilities as fate, the stars, and human choice). Ivo Kamps measures the importance of *Liebestod* for understanding the play by placing the topic of love in death in the wider context of early modern preoccupations with erotomania (love madness). Thomas Moisan describes an approach that makes students aware of the social constructions of Romeo's and Juliet's sexuality and the repressive effects these constructions have on the lovers' desires. Finally, Douglas Bruster suggests how instructors might clarify the perplexing comedy of *Romeo and Juliet* in a larger discussion of literary form.

The four essays grouped in the next section, "Literary and Contemporary Contexts," discuss teaching the play in an introductory drama course, in early modern historical and social contexts, in conjunction with other Shakespeare plays, and finally in relation to early modern ideas and practices of sexuality. Jennifer Low explains how Aristotle's *Poetics,* Sophocles's *Antigone,* Strindberg's *Miss Julie,* Genet's *The Maids,* and Caryl Churchill's *Fen* illuminate the nature of tragedy in *Romeo and Juliet*; Dorothea Kehler retrieves the circumstances and lives of early modern friars, nurses, and apothecaries so that students can appreciate the social dimension of tragedy; and Thomas H. Blackburn builds on Douglas Bruster's detailed comparison of *Romeo and Juliet* and *A Midsummer Night's Dream* by describing a pedagogy that places *Romeo and Juliet* in an enriching conjunction with Shakespeare's *Troilus and Cressida* and *Antony and Cleopatra.* Lastly, Nicholas F. Radel points the way for instructors to help students become aware that the main binary of heterosexuality and homosexuality does not resemble the more unified view of sexuality in the early modern period.

In the third section, "Modern Contexts," Cynthia Marshall explains how instructors can use the lyrics of rock and roll songs of the 1950s and 1960s to define not only the stylized tone and artificial terms of Romeo and Juliet's romance but also the timelessness of their love. Sara Munson Deats, by situating Romeo and Juliet's tragedy within a current American context of pressures "within masculine peer groups [. . .] and the failure of authority figures to mediate between young people and the establishment" (especially as these problems contribute to the increasing rate of teenage suicide), provides teachers with a way to stress these elements in the play and discuss the self-inflicted nature of Romeo's and Juliet's deaths. James Andreas concludes this section by showing instructors that teaching the play's bawdry and orality (as opposed to classical literacy) is not only central to the play's significance but also necessary to correct students' high school experience of a heavily censored, sanitized text of the work.

Essays in the following two sections focus on teaching important issues of the play's characterization, language, and texts. Selecting act 1, scene 3, of *Romeo and Juliet,* Michael Basile discovers new depths in Lady Capulet's character by detailing in a two-class outline the different emphases given to her words and deeds by Arthur Brooke, by Shakespeare in the 1597 and 1599 quartos of the play, and by Franco Zeffirelli and Baz Luhrmann in the two best-known film versions of the work. Paul J. Voss complements Dorothea Kehler's historical sketch of Elizabethan friars by arguing that the many-sidedness of Friar Lawrence makes this character an instructor's ideal vehicle for introducing students to the problematic relation between perspective and interpretation in

Romeo and Juliet. Karl F. Zender, by sensitively portraying the growth in character of Romeo and Juliet during the play and suggesting that Shakespeare gets us to love his lovers, provides teachers with an approach designed to counter students' objections that Romeo's and Juliet's conversions from boy and girl to man and woman are too rapid and thus unrealistic. Through several original, intricate examples, Joseph A. Porter models for instructors an approach to teaching the rich metaphors of the play in ways that quickly move beyond traditional textbook notions of figuration and that demonstrate how Shakespearean metaphor "can find northwest passages through the mind." Instructors desirous of teaching the play's language might supplement Porter's approach with strategies found in other essays. Zender traces Romeo's and Juliet's character growth by illustrating changes in their language in key pairs or sequences of scenes. Andreas contrasts the bawdry and oral (often vulgar) language of the play with the play's emphatic literate language. Radel and Moisan show how Romeo's and Juliet's language becomes conditioned by sexuality and desire. Kamps defines erotomania in terms of the excesses of the lovers' language, and Kinney introduces and develops his approach to the issue of authority in the play through fine close readings of the play's choruses and chorus-like speech. Finally, Jill L. Levenson introduces instructors to important texts of *Romeo and Juliet,* primarily those of the early quartos and 1623 Folio; to the bibliographic histories of the texts; and to the relations of the texts to one another. Her discussion provides a foundation for the several student textual assignments that she describes in the latter part of her essay.

Essayists in the last two sections of this volume offer approaches to teaching the play's dramatic technique and performance art as well as the play's transformations in other artistic media. James Hirsh proposes several classroom scenarios for overcoming students' preconceptions that the play is merely a sappy love story and for convincing students of the play's complex dramatic technique. His desentimentalizing exercises focus on Shakespeare's dramatic use of rhyme and poetic language (including whole and fragmentary sonnets) and on certain Renaissance stage conditions such as the balcony area in the rear wall of the stage and the repertoire company's doubling of parts. Stephen M. Buhler in his essay on the performance art of *Romeo and Juliet* describes engaging classroom exercises wherein students reenact five historical versions of a memorable scene in the play—"Romeo's abortive suicide attempt after learning of Juliet's anguished response to his slaying of Tybalt." By this means, "students can discover what kinds of challenges the play has historically presented to the expectations of performers and audiences, of editors and readers." Extending Basile's analysis of Zeffirelli's and Luhrmann's film versions of *Romeo and Juliet,* Robert F. Willson, Jr., gives instructors ideas about how to introduce students to these movies as well as to the 1936 MGM production of the play and help students realize that any performance of Shakespeare's tragedy reflects the values and practices of the culture producing it. The volume ends with R. Alan Kimbrough's invitation to teach Shakespeare's play in conjunction with three translations of the play: Leonard Bernstein's musical *West Side Story,* Charles-François Gounod's French grand opera *Roméo et Juliette,* and Sergei Prokofiev's ballet *Romeo i Dzhuletta.*

Every reader will have favorite approaches among the twenty above-described essays. Locating favorites can be a pleasure in itself.

READING STRATEGIES

Authority in *Romeo and Juliet*

Arthur F. Kinney

The first disturbing moment in *Romeo and Juliet* comes in the opening lines of the Chorus, which struggles to be evenhanded and sure in its outline of a play about "A pair of star-crossed lovers":

> Two households, both alike in dignity,
>   In fair Verona, where we lay our scene,
> From ancient grudge break to new mutiny,
>   Where civil blood makes civil hands unclean.
> From forth the fatal loins of these two foes
>   A pair of star-crossed lovers take their life;
> Whose misadventured piteous overthrows
>   Doth with their death bury their parents' strife.
> The fearful passage of their death-marked love,
>   And the continuance of their parents' rage,
> Which, but their children's end, naught could remove,
>   Is now the two hours' traffic of our stage;
> The which if you with patient ears attend,
> What here shall miss, our toil shall strive to mend. (prologue 1–14)[1]

My students and I begin our class discussions inquiring about the tone and stance of the Chorus. Unlike the choruses that appear in other Shakespeare plays to set the scenes and set forth the issues, this one gives away the whole plot. Why, I ask the class, might Shakespeare reveal the plot? To remind a preoccupied audience of a familiar story? To provide a kind of program guide for the uninitiated? Or, more likely, to give the plot an interpretation that seems always already there? If the last is true, what is that interpretation? Can we break open the closed sonnet form of this speech that like Shakespeare's other sonnets describes a situation and then sums it up in a couplet that seems to close off the ideas with the form? Such phrases as "fatal loins," "star-crossed lovers," "fearful passage," "death-marked love," and even "continuance of their parents' rage," we note, tell us not only what will happen but also what we should think about dramatic events. The deliberate parallel of "Two households" and "both alike in dignity" is echoed in "ancient grudge" and "new mutiny." Moreover, the phrases "civil blood" and "civil hands" (ends and means) seem to insist on balancing the past and the present that gives the opening of this play a static quality, a frozen sense of events that undermines narrative progression and dramatic development. Having read the chorus, why should we read the play? The most we can get out of the play is the how of the what, the details that, however we read and interpret them, we know will lead us to "death-marked love, / And the continuance of their parents' rage." The attempt of the younger generation to oppose their elders will wind up defeated, and the static situation in Verona will continue.

Not many students I know would settle for such a conclusion despite the preponderance of supporting evidence in these fourteen opening lines. So the search is on to prove me wrong, or at least to prove that Shakespeare is also doing something else. The something else, students discover, is in line 14: "What here shall miss." It is possible that the narrative summary here is incomplete, and so the judgments of the Chorus may be contingent. Rather than shut down the story of Romeo and Juliet, the Chorus opens it up. Yet if the Chorus, speaking on behalf of the actors, will by "toil [. . .] strive to mend" what is omitted from this twelve-line program note, does this suggest that what is omitted will only fill in the details of the outline already presented, interpreted, and, in a sense, evaluated? Or might the judgments, and therefore the narrative, of the Chorus itself be suspect—in need not so much of refinement as of alteration? We return one more time to the earlier lines, this time to look for too-easy generalizations, leaps in logic, or even inconsistencies. There is the uncertainty, for instance, of the undefined "ancient grudge" and, further, of how such a grudge could be an efficient cause for generations of strife. The past is hazy, the time span indefinite. Verona seems hardly "fair" in the picture the Chorus paints here; is there any reason for such a judgment to be sustained? Do the deaths of Romeo and Juliet "bury their parents' strife" as line 8 unequivocally states, or is there "continuance of their parents' rage" as line 10 unhesitatingly pronounces? It may be that these first fourteen lines are less pronouncement than rationalization, that the Chorus displays a troubling hope for change, a hope that is here posited only in Romeo and Juliet, "star-crossed lovers" whose "misadventure[s]" are nevertheless "piteous." And how are we to understand the "but" in line 11? If it means "if," then "their children's end" in fact "could remove" the "parents' rage." This would mean that "naught" is at least ambiguous, and the lovers' sacrifice of their lives for the prevention of future generations of feuding (and perhaps dying—"civil blood") is necessarily heroic ("piteous" and "star-crossed" then take on positive meanings). As fate's agents, Romeo and Juliet save Verona's future and so make the city "fair."

I open with this exercise for several reasons, among them that it teaches close reading. Armed with this skill, students are not readily accepting of glib critics who, over the years, have lifted phrases like "star-crossed lovers" out of context and made the play a simple tragedy of fate. Such critics may note that the meeting of Romeo and Juliet happens just when Romeo is despairing over Rosaline and Juliet is uncertain about marrying Paris or that Friar John arrives too late in Mantua with the crucial message about the state of Juliet in the Capulet tomb. Both these "fearful" circumstances, I point out, stem from deliberate human choices in the play. The first arises out of Benvolio's misguided counsel and Romeo's too-easy acquiescence (as well as, perhaps, out of Romeo's conventional and callow belief that he really is in love). The second arises out of another series of choices, in which Romeo and Juliet put all their trust in Friar Lawrence, and the Friar, in turn, puts all his trust in his own scheme. Pinpointing these moments in the play, we turn what seems at first to be certain and deterministic into what is, in fact, human and mistaken. Then we go on to see what it is in the characters themselves that allows such misjudgments. Having done that, we can return, perhaps for a final time, to the opening chorus to ask why it did not address the issue of choice or, if it did, why in the end this issue seemed unimportant. Here I introduce Shakespeare's lifelong concern with the relative merits of narrative and drama and with the need of his characters (and presumably of his audiences) to make up stories to explain, to understand, and finally to accommodate or accept events. The Chorus, I propose, pushes this play into parable; there is hidden below the play's surface a need for moral order based on just deserts, a fear of striving, and a desire for the ending of all strife (which seems connected to striving). If we find the Chorus's statement unsettling because it is too neat and too directed, then, I argue, perhaps this is because parables paper over troublesome matters. Thus the lesson the Chorus teaches is to use the opening lines not merely as a premise against which to test the rest of the play but also as a premise against which to test the unquestioned statements of characters in the play and then, in turn, to examine the play not for its events but for its choices. If authority in *Romeo and Juliet* does not inhere in the deterministic statements of the Chorus, where do we find the play's most reliable authority for understanding the play?

Probably by now—surely by now, in my experience—some student will remark that the Chorus reappears at the beginning of act 2. The second chorus also bears examination:

> Now old desire doth in his deathbed lie,
> And young affection gapes to be his heir;

> That fair for which love groaned for and would die,
>   With tender Juliet matched, is now not fair.
> Now Romeo is beloved and loves again,
>   Alike bewitchèd by the charm of looks;
> But to his foe supposed he must complain,
>   And she steal love's sweet bait from fearful hooks.
> Being held a foe, he may not have access
>   To breathe such vows as lovers use to swear,
> And she as much in love, her means much less
>   To meet her new belovèd anywhere;
> But passion lends them power, time means, to meet,
> Temp'ring extremities with extreme sweet.   (1–14)

The question is, has anything changed? The form of this chorus is identical to that of the first—the closed Shakespearean sonnet, in which three quatrains are brought to completion by a rhymed couplet. But the whole substance has changed, from plot to process. The time scheme has changed, from the vast and distant overview to the involvement of in medias res: "Now." Judgments in the lines are open to question: "That fair [. . .] is now not fair." "[L]ove's sweet bait" is associated with "fearful hooks," and the implication is that Juliet should be aware of this, as should Romeo. What appears one-dimensional in the first chorus now seems rife with disturbing paradoxes. Thus the verse "And she as much in love, her means much less" contrasts Juliet's present state with a more desirable past one. This line and the earlier line about Romeo, "Alike bewitchèd by the charm of looks," raise questions about the reality (and fallibility) of the two young lovers that remove them from simple parable. The sonnet's conclusion, in fact, puts the power of passion into opposition with time and means, suggesting drama rather than narrative. In "Temp'ring extremities with extreme sweet" statements have now become propositions. The Chorus arguably stops speaking because it has run out of information and is waiting until more actions unfold. The Chorus has been transformed, perhaps by the power of passion, from program note to playhouse spectator and auditor. The Chorus is no longer telling us but rather mediating for us and becoming like us. We join forces with the Chorus to mediate (that is, interpret and anticipate).

The next question I pose in class is this: if the Chorus moves from telling us to guiding us, what does it do next? The answer is that it disappears—a disappearance as startling as that in *The Taming of a Shrew* of Christopher Sly. Why, I ask, would Shakespeare dismiss the Chorus?

The answer we usually arrive at (the best we can determine) is that the role of the Chorus is subsumed by other characters in the play. Since that role is one of authority, a suitable candidate appears only three scenes later when Friar Lawrence, in the soliloquy at his first appearance, adopts the same knowing, oracular role the Chorus had. Having mediated between the initial Chorus and the actors, the second Chorus now merges fully into one of the major characters. The Friar clothes his distant view in terms as judgmental and moral as those of the opening Chorus; he too seems to summarize the play in fourteen lines:

> The earth that's nature's mother is her tomb.
> What is her burying grave, that is her womb;
> And from her womb children of divers kind
> We sucking on her natural bosom find,
> Many for many virtues excellent,
> None but for some, and yet all different.
> O, mickle is the powerful grace that lies
> In plants, herbs, stones, and their true qualities;
> For naught so vile that on the earth doth live
> But to the earth some special good doth give;
> Nor aught so good but, strained from that fair use,
> Revolts from true birth, stumbling on abuse.
> Virtue itself turns vice, being misapplied,
> And vice sometime by action dignified.   (2.3.9–22)

The Friar's speech is interrupted by Romeo's sudden appearance, and here timing is all: if Romeo were to enter earlier, he would overhear a warning from the Friar firmer than the one Romeo receives subsequently. (We spend some time in class discussing the possibilities of different moments when Romeo could appear to the audience but not yet to the Friar—and how the timing would affect Romeo's choice and consequently his power to choose.)

But a closer look at Friar Lawrence, even in his opening speech, also raises questions about knowledge and self-knowledge. "Within the infant rind of this weak flower," he notes, "Poison hath residence and medicine power" (23–24). He concludes:

> Two such opposèd kings encamp them still
> In man as well as herbs—grace and rude will;
> And where the worser is predominant,
> Full soon the canker death eats up that plant.   (27–30)

The Friar's sense of paradox here, however, is no greater than that of the maturing Juliet, who has just told Romeo that "I should kill thee with much cherishing" (2.2.183) if given the chance. The Friar, moreover, seems confused, for in claiming to exercise grace in dealing with the young lovers he in fact imposes his own rude will without hesitation or modesty. What begins in 2.3 as a chastisement of Romeo for his swift dismissal of Rosaline for Juliet only anticipates the swift way in which the Friar takes upon himself the task of ending the generations-old feud. He does not at first attempt to enter the civil realm of Prince Escalus, whose division of Verona by separating the Capulets from the

Montagues only prolongs the feud (1.1.84–106), but in fact he usurps that realm by attempting singlehandedly to end the ancient grudge himself:

> But come, young waverer, come go with me.
> In one respect I'll thy assistant be;
> For this alliance may so happy prove
> To turn your households' rancor to pure love. (2.3.89–92)

Having stressed to himself (and to Romeo) the paradoxes in nature, the Friar now forgets all possibilities of paradox when, paradoxically, he volunteers for the duty of the Prince. But this unholy matrimony of church and state—which dissolves in the play's final scene, when the Friar inversely confesses to the Prince and the Prince absolves him—is not the worst of the Friar's disregard for the law. Hearing the confessions of Romeo and Juliet as might a priest (but not a friar), Friar Lawrence marries them secretly, without the traditional banns, thus violating the sacrament of his church.

This act itself hangs on a nice paradox that, in my experience, leads to energetic class discussion. On the one hand, Catholic practices may be sacrificed here—the Elizabethan Shakespeare, writing for a Protestant England after the Reformation, sets evil practices in Catholic Verona. But, on the other hand, in Elizabethan England an alternative to the practice of pronouncing banns three times before the church service of matrimony was the practice known as *sponsalia de praesenti*, whereby vows were exchanged in the presence of a witness (and what better witness to such a pledge than a man of the church?). The vows, though subject to consecration at a later time, were held to constitute full marriage. The problem, of course, is that this premarital contract—on which the action of *Measure for Measure* also turns—is a Protestant ritual, not a Catholic one. (Here we often discuss the comparative authority of private and public vows, those secret and those revealed, for here too a choice is made irrevocably.) However we leave this discussion—which may be impossible to resolve fully, since knowledge in this play is always potentially paradoxical rather than parabolic—we note that in due course the Friar will attempt to master life and death by helping Romeo to a secret exile and by giving Juliet a potion that (as she makes clear in her soliloquy in 4.3) may literally be a matter of life and death. The Friar would not only be priest but also Prince and God.

Who then *has* the necessary authority in this play? Not the elder Montagues, for all their concern for their son, or the Capulets, for all their disregard for the opinions and desires of their daughter. Like the Friar, the two families are limited—the Montagues by hoping for a rosier world in the future, the Capulets by using force to achieve their way. Not the Nurse, whose earthiness is finally both too worldly and too banal. Not Benvolio, whose optimistic attitude, like that of Romeo's father, knows little doubt and naively concentrates on wishing Romeo well. Not in Mercutio, for all his wisdom about the dangers of dreaming (a pointed lesson for Romeo); when driven to accidental death, he would set an epidemic free indiscriminately: "A plague a'both your houses! [. . .] Your houses!" (3.1.108–10; cf. 92). Mercutio's condemnation is at best a throwback to the equivocation of the first Chorus. Not in Tybalt initially or in Paris finally, the latter of whom would forsake justice and mercy for vengeance.

Instead, authority rests—if it rests anywhere—in the tragic heroes themselves. Juliet's choice and dismissal of aid from her parents, then her confessor, and finally her nurse show that Juliet is driven back to her own best judgments as, holding the vial in her hands, she measures the consequences of a potion that may work or may fail. In each instance, she chooses constantly. (Seen in this light, the Chorus's insistence that she is "star-crossed" is woefully misguided.) Sequentially, but in a kind of parallel, Romeo's choice to face death by returning at once to Verona is embodied in his decision to pause in Mantua to visit an apothecary and choose, literally, his own poison. Here, as later in the tomb, he will, like Juliet, voluntarily choose death. They die by no authority but their own; if they take on themselves the sins of their fathers (their *births* were "star-crossed"), they also take on themselves responsibility for their choice to marry secretly in the Friar's cell.

There are always some students in the class who see this analysis as hairsplitting. The need for the lovers to die in this play is not entirely of their own choosing, the students argue, because Romeo and Juliet were born into an ancient grudge not of their making. But the characters' sense of responsibility seems central to the final actions of the play when the Friar, returning to his function as chorus, gives a synopsis of the play and offers himself as a sacrifice (5.3.267–68), seeming to know that his special role will save him. So it does, and when the Prince says, "We still have known thee for a holy man" (270), he excuses both the Friar and himself. Although this point too usually leads to impassioned class discussion, there would seem to be no other answer. The Prince excuses the Friar—lets him off without any civil punishment—because the Friar is "a holy man" and therefore, apparently, answerable to a different, higher authority. But the line also betrays the Prince, who surrendered his authority early in the play by failing to provide justice and prevent bloodshed. Finally, the two sets of parents vie in establishing memorials for the deceased lovers, beginning a variant of the feud all over again. The Prince's final pronouncement of "A glooming peace" (5.3.305) openly subscribes to this failure.

In stark contrast to their elders, the young lovers, lying dead, have made choices and exercised responsibility and punishment. If Romeo and Juliet's sense of justice (and love) does not teach any of those who remain on stage, their bodies lie there as silent emblems of authority and responsibility. If we attempt to stage this last scene in our minds—as I often ask students to do—we see that the characters crowd on the stage as they have in only two other scenes in the play: the masked ball and the fight between the Capulets and the Montagues in 1.1. (The latter scene contrasts with the fight in 3.2 where the chief Montague refuses to engage in combat.) In fact, Romeo does not fight in the first scene either (he is absent) and Juliet is in neither scene. Now that

Romeo and Juliet appear with all the others for the first time, their silent presence judges everyone else.

There is another way to look at the staging scenes in the play. Given a discovery space that might hold large props or suggest privacy, the three episodes necessarily at the rear of the stage, taking up the same theatrical space, are the bedroom scenes and the scenes in the Friar's cell (and the apothecary shop), and all are displaced by the large tombs at the end. The bedroom tempts the body, the cell tempts the soul, but both temptations are overcome in the graveyard when the lovers voluntarily reunite. In the end, the dead teach us, the living; Romeo and Juliet, through their actions, experiences, and choices, finally meld paradox and parable. But they do more—by embodying the tragic significance of their story, they make the play's final choric comment. They displace the earlier, more limited Chorus because their wider, deeper comment on the risk and cost of life is one that the Chorus never understood. The authority of Romeo and Juliet, we usually conclude, is the authority the play has been searching for.

NOTE

[1] Citations to *Romeo and Juliet* in this essay are from the J. A. Bryant, Jr., edition.

"I Love You Madly, I Love You to Death": Erotomania and *Liebestod* in *Romeo and Juliet*

Ivo Kamps

In the director Baz Luhrmann's 1996 film *William Shakespeare's Romeo and Juliet,* a production set in contemporary gang-infested Verona Beach, California, Romeo ingests some type of narcotic, dispensed to him by Mercutio just before crashing the Capulet masked ball. The white pill bears a red heart, and the immediate implication is that Romeo will fall in love (with Juliet) at the party. The concoction, however, is not a simple love potion. When Romeo arrives at the party, we see the drug's effect: for Romeo, the action takes place in slow motion, the room spins around him as the disco music blares, and the faces of other characters appear to him abruptly and grotesquely. Romeo is not himself, and he seems about to pass out as the drug's disorienting effects overwhelm him. We who are watching this scene know that Romeo will shortly meet Juliet and fall in love with her, and we are therefore encouraged to consider the possibility that Romeo's love for Juliet is drug-induced (like Demetrius's for Helena at the close of *A Midsummer Night's Dream*). Unfortunately, Luhrmann pulls back unambiguously from his provocative intimation when he has Romeo plunge his head into a basin of cold water, from which Romeo emerges clear-eyed and refreshed. Romeo's perception and state of mind, we are to infer, have returned to normal. The frenzied disco music has been silenced and now we hear a soulful song. Romeo and Juliet see each other and fall instantly and madly in love.

In a Western literary tradition that idealizes heterosexual love, *madly* of course means "deeply" and has an unmistakably positive connotation: Romeo and Juliet's love is pure, wholesome, and transcendent. Such love flourishes, according to Lysander and Hermia in *A Midsummer Night's Dream,* despite or, indeed, because of objections of relatives and differences in age and social class; it is the quintessentially human emotion that brings persons together and produces marriages and makes possible social reproduction. Over the years, even critics who take a less idealizing view of romantic love have argued that *Romeo and Juliet* ends tragically because love is defeated by fate, society (Davis 64), patriarchal values (Novy 99–109), the feud (Kahn), bad timing, the lovers' own "rashness" (Stauffer 30), or what have you. Even Norman Rabkin, who pronounces Romeo and Juliet's love impetuous, irrational, and self-destructive, insists that precisely those self-destructive elements form the "foundation and essence of a transcendent love" (183). Despite Romeo's and Juliet's deaths, their love is finally thought to have sufficient redemptive qualities to rise above its inherent detriments. (Jonathan Goldberg ["*Open Rs*"] and Dympna Callaghan have recently mounted cogent critiques of the idealization of romantic love in *Romeo and Juliet.*) Such approval is often expressed by apotheosizing Romeo and Juliet and suggesting that the manner of their deaths should be read as "sexual consummation and as rebirth" (Kahn 103 [*Estate*]). In a different context, even Michel Foucault—who is not given to idealizing love—asserts that if a certain type of love affair leads to death, "it is a death in which the lovers will never be separated again" (31). Now when I teach the play, I use the image of Romeo's drug-induced disorientation in Luhrmann's film as a starting point for reevaluating the love between Romeo and Juliet. I ask students to resist what most of them have been taught in high school—that Romeo and Juliet are a match made in heaven and that the play is the greatest love story ever told—and to consider that the love between the Verona youths is so antisocial and disease-like in nature that it is mad beyond rehabilitation. I ask them to see it as an instance of what was known in the Renaissance as erotomania or love madness.

Notwithstanding the widely affirmed nobility of love in the Renaissance, it goes almost without saying that anyone who read the Petrarch-influenced poetry of Thomas Wyatt, Philip Sidney, and many others or the medical treatises of André Du Laurens (1599) and Timothy Bright (1586) or saw a play like Shakespeare's *A Midsummer Night's Dream* would be aware of the association of love and madness. That the subject of love madness remained current throughout the late Elizabethan and early Stuart periods is evidenced by plays such as *Hamlet* (1601) and John Fletcher's *The Mad Lover* (1617?) and by prose treatises such as Thomas Walkington's *Opticke Glasse of Humors* (1607), Robert Burton's *The Anatomy of Melancholy* (1621), and Walter Bruel's *Praxis Medicinae* (1639). But the subject's most vivid and explicit treatment is found in the physician Jacques Ferrand's *Erotomania* (1612), which, though not translated into English until 1640, analyzes in a pseudomedical context ideas about love madness that circulated widely during the second half of the sixteenth century.

Ferrand describes falling in love as follows:

> Once love deceives the eyes, which are the true spies and gatekeepers of the soul, she slips through the passageways, traveling imperceptibly by way of the veins to the liver where she suddenly imprints an ardent desire for that object that is either truly lovable, or appears so. There love ignites concupiscence and with such lust the entire sedition begins. [. . . L]ove turns directly upon the citadel of the heart, and once that salient stronghold is made subject, *she attacks the reason and all the noble forces of the brain* so vigorously that she overwhelms them and *makes them all her slaves.* Then all is lost: the man is finished, *his senses wander, his reason is deranged, his imagination becomes depraved, and his speech incoherent.* The poor lover thinks of nothing but his idol. [. . .] You will see him crying, sobbing, and sighing, gasp upon gasp, and in a state of perpetual inquietude, fleeing all company, preferring solitude and his own thoughts [. . .]. (*Treatise* 252, emphasis added)

Ferrand's account of love's assault—"a kind of poison" (229)—on the human psyche is based on traditional Renaissance conceptions of health. By entering the liver and spurring the overproduction of blood, love causes an imbalance in the ratio between the four humors—blood, choler, phlegm, and melancholy— present in the body. Minor imbalances do not have profound consequences; they merely determine a person's complexion (the predominance of blood, for instance, produces a sanguine temperament; see Du Laurens 84). A great abundance of or deficiency in one of the humors, however, has an adverse im- pact on the organ or organs nourished by the humor and can eventually cause severe physical and mental illness. Such humoral imbalance can result from a purely physiological origin (88), but it can also result from reason's failure to regulate the passions properly. "Concupiscible passions arise when the imagina- tion or the reasonable will perceives or conceives an object which appeals to it as pleasing and repellent. If the object is pleasing, the motion *love* is aroused. [. . .] From love arises *desire*, the inclination to possess whatever one loves [. . .]" (Babb 4). Typically, a passion coming from the sensible soul is amplified by a humoral response. When one falls in love, the liver produces additional blood, which raises the body's heat and moisture (the attributes of blood). When the soul functions properly, reason, which has the ability to determine a passion's appropriateness, either initiates or authorizes the passion. It is also possible, however, for the humors to "stimulate passion without authorization of any mental faculty" (12). Lack of authorization can then lead to an excess of passion and can cause fever, frenzy, and even hallucinations. If the love-mad person is not cured, he might become "melancholy, foolish, misanthropic, maniacal, and lycan- thropic" (as we see in Webster's *Duchess of Malfi*) (Ferrand 229; see also Du Laurens 89). In the most severe cases, the victim can go "stark mad" (Babb 136).

In discussing the love between Romeo and Juliet, however, I do not simply want to show that their passions override their reason—although an excess of passion plays a key part in their journey into madness. In addition to consider- ing physiological (humoral) and psychological (passion) approaches, I also look at Romeo and Juliet's love madness from social and, to a lesser extent, religious standpoints. The social dimension of madness ranks as most important here be- cause, no matter what the ultimate nature of madness may be (if in fact mad- ness has an ultimate nature), it is more clear than ever after Foucault's *Madness and Civilization* that public, religious, and medical perceptions of what mad- ness is, and how it should be treated, change. Madness has a (social) history.

David Ingleby points out that there are three prevailing models for identify- ing and thinking about madness. First, there is the disease model, which "re- gards underlying physical pathology as the core of true 'mental illness.' " This view has its roots in the ancient world and is manifest in the Renaissance hu- moral theories of Timothy Bright, Robert Burton, Thomas Walkington, Philip Barrough, and others. The second model defines mental illness as a "deviation of *moral* conduct," which, as one might expect, in the Renaissance is persistently linked to questions of religion. The third model holds that "criteria of *intelligi-bility* are central to the ascription of mental illness." The fundamental distinction between the second and third model is that the latter "proposes that the mentally ill do not deviate from the norms of *morality* so much as of *rationality*" (124, emphasis added). However, it is easy to see how these two models can become conflated when what a society finds intelligible is also what it considers moral, and vice versa. The act of suicide, for instance, was viewed in Shakespeare's day both as an immoral and irreligious act and as an irrational act—indeed, as an act of madness. Things become even more complicated when we recognize that standards of both morality and rationality change over time and that therefore all judgments of madness are inherently social in character. Of course the disease model itself, especially the theory of humors, can also be viewed as an elaborate metaphor designed to give physiological grounding to medical judgments that were not based on valid physiological testing.

Another point of confluence among these three models of psychiatry is their understanding of the relation between madness and identity. If humoral balance and moral and rational behavior stabilize and solidify one's social identity, by making one recognizable to others and constituting a social self, then a serious deficiency in any of these areas is likely to give the impression that one is, to paraphrase Robert Burton, beside oneself (Babb 136). We perceive just how vital the link between social identity (or "subject position," as Catherine Belsey has termed it [*Subject* 5]) and sanity is when we witness the loss of social identity. King Lear's voyage into the gorge of madness starts with a disavowal of his crown and the surrender of his power; both crown and power have shaped his identity in crucial ways. "Only we shall retain / The name and all th'addition to a king" (Folio 1.1.133–34), the king declares, unable to recognize that a name without significant power to prop it up means nothing in the world of realpolitik.[1] "This is not Lear," a befuddled Lear soon asserts. "Who is it that can tell me who I am?" (Folio 1.4.191, 195). The identity crisis following sociopolitical change eventually results in madness. Similarly, Ophelia goes mad when the subject positions usually available to a young aristocratic woman are taken from her. Her father and brother, the king, and Hamlet all use her for their own purposes, destroying her social identity as obedient daughter and sister and as future wife. Apparently, characters like Lear and Ophelia have no recesses of inner strength (a sense of self that is generated from within) on which they can draw in the midst of crisis. Madness ensues. In *The Comedy of Errors,* we see Shakespeare's comedic approach to the same issues. Throughout this play, the Antipholus brothers are mistaken for each other. They look like themselves but do not act like themselves and are accordingly deemed mad by those around them (see 2.1.56, 4.1.93, 4.3.76)—a quack exorcist is eventually brought in to cast out the devil (4.4). That the Antipholuses are not actually mad is not the issue; the society around them is ready to diagnose as insane those persons who fail to perform the identity by which they are known in their community.

The main challenge in discussing *Romeo and Juliet* as a play trafficking in madness is that, unlike Lear and Ophelia, neither Romeo nor Juliet ever lapses into the virtual incoherence and disjointed speech commonly associated with madness on the Renaissance stage (see Neely 323–25). The reason for this difference is that love is a socially endorsed form of madness that has its own Petrarchan or courtly language. Nonetheless, a strong case can be made that Romeo and Juliet's love for each other qualifies as madness in the context of the three models just discussed.

If we take Ferrand's description of love madness as our starting point for considering love in *Romeo and Juliet*, few would deny that Romeo's love for Rosaline exhibits most if not all of the traits Ferrand enumerates. Though Romeo's speech is not incoherent, Romeo appears distracted during his encounter with Benvolio and shows all the signs of one whose liver has been visited by love: he groans (1.1.193), thinks himself ill (196), speaks of tears and sleeplessness (185, 174), is secretive (142), seeks solitude whenever possible, and wanders nightly through the sycamore grove outside the city walls. "Tut, I have lost myself. I am not here," Romeo says, echoing Lear and Robert Burton. "This is not Romeo; he's some other where" (1.1.190–91). And we may glimpse the depravity of imagination to which Ferrand refers when Romeo reveals that Rosaline will not "ope her lap to saint-seducing gold" (1.1.207). Apparently Romeo has made the offer. He self-diagnoses his love as "A madness most discreet, / A choking gall and a preserving sweet" (1.1.186–87). He later retracts that diagnosis only to reveal that he is "bound *more* than a madman is; / Shut up in prison, kept without my food, / Whipped and tormented" (1.2.53–55, emphasis added). Indeed, just as Ferrand describes it, Romeo's reason has been overcome by love, and Romeo has become love's abject slave.

So while there is no doubt that love for Rosaline brings Romeo the psychic torment and physical illness commonly associated with love madness, critics have come to Romeo's (and love's) rescue by arguing that Romeo's love for Juliet is more mature than this Petrarchan passion for Rosaline is and that his love for Juliet returns him to mental health (see Hapgood, *Shakespeare* 84–85; Marsh 50–51). As Ronald Knowles argues, the opposite may in fact be true, namely that Romeo's love for Rosaline, which is played down in Shakespeare's source, undermines the purportedly ideal love for Juliet (74–75). If Romeo's claim to be beside himself with love for Rosaline is a sign of his social isolation and love madness, then his love for Juliet constitutes a far greater assault on his identity. For Romeo and for Juliet—representatives of enemy clans—to denounce their names and form a relationship with each other is to cast off their social identities and future places in Verona and family life. As we can see by Capulet's treatment of Juliet when she refuses to marry Paris (a refusal that makes her completely unintelligible to her parents), Romeo and Juliet's relationship turns the lovers into exiles who will no longer be acknowledged as members of their respective families.

Moreover, as Ferrand and other Renaissance physicians maintain, it is not only obsessive love of the unrequited variety that contains elements of madness. Even when a relationship is reciprocal, "lovers necessarily suffer some degree of mental derangement" (Babb 136). They are "mad-men [. . .] fools [. . .] beside themselves" (Burton qtd. in Babb 136). Ferrand, for instance, strongly agrees with Cicero that even an ideal love relationship contains "elements of interest or of lust, and that above all men 'must be warned of the madness of the passion of love. For of all disturbances of the soul there is assuredly none more violent. [. . . T]he disorder of the mind in love is *in itself* abominable'" (Beecher and Ciavolella 113, emphasis added). Love is deemed a pathology because it is considered an unnatural state of being. "For were love a matter of nature all men would love, as well as always love and love the same object" (Cicero qtd. in Beecher and Ciavolella 113). Like many Renaissance medical writers, Ferrand follows classical authority and asserts "that love or erotic passion is a form of dotage, proceeding from an inordinate desire to enjoy the beloved object" (238).

In the play, Benvolio confirms the inherent pathology of love when he counsels a cure for Romeo's ailment and describes the next woman in Romeo's life as a "new infection to thy eye," which will cause "the rank poison of the old" to die (1.2.49, 50). The disease called love cannot be cured; it can only be replaced by the next infection, which will of course be Romeo's love for Juliet. The only difference, therefore, between Romeo's love for Rosaline and his love for Juliet is that the former is unrequited and has had time to turn to melancholy love sickness (Romeo's obsessive thoughts about Rosaline have consumed heat and moisture), whereas the love for Juliet, because it is reciprocated, will for the time being remain sanguine (see Babb 134). But Romeo's passion for Juliet is just as excessive and dangerous to his mental health as was his passion for Rosaline. It is the same "overwhelmingly powerful [. . .] erotic impulse [that] impels men headlong into folly and evil" (Babb 133).

This "inordinate desire" is given voice by Juliet just before the wedding ceremony when she proclaims, "[T]rue love is grown to such excess / I cannot sum up sum of half my wealth" (2.5.33–34). The same mad intensity is evident when Romeo, pressing the Friar to haste, urges, "Do thou but close our hands with holy words, / Then love-devouring death do what he dare— / It is enough I may but call her mine" (2.5.6–8). The Friar sees the potential for utter self-destruction in Romeo's haste and reckless desire and cautions, "These violent delights have violent ends, / And in their triumph die like fire and powder, / Which as they kiss consume" (2.5.9–11). That madness could lead to suicide was widely understood in the Renaissance (MacDonald 132–38), and that Shakespeare knew as much is clear from the gravediggers' scene in *Hamlet*.

From the church's and society's points of view, of course, Romeo's passionate claim runs counter to the very purposes of marriage, which are to regulate human sexuality and to promote the ordered reproduction of social formations (that is, the orderly transfer of title, wealth, privilege, and property; see Callaghan 59–62). Indeed, especially in aristocratic circles, love had to exist in the service of social and religious interests. "If love is directed by reason and if it has social and religious sanctions, it is conducive to man's physical and spiritual welfare" (Babb 133). Despite the Friar's willingness to marry the young lovers, it is clear that they lack social as well as religious sanction. As Rabkin (182–83) and others have observed, Romeo and Juliet's love is from its inception cast in idolatrous terms, underscoring their obvious lack of devotion to Christianity and strongly insinuating a heretical dimension to their relationship (see 1.5.90–107; note that here too Romeo's love for Juliet echoes his love for Rosaline—see 1.2.88–93). Romeo, in fact, appears to be saying that the very instant of marital union will make his life complete. (Note that Othello makes a similar observation but that Desdemona's response indicates that she hopes they will have a long life ahead of them [2.1.190–92].) We have already suggested that Romeo and Juliet's decision to abandon their names and to shed their clan identities constitutes a form of social madness, and Romeo's view of the social institution of marriage has to be considered part of that madness. Of course at this point there is nothing especially surprising about Romeo's eager association of love and death; we saw him make this association as early as the balcony scene. And Juliet did so even earlier than that. At the end of the Capulets' banquet, before she knows that Romeo is of the house of Montague, she exhorts, "If he be marrièd, / My grave is like to be my wedding bed" (1.5.131–32).

However, it is also clear that Romeo does look beyond the marriage ceremony itself (though we need not doubt the earnestness of his attraction to "love-devouring death") as he fervently anticipates sexually consummating his relationship. The Friar understands as much and says, "[Y]ou shall not stay alone / Till Holy Church incorporate two in one" (2.5.36–37). Now it was a common assumption among Renaissance physicians that sexual activity would lessen desire and cure love madness (Babb 137). But after Romeo and Juliet have sexual intercourse, there is no indication whatsoever that Romeo has achieved humoral balance—that his passion for Juliet is any less excessive than it was—or that he will become reintegrated into the fabric of society. Almost immediately after consummation, Romeo again announces his readiness to die: "Let me be ta'en, let me be put to death. / I am content, so thou wilt have it so" (3.5.17–18). In fact, if it were not for the Friar and Nurse, Juliet and Romeo would have been dead before the beginning of the fifth act (see 3.3.106–07, 4.1.53–54). Teetering on the brink of suicide, contemplating death at the slightest provocation, Romeo and Juliet are so overwhelmed by their passion that they are profoundly helpless and altogether unable to function on their own.

On the whole, however, critics have suppressed love's madness and instead focused on the lovers' deaths as a *Liebestod* in which love somehow overcomes death. Romeo and Juliet themselves do not seem to consider death the absolute end. As Coppélia Kahn has argued, the manner of Romeo's and Juliet's deaths "bring[s] together the idea of death as sexual consummation and as rebirth" (103 [*Estate*]). Romeo, on drinking the poison, says, "Thy drugs are quick" (5.3.120). If we take "quick" to mean "life," then Romeo's equating poison with life is consistent with Juliet's calling the same poison a "restorative" when she kisses Romeo's lips (5.3.166). Stephen Greenblatt suggests that "restorative" refers to "both the kiss, which is healing, and the poison, which restores them to each other" (*Norton Shakespeare* 936).

But if Romeo and Juliet do not see death as the end, how are we to envision what awaits them? Is it possible that they are completely self-deceived and that nothing awaits them? We have already seen that they worshipped love in the language of religion and that they paid little attention to religion itself. Given both social and religious prohibitions against suicide, they cannot reasonably expect to enter heaven. Nor is there any indication that they anticipate going to hell (or to heretical limbo, for that matter). What does lie beyond death for the lovers? The protagonist of John Fletcher's *The Mad Lover* contemplates cutting out his heart in the hope that he and his beloved will be together in Elysium, but Romeo does not appear to have such a vision. *"Here, here* will I remain / With worms that are thy chambermaids," he says next to what he believes is Juliet's corpse (5.3.108–09, emphasis added). Juliet, likewise, offers no image of a life beyond death, yet she calls the poison on Romeo's lips "a restorative." How are we to square the language of consummation, rebirth, and renewal with the absence of even the slightest hint of what is next? One explanation is that when Romeo and Juliet each believe the other dead, passion completely clouds the lovers' senses. Madness, Foucault points out, can take the form of "desperate passion": "love deceived by the fatality of death [. . .] has no other recourse but madness. As long as there was an object, mad love was more love than madness; left to itself, it pursues itself in the void of delirium" (30). Indeed, perhaps Romeo and Juliet do not plan to go anywhere; perhaps their suicide is merely the final logical retreat into the vortex that is their love madness.

Delirium is the inevitable result of a process of isolation that begins long before the scene in the tomb. Already in the balcony scene, Romeo and Juliet's love manifests itself as secret and all-consuming; though not yet ominous, the process of withdrawal from the world begins. Romeo and Juliet quickly become like John Donne's lovers in "The Sun Rising": "She is all states, and all princes I; / Nothing else is" (lines 21–22). They become each other's world, and "they divest themselves of the world as of a thing of no value" (Rabkin 186). But after Romeo kills Tybalt the choices become difficult. In killing Tybalt, Romeo momentarily reenters the world of clan loyalty, but he quickly regrets his act. Juliet chooses Romeo over loyalty to her kinsman and follows her choice with a rejection of her parents and, ultimately, of the Nurse, who breast-fed and raised her. Delirium begins to set in soon after Romeo's enforced banishment separates the lovers. Passion, lacking a love object, turns back on itself—reducing their world yet further—and manifests itself in helplessness, attempted suicide, and despair. Therefore, we can look at Romeo's and Juliet's suicides in two ways (which really mean the same thing): either the lovers leave a world they have long since left behind, or their suicides do not constitute a departure at all— they merely give in to the delirium of love and enter its ultimate isolation.

But how exactly does madness relate to death? Or, to put the question more accurately, what is the relation between the awareness of death and the awareness of madness? Common sense suggests that death supersedes madness, but Foucault offers a different, counterintuitive answer when he writes that "madness is the *déjà-là* [already there] of death." What he seems to mean by this is that toward the end of the Middle Ages there occurs a shift, or "torsion concerning people's attitudes toward death." Up until that moment, "the theme of death reigned alone. [. . .] What overhangs all human existence is this conclusion and this order from which nothing escapes." Toward the end of the fifteenth century, however, "this enormous uneasiness [about death] turns on itself; the mockery of madness replaces death and its solemnity" (15). This mockery is reflected in such works as Pieter Brueghel's *Dulle Griet,* Hieronymus Bosch's *The Cure of Madness* and *Ship of Fools,* Brant's poem *Das Narrenshiff,* and Erasmus's *Praise of Folly*—to name just a few—and signifies that human beings have shifted from contemplating death as "that necessity which inevitably reduces man to nothing [. . .] to the contemplation of that nothing which is existence itself" (Foucault 15–16). In the process, death loses much of its potency because it is now understood that "life itself was only futility, vain words, a squabble of cap and bells" (16). In other words, when life and all its activities are experienced as absurd, then the loss of life (to death) is no great loss indeed. Madness becomes the central experience as we act in and plan and live our lives in the face of absurdity—in the face of the nothingness of existence—and in the face of death. Madness becomes the insight or experience that shapes our sense of death; it becomes the *déjà-là* of death.

Although Romeo and Juliet do not embrace madness as a defense against death in the way Foucault describes, it does seem that their excessive passion produces such an extreme and irrevocable isolation from the world that the world ceases to have meaning for them. Neither of them considers a path out of the tomb back into the world of the living. Not love for family or love for friends or love of God or the promise of new love can bring them back. It seems that if, according to Foucault, madness becomes the determining signifier in the "contemplation of that nothing which is existence," we could say that Romeo and Juliet reach this same point of madness but by a different road: as the world loses meaning and as they lose the object of their desire, the madness—the madness that is inherent in all love and that flourishes as the desire for the object grows more inordinate—is all that remains.

During the play's final scene we witness the reappropriation, or, should we say, the resocialization, of the young lovers by the parents and Prince Escalus. As the opening Chorus predicted, the death of Romeo and Juliet has brought peace between the families and peace to Verona, turning the earlier clan-like rejection of the Prince's authority into acceptance, a transformation that is necessary for the functioning of the centralized protomodern state. The Prince stresses that with the death of Romeo and Juliet heaven itself has punished the Montagues and the Capulets for their uncivil broils. The assertion serves the Prince's authority and also places Romeo and Juliet's love within God's providence. The penitent fathers vow to raise golden statues to commemorate publicly the sacrifice of the children for the social good. But how would this public display strike Romeo and Juliet? Nowhere in the play do Romeo and Juliet view their love as a means of bringing the families together. Indeed, even in death Romeo and Juliet's love remains profoundly unintelligible to their parents. The only way to make Romeo and Juliet sane and to make their love "restorative" is to mourn the loss of the young lovers and to reappropriate their love for the moral and rational agenda of civilized Verona, where the Prince asserts his legal and ideological power over feuding families.

Contemporary interpreters of the play not only rehabilitate the lovers but also embrace and refashion the love madness itself. Luhrmann has Romeo and Juliet die in a candle-lit church and so sanctifies their love (and death). As Luhrmann's camera pulls back from the dead bodies, we get a close-up of the inscription on Juliet's ring, which reads, "I love thee"—implying that the love somehow continues. The scene ends with a still image of Romeo and Juliet kissing under water, taken from the balcony scene. The lovers look tranquil and happy in their embrace; their love is frozen in mid-action—a sad but romantic moment for the audience to linger on. We are encouraged to read their death through an image of their life and love and to feel some redemption. If we take the bait (and many of us have) we may be responding to our own wishful desire that passionate love and marriage are compatible—that love "grown to such excess" can be contained by a social institution—and forgetting that such a desire was far less paramount in aristocratic circles in Elizabethan England (see Stone, *Family* 70). Shakespeare and many of his contemporaries acknowledged the madness in love; but for many modern interpreters not even self-destruction can dampen our relentless glorification of love madness. Love, it seems, remains one of the last bastions of modern life that we are unwilling to demystify.

NOTE

[1] Citations in this essay are from *The Norton Shakespeare.*

"Now Art Thou What Thou Art"; or, Being Sociable in Verona: Teaching Gender and Desire in *Romeo and Juliet*

Thomas Moisan

That gender has a good deal to do with the tragedy of *Romeo and Juliet,* that *Romeo and Juliet* derives its tragedy in no small measure from the relation between the love of the eponymous protagonists and what is expected of them, or what they expect of themselves, as a male and female in Verona, has been a thesis often and in various forms compellingly rehearsed in recent criticism of the play. To heed such criticism and teach *Romeo and Juliet* with an ear for what gender can tell us about the nature of its tragedy has, as Joan Ozark Holmer notes, enriched the possibilities of the play for students ("Practices" 191–92). For one thing, to do so helps students parse the tragedy in social terms, inviting them, for example, to view Romeo and Juliet not simply as male and female but as male and female in—or, to recall the pointedly anthropological title of Coppélia Kahn's influential piece, "coming of age in"—Verona. Nor is this identification of sexual identity with social prescription a mere imposition of late-twentieth-century psychosocial theory on an early modern text. Indeed, we hear this identification articulated in a celebrated instance within the play by one of Verona's two foremost social-psychological theorists, Mercutio: momentarily pleased with Romeo for acting like one of the guys, Mercutio intones in holistic and mystificatory benediction, "Now art thou sociable, now art thou / Romeo; now art thou what thou art, by art as well as / by nature" (2.4.89–91). And, of course, we hear it in an equally notorious malediction by the other, less secularly humanist social-psychological theorist, Friar Lawrence: momentarily displeased with Romeo for his reluctance to patiently accept the dilemma that Friar Lawrence himself has had a significant hand in creating, the Friar hits, as it were, below the belt, taking Romeo's behavior as evidence of not acting like one of the guys and, thus, of acting unnaturally:

> Art thou a man? Thy form cries out thou art;
> Thy tears are womanish, thy wild acts [denote]
> The unreasonable fury of a beast.
> Unseemly woman in a seeming man,
> And ill-beseeming beast in seeming both [. . .].
> (3.3.109–13, bracketed word in original)

In turn, in the degree to which the action of the play seems to draw notions of identity (including sexual identity) and social expectation into a combustibly conflictual nexus, rendering it impossible, for example, for Romeo both to do what Verona expects of a man and to love Juliet in Verona, the consideration of gender offers students an interpretative alternative to the classic, Aristotelian decorums for tragic action and character against which the play had long been rather invidiously measured. To allot gender a role in what makes this tragedy tragic is to liberate our teaching of *Romeo and Juliet* from such narrowly generic questions as whether the play's tragic instrumentality is overly dependent on the aleatory; whether the play's protagonists are not so much tragic as pathetic victims of Fortune and poor timing, dramatic scions of—if less tragically mirthful than—Pyramus and Thisbe; and ultimately whether this play is less mature and, by implication, less satisfactory than those we associate with Shakespeare's tragic maturity, *Hamlet,* for example, and Shakespeare's Jacobean tragedies.

Still, though the consideration of gender provides students with a social calculus with which to delineate the tragedy of *Romeo and Juliet,* this approach is not unproblematic. For it could be asked whether, in deposing Fortune or bad luck as the primum mobile of the tragedy, the attention to gender that has marked recent criticism of the play runs the risk of enshrining a mystificatory and reductive determinism of its own. If we accept, for example, Susan Snyder's powerful account of the powerful control of ideology and the feud over gender roles in Verona ("Ideology" 88–92) or concur with Jonathan Goldberg's argument that "what the ending of the play secures is a homosocial order" ("*Open Rs*" 219), are we not being asked to see Romeo and Juliet once again as victims of a controlling social order that has no place for their love or for their subjectivity as lovers and characters? In rejecting what Verona and its feud ordain for its male and female children, have Romeo and Juliet been given no choice but to die, not Fortune's fools, to paraphrase Romeo, but society's pawns?

That the answers to these questions are not uncomplicated testifies to the fact that *Romeo and Juliet* has long been perceived in the theater and in the classroom to have a power that transcends a paraphrase of the play's pathetic premises, a power derived at least in part, I would contend, from audiences' and students' recognition in the play of the force of desire: immanent, ineluctable, nonnegotiable, and—as the recurrent ability of the play to evoke current events and the most powerfully self-destructive impulses of adolescence demonstrates—subversive and dangerous.[1] In what follows I argue that in *Romeo and Juliet* gender and desire are integrally, but intricately, related and that to examine the inscriptions and prescriptions of gender in teaching *Romeo and Juliet* is inevitably to bring gender and desire into a tangency that highlights the irruptive force of desire and the repressive function of gender. Indeed, even as we are led to see gender as a socially constructed and ordained decorum, as a set of expectations that, to recall the mystificatory rhetoric of Mercutio's and Friar Lawrence's formulations, elides sexual identity and social behavior, placing what we are by art in apposition to what we are by nature, we are simultaneously made aware of, to recall Goldberg's word "energies" ("*Open Rs*" 226), forces erotic and libidinal that resist the prescriptions of gender. In fact, what may get lost in deterministic readings of the play, in the Althusserian sense of ideology as omnipresent and inescapable, is the possibility that Romeo and Juliet's love is not only a casualty of the way things are in Verona but also a danger to it.

To look at *Romeo and Juliet* through the lens gender provides is ultimately to invite students to consider the ambivalent relation of the play to the very structures and ideology the play would seem to represent. Exposing gender as a powerful but vulnerable patriarchal construction designed to repress or contain volatile realities, over which the structures and strictures of gender and patriarchy are ultimately powerless, the play simultaneously mystifies its own inability to explain those forces that would undermine the patriarchal order. The play persistently retreats, like Romeo in his Petrarchan oxymorons, into a discourse of conundrums: witness the paradox of civil blood making civil hands unclean with which the prologue describes life in Verona (4) and the paradoxical cohabitations and contiguities Friar Lawrence ponders in his garden—poisons and medicines in herbs, grace and rude will in humankind (2.3.23–28). Indeed, departing a bit from readings that take Romeo and Juliet's love as something opposed to, stolen from, and a casualty of the patriarchal, masculine violence metonymized in the Capulets and Montagues' feud (Gohlke; Kahn; Novy), I offer students the alternative that if we see both Romeo and Juliet's love and the violence of the feud as phenomena that, like death, are impervious to patriarchal control, then the love and the feud, though circumstantially opposed, become uncannily parallel symptoms of the imponderables at the heart of human experience from which the play derives its sense of tragedy.

For evidence of how gender is implicated in the social structure of Shakespeare's Verona, we do not, of course, have long to wait. Initiating the rich social cacophony that constitutes the opening scene of the play, the exchange between the Capulets' loyal retainers Sampson and Gregory turns the question of what it means to be "civil" in Verona into a seminar on what Robert Appelbaum has called the "ambivalent prosthetics of masculinity" (252), namely, to stand or to stir? How richly this passage serves as a paradigm for the semiotics of gender and sociability in the play! Adumbrating other exchanges between young men who seem not to have much to do with their time, the dialogue affords an inventory of all the things likely to happen when young men get together in unspecified outdoor sites in Verona, or what Benvolio later calls "the public haunt of men" (3.1.50): they pun, distinguishing themselves as males by differentiating themselves from females, and their puns veer allusively toward sexuality and violence; they play, and their play merges seamlessly with actions freighted with heavy consequences. A linguistic economy unites their sexual and martial selves into one masculine identity, making them what they are, by art as well as by nature, and enabling them at once to keep their "tool" and "naked weapon" "out" (1.1.31, 33) and to elide the boundary between sexual fantasy and "naked aggression." Ludic and trivial, Sampson and Gregory impart some of their triviality to their masters and social superiors who follow them directly onstage in that, as Kahn has noted, the latter parody their inferiors by taking up the brawl Sampson and Gregory have helped to reignite (174 [Lenz, Greene, and Neely]). And inasmuch as the lethal feud is sustained by such lightweights as these, the feud itself, to anticipate one of Romeo's phrases, assumes a "heavy lightness" (1.1.178) and becomes one more of the oxymorons that make life in Verona what it is.

Still, one other truth about gender, or, rather, the genders, in Verona that students can hear heralded in this opening exchange—and it is a point so obvious as generally to go unnoted in criticism—is how rigidly and profoundly the sexes in Verona are segregated. Here, of course, we might say that Shakespeare takes his cue from his putative source, Arthur Brooke's *Romeus and Juliet,* a poetic narrative in which the protagonists exist for long stretches in relative isolation, attenuated mainly by the confessions each shares with a confidante, and surrogate parent, of the same sex—Romeo's "ghostly sire" (line 559, Munro ed.), Friar Laurence, and Juliet's Nurse (341–47, 557–60, 565–86, 619–30). Yet in translating Brooke's verse narrative into the scenic divisions of the stage, Shakespeare creates units of dramatic action that, in giving us a far more vivid sense of Verona as a living, breathing—if somewhat dysfunctional—social organism, divide that organism as much by gender as by hierarchies of rank and status. Indeed, rather like the "[t]wo households, both alike in dignity," whose feud is the donnée of the play (prologue 1), males and females in *Romeo and Juliet* do not mingle much in public and, not coincidentally, when they do mingle it is in moments of chaos or some other form of social disorder. Both sexes appear, for example, in the terminal stages of the riots in acts 1 and 3 and in the turmoil that attends the carnage in the Capulets' tomb in act 5. The sexes also mingle, of course, at Capulet's masked ball, an event that, by Capulet's own description, is very much about a setting aside of rules. At the ball, such social niceties as those governing who may have a special claim to whom are suspended in favor of a more open invitational and empirical wooing process (1.2.20–33), the disruptive consequences of which need no recapitulation. And when, in quest of Romeo, Juliet's Nurse happens on a group of males hanging out, her appearance is greeted by Romeo as well as by his friends with hilarity and verbal abuse and insinuation about her likely profession (2.4.101–44). Nor is it only when a female enters a male domain that the play reaffirms this segregation by gender. When in a paroxysm of domesticity and micromanagement Capulet concerns himself with culinary details for the upcoming nuptials of his daughter and Paris, the Nurse, with a freedom of address she nowhere else displays toward Capulet, conflates slurs on his gender and social status in a single epithet of social derision, dubbing him "cot-quean" (4.4.3–8).[2]

And, indeed, to remind students that in contemporary performance the two sexes would have been represented onstage by actors of the same sex only sharpens their sense of the social taxonomies dividing Verona's physical space into gender-coded, homosocial realms, realms that acquire definition only when their boundaries are violated. In turn, students are quick to speculate on what else these divisions may tell us about the relations of the sexes in the play. Though students are not particularly interested in gender as an abstract concept, they are interested in the roles played by gender and desire in shaping those relations—or, rather, those nonrelations. After all, apart from Romeo and Juliet, men and women in this play seem not to have relations, at least not intimate relations; on the contrary, they glance at and away from one another along a frontier of emotional sublimation and rhetorical double-dealing. To be sure, as we saw in Sampson and Gregory's dialogue, men talk about women and sex a fair amount, though, of course, they do so punningly, as if allowing the drift of language to carry them to topics they are not supposed to discuss. And when references to women arise, one may question whether they do so from the force of desire or from the desire for argumentative force. The exchange between Gregory and Sampson unfolds less as a dialogue than as a verbal joust, in which contra Gertrude, there is less matter and more art. Their exchange is a forerunner (for duller wits) to the virtuoso competition in paronomasia we will hear later in the wild-goose chase staged by Mercutio and Romeo, their verbal jousting a part of the rhetorical educational tradition that located masculinity, as Walter Ong has argued, in verbal prowess (129–39), or what John Donne calls his "masculine perswasive force" (Elegies, "On His Mistris," line 4). One may well cite the misogyny in the crude and sexually violent verbiage about women that segues into the crude and violent clash with employees of the Montagues. The abuse of women in this patter lies not in any emotional vehemence Sampson and Gregory display but in their detachment. The rape they envision is matched by the rhetorical rape they perpetrate in seizing on women as tropes and translating women into general categories ("weaker vessels [who] are ever thrust to the wall"), into accessories by alliteration to the Montague clan ("any man or maid of Montague's"), and lastly into metonyms for the violence Sampson will visit on the Montagues: " 'Tis all one" (1.1.16, 12, 21).

This opening exchange offers but a snapshot of the emotional ethos in which Romeo and Juliet live, move, and have their being and in and against which they take their love. The exchange represents Verona as a world in which men evince their masculinity in their proclivity for divorcing sexual reference and emotion and for sublimating feelings of desire through an array of rhetorical devices. The Verona of *Romeo and Juliet* is a world students can savor for its remarkable emotional dishonesty, a world where efforts at displacement tend to be most successful at revealing their own strenuousness, marginalizing desire while simultaneously keeping it visible on the margins of discourse, never fully dispelling its emotional residue. Exemplary is the frequent use of puns or double meanings, which, in imbedding sexual valences among the competing possibilities, keeps these valences diffused and unacknowledged but ever present. "Peace, peace, Mercutio, peace! / Thou talk'st of nothing" (1.4.95–96): in halting Mercutio's revery on Queen Mab just as Mercutio has made reference to sexual copulation, Romeo's characteristically repressive intervention undoes itself with its own cleverness. Though the allusion to female genitals conveyed in the secondary sense of "nothing"—a pun into which Romeo strayed earlier in the play (1.1.182)—indicates precisely what Romeo seeks, as it were, to abort in Mercutio's monologue, the very secondary-ness of the allusion has the effect of keeping open by suggestion, indeed, italicizing, a subject Romeo wants to change. Like other instances of men's erected wit in the play, this one keeps repression and suggestions of desire in a liminal embrace.

In his rhetorical virtuosity, no one in the play is more masculine—or more liminal—than Mercutio; that is, no one invokes with greater urgency the powers of "masculine perswasive force" at once to exorcise desire, only, then, to make us feel more keenly its encroachment. We feel the repressive force of Mercutio's wit in the verbal foreplay to his lethal exchange with Tybalt. Here Mercutio deflects the sexual potential in Tybalt's remark, "Mercutio, thou consortest with Romeo," by purposefully mis-taking "consort" in its musical sense, thus turning Tybalt's derision of Mercutio and Romeo's relationship into a slur on their social standing: "Consort! what, dost thou make us minstrels?" (3.1.45, 46). In the fullest discussion to date of Mercutio and the implications of his masculinity, Joseph Porter maintains that "Mercutio's essential subtextual address is to Romeo, and it is a Mercurian summoning away from love to the fellowship of men, guarded with warnings of the consequences of not heeding" (*Shakespeare's Mercutio* 114). In Porter's reading, the Queen Mab speech is aimed by Mercutio at "changing the subject away from Romeo's woes" but gets "carried away" by its "oracular" self-absorption (105), careening, in the process, into that territory which, we have seen, Romeo peremptorily declares to be "nothing." Actually, Mercutio, with Romeo's help, does a better job of changing the subject several scenes later (2.4.37–101). On the morning after the fateful night of the ball, a conversation that begins with Mercutio's taxing Romeo for his effeminizing enthrallment to love finds the two friends engaging each other in a wittier version of the sort of contestation we encountered between Gregory and Sampson. One would expect students to find this wild-goose chase of an exchange easy to resist, so dependent is its wit on the secondary and tertiary meanings of words unfamiliar in their primary sense; still, students find pleasure in the pleasure Mercutio and Romeo derive from each other and in the game of contorting each other's words to create a deconstructionist's delight, a metadiscourse that calls attention to the power of words to forge their own connections while making reference to, well, nothing—in its primary sense:

> MERCUTIO.   Sure wit! Follow me this jest now, till thou hast worn out thy
> pump, that when the single sole of it is worn, the jest may
> remain, after the wearing, soly singular.
> ROMEO.   O single-sol'd jest, soly singular for the singleness!
>
> (2.4.61–66)

In an act that opened with Romeo deserting his male companions and urging his "dull earth" to "find thy centre out" in the person of Juliet (2.1.2.), the flight of the wild-goose chase is spectacularly centrifugal. And yet it is Mercutio who brings the chase back to its point of origin; having reprimanded Romeo at the outset about love, Mercutio cannot refrain from homilizing on the subject at the end, even as he seals Romeo, as we have seen, in the tribe of the sociable (2.4.88–93).

Still, is there no space in the aggressively masculine world of Verona for feminine discourse? When women are with other women what do they have to talk about, and does their discourse show the same anxieties about desire that we have heard among the males? Showing his penchant for controlling all discourse, Mercutio, of course, presumes to answer for women, or, at least, for "maids" (2.1.36). He suggests, rather parenthetically and with a touch of uncharacteristic faux delicacy, that "when they laugh alone" the thoughts, or at least the language, of maids evince the same preoccupations and inflections we have by now come to associate with males in general and with Mercutio in particular. Fantasizing about Romeo fantasizing about his beloved, Mercutio imagines Romeo sitting "under a medlar tree" (2.1.34), wishing

> his mistress were that kind of fruit
> As maids call medlars, when they laugh alone.
> O, Romeo, that she were, O that she were
> An open[-arse], thou a pop'rin pear!   (2.1.35–38)

Now, how Mercutio would know what maids call medlars when they laugh alone we cannot say; nothing in his references to love and sexuality would suggest that he enjoys intimacy with the opposite sex. Still, and acknowledging the sexual and textual vagaries of the anal reference to which Goldberg has called attention recently ("*Open Rs*" 229–30), I find no less interesting in this moment the implications of its virtuosic indirection, its blend of a double ventriloquism and preterition that gives Mercutio license to vocalize what he puts into the mouths of maids and what he has taken from and put into the mind and mouth of Romeo. This is one of the crossover moments, like the Queen Mab speech, that, at least in twentieth-century representations, have given Mercutio hints of the histrionic flamboyance and gender bending of the shaman or performance artist—witness Mercutio's over-the-top drag performance at the Capulets' ball in Baz Luhrmann's recent film.[3] And yet, as we listen to Mercutio, avatar of masculinity, pretend to negotiate the private recesses of what maids say when they laugh alone and what Romeo wishes for under a medlar tree, we are also reminded at once of the frail partitions on which distinctions between genders in the play depend and of how sexuality and repression interact uneasily to maintain those partitions.

Earlier in the play, of course, we have already witnessed this unease in women's discourse with one another, in the scene in which Lady Capulet, with the Nurse at hand, conveys to Juliet Paris's proffer of matrimony (1.3). This is a scene remarkable for its centrifugal stresses and for the discomfort and fissions the proffer either reveals or causes. Least uncomfortable, it would seem, is the Nurse. While not, and not having been for some time, a maid, the Nurse is not reluctant here to refer to sexuality with an earthiness consistent with the vocabulary Mercutio attributes to maids "when they laugh alone." But even in telling and retelling the joke about Juliet's early discourse, the Nurse can claim, *modulo* the addition of some anatomical embellishment from the barnyard, only to be reporting the (conveniently unverifiable) discourse of others—her deceased husband and the almost but not quite infantine Juliet:

> And yet I warrant it had upon it brow
> A bump as big as a young cock'rel's stone—
> A perilous knock—and it cried bitterly.
> 'Yea,' quoth my husband, 'fall'st upon thy face?
> Thou wilt fall backward when thou comest to age,
> Wilt thou not, Jule?' It stinted and said, 'Ay.'   (1.3.52–57)

While Juliet peremptorily checks the Nurse's own efforts to insinuate sexual desire by ventriloquism—"And stint thou, too, I pray thee, Nurse, say I" (1.3.58) —Lady Capulet would rather talk about books. That is, faced with the task of saying why Juliet should be thrilled to accept Paris's offer (an offer Lady Capulet has seemed uncomfortable in delivering and Juliet uncomfortable in receiving), Lady Capulet textualizes desire, rendering passion as something akin to bookbinding, with Juliet playing the part of a book cover (87–94).

In textualizing Juliet's sexual self and repressing the vision of female sexuality the Nurse has so generously evoked, Lady Capulet writes Juliet into the Petrarchan discourse in which Romeo is so snugly encased and which, students quickly recognize, is as much about keeping lovers apart as it is about bringing them together, turning even kissing, as Juliet acutely observes in her critique of the kisses Romeo has bestowed on her at their first encounter, into something to be done "by th' book" (1.5.110). In this poetic ethos, Romeo and Juliet encounter each other initially through gendered decorums of words and movements and are retailed as disembodied collections of a limited number of body parts, their interaction an intricate exercise in metonymy and synecdoche. Indeed, noting that there is no stage direction that has Romeo remove his mask in approaching Juliet, Ronald Knowles has quipped that "if Romeo remains masked until the kiss, it means that Juliet has instantly fallen in love with a visor and a quatrain" (75).

" 'But ah,' Desire still cries," Philip Sidney's Astrophil ruefully observes, " 'give me some food' " (71.14). As we know, desire not only articulates its appetite but also sets about to satisfy it rather quickly in *Romeo and Juliet*, yielding Romeo twice the number of kisses, students find it instructive to learn, in little more than a sonnet's worth of dialogue than Sidney's Astrophil achieves in almost a thousand lines of Stella-gazing and wheedling. As Gayle Whittier has demonstrated, *Romeo and Juliet*, which writes itself and its protagonists into the lexicon and decorums of the Petrarchan sonnet, collapses the stasis of that poetic world into the onrushing events and "uncomfortable time" of the play's dramatic action (32–33). And even as dramatic action vies to displace poetic control, so desire threatens the decorums of gender and the social grammar of the play, voicing itself, in Juliet's plaintive apostrophes in the balcony scene, as an instrument of social disintegration: " 'Tis but thy name that is my enemy; / Thou art thyself, though not a Montague" (2.2.38–39). Here students can recognize the socially disruptive force of passion in the inversion of the Petrarchan norm, as Juliet turns the conventional enumeration and idealization of the lady's parts into an exercise in material dismemberment, isolating the name Montague as an abstraction by divorcing the name from all the parts of Romeo's body with which being a Montague has nothing to do, the sexual suggestiveness of Juliet's inventory rendered audible by its abrupt detour into unspecificity: "What's Montague? It is nor hand nor foot, / Nor arm, nor face, [nor any other part] / Belonging to a man" (2.2.40–42, brackets in original).

François Laroque has commented on the ways in which the language and respective positioning of Romeo and Juliet in this scene reverse and, thus, subvert gender roles in the play; with Juliet literally "on top," Romeo "is thus spatially dominated by Juliet and this places him in an inferior, passive position" (29–30). And, indeed, this image of Romeo rendered passive by love is only amplified by the erotic violence of Juliet's prothalamic hymn to night in 3.2; here Juliet's vision of the stellification through dissection she would like Romeo to undergo "when I die," suggests that, whatever delights may await Romeo in the stars, consummation might not be beneficial to his sublunary health (21–25).

Still, what are we asking our students to see in such images? In part, of course, these images associate desire with female desire, drawing on deep veins of contemporary misogyny to suggest that desire is dangerous because it subjects one to the voraciousness of female sexuality. Thus it could be said that in the very process of representing the subversion of gender roles, images of desire in this play bear a recuperative force and reinforce the assumptions of difference on which the notion of gender depends. In this way, the play evokes, and might seem to affiliate itself with, the social moralism and misogyny of its likely source, Brooke's poem, which in its prose epistle, "To the Reader," offers the narrative to follow as a cautionary fable depicting "unfortunate lovers, thralling themselves to unhonest desire [and] neglecting the authority and advice of parents and friends" (lxvi) but which, in subsequently characterizing Juliet as a "wily wench" and "jennet" (717, 723), relies on the pre-fitted epithets of literary misogyny.

At the same time, however, in calling our attention to gender roles as roles, as constructions that reveal one to be what one is as much by art as by nature, the play bears an obviously subversive potential. For a reminder of that potential we can point to a recent off-Broadway production in which a quartet of male actors play male students who put on *Romeo and Juliet* as a diversion, in the process eliding, or exposing as fragile, the boundaries between male and female and between reality and make-believe (Marks). It is not, of course, only through such examples of late-twentieth-century gender-bending theatrical practice that students can grasp the subversively rhetorical representation of gender in Shakespeare's text. For gender repeatedly assumes a reactionary function in the play, becoming less something that one always is than something to be invoked at moments that threaten patriarchal discipline and discourse. I have argued elsewhere, for example, that ideology of gender is especially conspicuous, and figures like Capulet and Friar Lawrence are particularly paternalist and "masculinist" in their prescriptions, at those moments when rude feelings and inexorable realities irrupt to elude those prescriptions and challenge that ideology (Moisan, " 'O Any Thing' " 131–32). And, indeed, we never feel more keenly the improvisatory character of gender than when gender is applied to something that is neither male nor female, especially to the ultimate inexorable reality in the play, death. If sometimes death is accepted as something, albeit sad, that happens (3.4.4), at other times, when death frustrates patriarchal or male prerogatives, it gets personified as a male, and an obnoxious and sexually predatory one at that, and, thus, is rendered recognizable, if not manageable, by being engendered. So it is that in the remarkable "lamentations" scene we encounter death as the rapist and importunate son-in-law who has deprived Capulet of his daughter and of his right to bestow her in marriage (4.5.35–39); as the "detestable" figure who displaces Paris and leaves him feeling, among other things, "beguiled" (4.5.55–56); and later as the conquering antihero and amatory rival Romeo apostrophizes in the Capulets' tomb (5.3.87–105).

Ultimately, however, to consider the representation of gender in *Romeo and Juliet* and the play's tendency to invoke gender as a means of rationalizing the inexplicable and uncontrollable is to sense the difficulty the play has in explaining itself. We sense this all the more at those moments at which the play draws our attention to the conflict—so often noticed in recent criticism—between Romeo and Juliet's love, on the one hand, and what it means to be masculine in Verona, on the other. "O sweet Juliet," Romeo declares at, perhaps, the most conspicuous of these moments (3.1.113), when Mercutio has been mortally wounded, "hurt under [Romeo's] arm" (3.1.103), "Thy beauty hath made me effeminate, / And in my temper soft'ned valor's steel" (114–15). Responding to this passage, students cannily hear in it the inflections of self-exculpation and ask whether one trait essential to being masculine in Verona is an instinct for shifting the blame to women when one's masculinity has failed one. Even more cannily, they wonder how much weight we are to assign gender as a source of tragedy in the play when, only twenty lines or so later, Romeo has come up with a more numinous, if more nebulous, entity to blame, self-pityingly declaring, "O, I am fortune's fool!" (136). Gender, that is, becomes one of a number of discourses auditioned in the search for an interpretative paradigm.

Here again, to be sure, the play could be said to absorb and put in Romeo's mouth some of the excuse mongering and finger-pointing of Shakespeare's source in Brooke, who, as if not fully sure of the generic demands of his story or of whether he is obliged to make someone or no one responsible for its "tragical matter," has his narrator distribute blame widely to take no chances. Part moralistic censurer of wickedness and "unhonest desire," carping at "drunken gossips," "superstitious friars" ("To the Reader" lxvi), delusional, lustful lovers (429–32), and, as we have seen, wily wenches (717) and jennets (723), part sentimentalist and Boethian fatalist, decrying the cruel spins of Fortune's Wheel (935–46), Brooke indulges his craving for accountability in the detailed recitation of penalties Escalus metes out at the end of the poem (2985–3004).

In Shakespeare, however, the retributive desire of Escalus to affix responsibility through an assignment of penalties and pardons gets deferred, the deferral at once an indication of the play's need to explain itself and an acknowledgment that any explanation will have managed to elude the bounds of the play. Even as the play defers and diverts attention from the kind of sentencing tribunal that preoccupies Brooke, however, we must ask what it is that Shakespeare leaves onstage instead. The critic Nicholas Brooke once termed *Romeo and Juliet* a "spectacle of human experience" (256); what we see onstage before the Prince calls everyone off could as easily be called a spectacle of recuperation, in which the surviving patriarchs vie with each other in one last attempt to circumscribe Romeo and Juliet in death within the social decorums the lovers transgressed in life. In addition to noting the implications for Verona's future in the competitive edge to the patriarchs' rapprochement here, students find in the patriarchs' "civil" public-works plans a disquieting and repressive materialism that would transform the passionate, flesh-and-blood lovers into his-and-her statues, equally "rich" and the best of their kind in town (5.3.298–304)! Here the social order, having failed to control the passion of the lovers, would control the representation of that passion and in this way mirror the mimetic activity of the play itself. At the same time, the diversionary effect of the patriarchs' lurch toward social reconciliation offers a simulacrum of the role the social prescriptions of gender perform throughout the play. Indeed, as Escalus declares victory and withdraws, pulling everyone offstage to have "more talk of these sad things" (5.3.307), he only frames the silent space onstage as the site of the destructive "extremities" of desire, the power of which the prescriptions of gender in *Romeo and Juliet* serve both to conceal and to reveal.

NOTES

[1] See Holmer ("Practices" 192–93) and Barbara Hodgdon ("Absent Bodies" 341–45) for comments on the relation of the study and performance of *Romeo and Juliet* in recent years and heightened concerns over the social implications of the play.

[2] In notes on this passage, both G. Blakemore Evans in the New Cambridge edition of the play and Brian Gibbons in the second Arden edition cite the doubt raised by one commentator that this line could be the Nurse's, given its insubordination. But both Evans and Gibbons defend the ascription: for Evans the remark merely bespeaks the

Nurse's "privileged" and, thus, protected position in the household (167); for Gibbons the Nurse's comment is of a piece with the normal "vulgarity" of her language, while her exchange with Capulet is "wholly consistent with the presentation of the domestic affairs and manners of the Capulet household" (207).

[3] Though clearly more adherent to the boundaries of gender than in Luhrmann's film, associations of Mercutio's theatrical flamboyance with complexities in his sexual representation are not inaudible in older film versions of the play. Porter cites the blending of "effeminacy" and "phallic zaniness" in the earringed John Barrymore's Mercutio in the George Cukor version (189), while both Porter (*Shakespeare's Mercutio* 191–92) and Jack Jorgens discern in what Jorgens calls the "mercurial showmanship" (84) of John McEnery's Mercutio in Franco Zeffirelli's film a deep and suggestively sexual attachment to Romeo.

Teaching the Tragi-comedy of *Romeo and Juliet*

Douglas Bruster

From the opening chorus that gives away the story's tragic ending to the final couplet of the play—"never was a story of more woe / Than this of Juliet and her Romeo"—*Romeo and Juliet* seems conscious, even assertive, of its status as a tragedy. Yet as many critics have pointed out, few of Shakespeare's works show more tension between their primary genre and the other genres that shape their dramatic worlds. So free was the matter of writing plays during the early modern period in England, of course, that we can describe most of the era's dramatic works as being of mixed genre. Nevertheless, Shakespeare's story of woe offers a special challenge for readers interested in literary form, because within this celebrated work lies a comedy that both interacts with the tragedy of *Romeo and Juliet* and lends the play much of its power. This dual generic nature makes *Romeo and Juliet* an extremely valuable document with which to introduce the relation of literary convention and meaning. Accordingly, this essay begins with a brief account of the comedic elements in *Romeo and Juliet* and goes on to discuss literary form as it pertains to teaching Shakespeare's plays. It then describes various teaching exercises involving the role of comedy in *Romeo and Juliet,* closing with suggestions for further reading in genre criticism and theory.

While *Romeo and Juliet* offers us a tragic story, it does so with a variety of comedic elements. With respect to plot, characters, and atmosphere, the play is as much a comedy as it is a tragedy. For example, like many comedies, *Romeo and Juliet* takes as a primary theme the nature of desire. This theme is explored through a plot that is structurally, if not finally, comedic; the play's fundamental situation—two young lovers separated by disapproving parents—is the starting point for many comedies, including *A Midsummer Night's Dream,* and is a part of such plays as *The Merry Wives of Windsor, Cymbeline,* and *The Winter's Tale.* Comedic serving characters, who help the lovers get past their parents' resistance, are here represented by Juliet's Nurse and Friar Lawrence. The Friar is of a higher social station than the Nurse is, but, like her, he becomes both a collaborator and a surrogate parent of a young lover.

Comedic perspective joins comedic function in Mercutio. Broad in character like the Nurse, Mercutio is a witty and loquacious gallant whose satire helps establish a knowing viewpoint in a play that contains many farcical moments. The play opens, for instance, with a slapstick encounter between servants of the Montagues and Capulets; the servants' names (including Sampson, Gregory, and Abram) almost parodically indicate their nonheroic status and natures. The play continually asks us to take certain matters less seriously than face value would warrant. One finds examples of this in the response to Juliet's "death" by the Capulets, the Nurse, and County Paris (4.5.14–90) and in the musicians' banter with Peter at the close of this scene. Capulet indicates, at this moment, a shift in what we might call the genre of the characters' collective experience:

> All things that we ordained festival,
> Turn from their office to black funeral:
> Our instruments to melancholy bells,
> Our wedding cheer to a sad burial feast;
> Our solemn hymns to sullen dirges change;
> Our bridal flowers serve for a buried corse;
> And all things change them to the contrary. (4.5.84–90)

Yet because we have been privy to the comedic plans of the young lovers and their accomplices—plans that have included furtive messages, a secret marriage, a concealed rope ladder, and a sleeping potion—we see Capulet's pronouncement as premature if not mistaken. Contrary to what Capulet states, things have not changed "to the contrary" but remain contrary to what they seem. Whereas Capulet describes a tragedy, we feel that the lovers and Friar Lawrence are still ensconced in the safety of a comedic plot. Our reception of the grief displayed in this scene, then, is structured by a knowing sophistication, a sophistication akin to that of Mercutio, that has earlier been a large part of Mercutio's character. This knowingness is integral to what Bertrand Evans has described as the "discrepant awareness" involved in comedy, where audience members know more about the characters and the characters' situation than do the characters themselves (*Shakespeare's Comedies*).

Romeo and Juliet is comedic in many ways. Its juxtaposition of comedy and tragedy helps deepen the latter and may explain why Shakespeare chose to emphasize, in his opening chorus, the tragic ending of the play: without this forewarning, audiences and readers unacquainted with the source story—and perhaps even those who knew it—could well resent the playwright for arbitrarily enforcing a cruel ending on the story's protagonists. By giving the grim conclusion of his story in advance, Shakespeare helps absolve himself of such culpability.

It should be pointed out here that the word *tragi-comedy* in this essay refers to the general sense we find Sidney using in his *Apology for Poetry*. Complaining that certain English plays mingle "kings and clowns," Sidney inveighs against the plays' "mongrel tragi-comedy" (77). Sidney does not mean that the tragic and comedic should never be mixed: as he confesses, such authors as Apuleius and Plautus combined the two in their works. Sidney's objection is, instead, to the indecorous, even crude, admixture of dramatic elements and registers. John Fletcher provides a more technical definition of the term in the often-quoted preface to *The Faithful Shepherdess:* "A tragi-comedy is not so called in respect of mirth and killing, but in respect it wants deaths, which is enough to make it no tragedy, yet brings some near it, which is enough to make it no comedy" (497). Obviously, *Romeo and Juliet* is closer to Sidney's definition than to Fletcher's. Mixing slapstick, farce, clowns, and comedic energy

(Fletcher's "mirth") with the deaths of six of its speaking characters (Fletcher's "killing"), the play is a hodgepodge of literary kinds.

Teaching *Romeo and Juliet* in relation to this diversity of kinds may appear old-fashioned in these days of new historicism and politically oriented criticism. Arguably, though, the play's dedication to issues of sexual desire and the dynamics of family life makes *Romeo and Juliet* potentially less rewarding to those interested in pursuing literature from an intensively historicist or political point of view. The continuing popularity of *Romeo and Juliet* with young audiences— especially in filmed productions—suggests that the play's issues are as germane to contemporary culture as they were to Elizabethan England. While not transcending its own time and place, then, *Romeo and Juliet* seems less anchored to its era than do many other Elizabethan plays. Perhaps the most rewarding approach to grounding this play in the contexts of the early modern era is to emphasize the play's mingling of contemporary literary kinds. In this approach the interests of what Heather Dubrow has called the "New Formalism" in early modern studies (*Eden* 266) coincide with the shapes of Shakespeare's tragedy, reminding us that what and how a play means depend greatly on its relation to literary conventions and its negotiation of the genres those conventions help to define.

Teaching *Romeo and Juliet* from a formal perspective means introducing terms with which many students may have only a passing acquaintance. Of course, as experienced consumers of popular culture, today's students possess highly sophisticated knowledge about the workings of genre in contemporary texts (from films and television programs to novels, poems, paintings, photographs, and popular songs). But however savvy students may be, often they do not see how their knowledge of rules and conventions may help them understand texts from other times and places. Thus the following exercises are designed to draw on students' latent familiarity with genre and generic conventions, bringing knowledge and skills students already possess to bear on the function of form in *Romeo and Juliet.* Such exercises work well if one teaches the play alongside other dramatic works, since genre is a horizontal notion that depends on other texts, like and unlike the text in question, for elucidation. Ideally, one would teach the play in close conjunction with *A Midsummer Night's Dream*—written, it is believed, in 1596, perhaps in the same year as *Romeo and Juliet.* Yet material in *Romeo and Juliet* itself makes it possible to emphasize form whatever the course syllabus.

One way to introduce the idea of genre to students is to begin with their knowledge of artistic categories. This type of introduction can be preferable to a lecture that expounds on genre in the early modern era, since working with students' own experiences helps show students that genre remains a central mode of understanding aesthetic objects. Thus an introductory exercise on genre might start before the first course meeting on *Romeo and Juliet.* An instructor might ask students to come to the next class meeting prepared to offer a personal or dictionary definition of the word *genre* and to supplement this definition with examples drawn from contemporary culture. That is, an instructor might ask students to think of places where generic distinctions are made. These might include both real and textual locations. Students might suggest, among other places, video stores, bookstores, film and television listings, and online library catalogs. At the following class meeting, students might report on a variety of generic distinctions. One bookstore might make a distinction between classics and fiction. A video store might divide its holdings into such genres as drama, comedy, science fiction, and documentary and, further, into children's and adult videos. Movie reviews in a newspaper might be even more specific, speaking of "a futuristic thriller," "a live-action feature," "a contemporary comedy," or "a dark love story."

An instructor could begin by asking the class to define, as a group, the term *genre,* then open a general discussion of the various categories that students have uncovered in their individual investigations. A number of questions might be posed: How are these various categories construed? For instance, what leads a video store to categorize a particular film as a drama rather than a comedy? What makes a film a children's film? a documentary? a western? What rules seem to govern the narratives of such films? What might a film's classification suggest about the store's understanding of its films? of its customers and their assumptions? Could one use other classification schemes as well? If so, what might they look like?

At this point, when students begin to see how strongly notions of category and type structure our relations to art, an instructor might ask the class to move from the idea of genre as an aid to consumption to the idea of genre as an influence on production. That is, granting that generic classifications help us select the aesthetic objects we are interested in (including books, films, poems, and paintings), what might it mean for artists to have such categories or genres in mind as they produce their works of art? Here one might invoke the idea of *convention* to lend nuances to the class discussion. Students often quickly recognize that various dramatic genres differ in their endings: that comedies usually end happily and that tragedies end unhappily. Further discussion might lead to explicit definitions of "happy" and "unhappy"—a happy work typically includes some kind of romantic alignment, and an unhappy one some form of serious bodily harm, including death.

An instructor might suggest that these endings are generic conventions, briefly define the term, and then ask students to identify other conventions from various genres. Because students are likely to be more familiar with film than with drama, one might ask them about conventions in romantic comedies, horror films, or westerns. Plot is, of course, important to many genres and is likely to be prominent in student responses. However, to avoid accounts that center exclusively on plot, an instructor might at this point try to categorize students' insights into generic conventions. For the sake of efficiency, an instructor could focus discussion on one genre in particular. What kinds of characters, actions, settings (including placement in a particular era), dialogue, music, and costumes typically occur in this genre? What kinds of actors are typically cast in various roles? What kinds of people usually make up the primary audience for such films? What do audiences experience during these films? Laughter? Tears? Fright? Arousal? How are these bodily experiences related to what happens to the bodies of characters in such works? These are only a few of the questions that one might raise about genres with which students are familiar. By building on students' experiences of contemporary film genres, the instructor can enhance their understanding of the genres of early modern drama.

At some time during these introductory discussions, an instructor may wish to provide background on how early modern readers and writers understood genre. Here it may be relevant to delineate conceptions of comedy and tragedy, exploring how *Romeo and Juliet* relates to these genres. One might make an initial distinction with the help of Aelius Donatus's definitions of comedy and tragedy. Donatus, an early editor of and commentator on Terence, offered what one might call meteorological definitions of comedy and tragedy: where comedy begins with turbulence and ends in calm, Donatus said, tragedy begins with calm and ends in turbulence (Nugent). This pattern of definition is replicated, with new attention to the calm and turbulence of the body, in Cyril Tourneur's *The Atheist's Tragedy*, where D'Amville remarks, "Here's a sweet comedy. 'T begins with *O Dolentis* and concludes with ha, ha, he" (2.4.84–85). If genre was held to affect bodies in various ways, it could also involve certain kinds of bodies, or rather the bodies of certain classes of characters. The pattern of tragedy that focused on the fall of significant figures, often princes or governors, is called *de casibus* tragedy after Boccaccio's *De casibus virorum illustrium* ("On the Fall of Illustrious Men"). Most often early modern readers and writers defined tragedy as involving the deaths of significant persons (although a vital subgenre, domestic tragedy, focused on persons of the middle orders). Further, a dedication to decorum led many to believe that certain subjects called for appropriate aesthetic vehicles; tragedy required a grave and stately style of presentation and a serious discursive register.

Significantly, *Romeo and Juliet* appears from the outset to involve a different paradigm of tragedy. The farcical quarrel that begins the play asks us to see the world of the Montagues and Capulets as a prosaic, even comedic, place. The romantic relationship between the title characters calls up not *de casibus* tragedy but a form of romantic tragedy that Shakespeare knew from the classics and from Chaucer's *Troilus and Criseyde*. Shakespeare articulates various permutations of this form of tragedy in an exchange between Hermia and Lysander in *A Midsummer Night's Dream*:

> LYSANDER. Ay me! for aught that I could ever read,
>   Could ever hear by tale or history,
>   The course of true love never did run smooth;
>   But either it was different in blood—
> HERMIA.   O cross! too high to be enthrall'd to low.

> LYSANDER. Or else misgraffed in respect of years—
> HERMIA.   O spite! too old to be engag'd to young.
> LYSANDER. Or else it stood upon the choice of friends—
> HERMIA.   O hell, to choose love by another's eyes!
> LYSANDER. Or if there were a sympathy in choice,
>   War, death, or sickness did lay siege to it.   (1.1.132–42)

An often noticed point of resemblance exists between this exchange and one in *Romeo and Juliet*. In the lines that follow those quoted above, Lysander analogizes the ephemerality of love to the brevity of light from lightning after dark, a phenomenon that is finished almost as soon as it commences. Juliet makes this analogy as well in saying that her contract with Romeo "is too rash, too unadvis'd, too sudden, / Too like the lightning, which doth cease to be / Ere one can say it lightens" (2.2.118–20). In Juliet's speech we can hear versions of Hermia's *too's*—"too high," "too old"—and gain the sense that love tragedies are the product less of moral excess than of social situation and the accidents of desire.

It is in relation to both the social basis of love tragedy and the emphasis of such tragedy on desire that an understanding of comedy in early modern England becomes helpful, for comedy was the dramatic vehicle most often associated with passion and desire. Sometimes performed on the occasion of a wedding or other festival, comedies frequently took romantic themes as their focus and could include the temporary inversion of established social order. Here the influence of Plautus and Terence, whose plays typically involved an *adulescens amans*, or young lover, and his *amica*, or beloved, was clear. Such Roman New Comedy plots also featured parents as blocking figures, obstacles to be bypassed with the help of a *servus*, or servant figure. In contrast to formal tragedy, comedy in early modern England usually involved characters from the middle and lower orders of society. As George Puttenham remarked in *The Arte of English Poesie* (published in 1589), comedy involves

> the matters of the world [. . .] but never meddling with any Prince's matters nor such high personages, but commonly of merchants, soldiers, artificers, good honest householders, and also of unthrifty youths, young damsels, old nurses, bawds, brokers, ruffians and parasites, with such like, in whose behaviors lieth in effect the whole course and trade of man's life, and therefore tended altogether to the amendment of man by discipline and example.   (32)

As Puttenham's final clause reminds us, comedy was sometimes held to cure, by its examples of the ridiculous, audiences' and readers' propensity to err. One might note in this regard Sidney's feeling that comedy should show the "common errors of our life, which [the playwright] representeth in the most ridiculous and scornful sort" (44). One could consider as well the opinion of Thomas

Elyot, who describes comedy as a genre in which we may behold "the prompt-ness of youth unto vice; [. . .] the deceit of servants; the chances of fortune con-trary to men's expectation" (48). Elyot reads comedy as a cautious parent might; one needs, he implies, to watch children and servants carefully. In his caution, Elyot anticipates the energies of *Romeo and Juliet,* where youths are drawn to-ward each other by a passion that avoids vice only through a secret marriage, where servants deceive their masters, and where fortune falls "contrary to men's expectation." What this arrangement of plot and persons suggests is that *Romeo and Juliet* is what comedy looks like when filtered through the fears of a parent.

It is worth posing, as questions for class discussion, whether individual gen-res can imply attitudes toward human behavior and whether genres are struc-tured by assumptions about life, society, and the function of families, among other matters. Here a comparison of *Romeo and Juliet* with *A Midsummer Night's Dream* can be illuminating. Each play can be read as the obverse of the other—like the twin masks of comedy and tragedy in classical iconography. The two plays appear to use the same basic material, though to various effect and with differing conclusions. As we have seen, Hermia and Lysander rehearse a version of how their love might end in a tragic way. Even as an enraged Capulet threatens Juliet with expulsion from the family and a life in which she might "hang, beg, starve, die in the streets" without his "acknowledg[ment]" (3.5.192–93), so does Egeus in *A Midsummer Night's Dream* call for the enforcement of a law that would command his daughter's obedience or death (1.1.41–45). An instructor could ask students about the role of these irate fathers. What func-tion do they have in their plays? Is Capulet given more motivation for his resis-tance than Egeus is? Or are Capulet's actions equally arbitrary? The roles of paternal fiat and of youthful disobedience might also be considered in relation to critical pronouncements about patriarchy in early modern society. How suc-cessful is patriarchy at enforcing obedience in these plays? Does comedy have a certain skepticism about power—whether based on age, gender, or bloodline?

Other points of contact between *A Midsummer Night's Dream* and *Romeo and Juliet* might be noticed in the characters of Mercutio and Puck and even in Mercutio's bravura description of Queen Mab (1.4.53–95). Is Mab a kind of sis-ter spirit to Puck in her fondness for addressing human libido? The love juice of *Dream* facilitates the comedy that follows; the sleeping potion of *Romeo and Juliet* might usefully be discussed in relation to what it is meant to do as well as to what happens when it misfires. Perhaps the most fruitful discussion based on these plays will arise from reading the mechanicals' play-within-the-play, "Pyramus and Thisby," alongside *Romeo and Juliet.* Although the playlet misses a tragic effect because of the manner in which it is performed, its structural similarities to *Romeo and Juliet* might be considered at some length. Like the story of Romeo and Juliet, that of Pyramus and Thisby involves ardent young lovers of neighboring families that disapprove of the lovers' relationship. The mechanicals' play, of course, literalizes the rift between "these two neighbors"

(5.1.206–07) by employing Snout as a wall. It might be asked what it means for Romeo and Juliet to be separated by just such a wall. Is a wall between lovers essentially a comedic device, a concrete realization of the way comedy functions—by establishing an impediment to eros that must be circumvented? Or do the different outcomes of these two stories suggest that conventions are in themselves neutral and that genres are established only by—or primarily by—the ends of works, by whether the characters live or die?

Attempting to answer this question can prove a valuable classroom exercise. An instructor might begin by rehearsing some of the generic markers raised in previous discussions, from the social class of a drama's characters and the form or forms the characters' speech takes to the play's themes, actions, and plot outcomes. The instructor might then ask the students whether it would be possible to rewrite *Romeo and Juliet* as a comedy. Which, if any, of the play's generic markers would have to be changed? One might make useful reference here to Nahum Tate's revision of *King Lear* (1681), which provided a happy ending to Shakespeare's tragedy and enjoyed great popularity through the early nineteenth century. Even more to the point is the recollection of John Downes, a longtime prompter in the Restoration theater. In his *Roscius Anglicanus*, published in 1708, Downes remembered that

> [t]his Tragedy of *Romeo and Juliet,* was made some time after into a Tragi-Comedy, by Mr. *James Howard,* he preserving *Romeo and Juliet* alive; so that when the Tragedy was Reviv'd again, 'twas Play'd Alternately, Tragical one Day, and Tragi-comical another, for several Days together [. . .].   (C3v)

Although we do not possess Howard's "Tragi-comical" revision of *Romeo and Juliet,* Tate's *Lear* gives us an idea of how readily one may transform a tragedy by means of a happy ending.

Students often point out that *Romeo and Juliet* might end happily if Friar John were not to be prevented from delivering Friar Lawrence's message to Romeo in Mantua (5.2.1–20). In this scenario, Romeo returns to the Capulets' tomb in time for Juliet's awakening, both families recognize the lovers' marriage, and the feud is resolved as the couple appears poised to live happily ever after. Just as often, however, students then recall that Romeo has been banished for slaying Tybalt, who in turn killed Mercutio. Mercutio's death seems more out of place in a comedy than does that of Tybalt (whose absence from the play is rarely regretted by students). Dryden was aware of this when he wrote, in "An Essay on the *Dramatique Poetry* of the Last Age," that

> *Shakespeare* show'd the best of his skill in his *Mercutio,* and he said himself, that he was forc'd to kill him in the third Act, to prevent being kill'd by him. But, for my part, I cannot find he was so dangerous a person: I see

nothing in him but what was so exceeding harmless, that he might have liv'd to the end of the Play, and died in his bed, without offence to any man.   (215)

Dryden's remarks show us Shakespeare's awareness of the danger that Mercutio posed to the genre of tragedy in *Romeo and Juliet*. Where a comedy might indeed have Mercutio live "to the end of the Play," Shakespeare's play becomes a tragedy only by killing him. A discussion of Mercutio's role in the play and of the relation of his character to genre might include not only the blunt truth of his death but also the quintessentially comedic nature of his character—his satirical but positive orientation to the bustle of life in the play and his unrealized potential as a comedic accomplice.

After imagining what it would involve to rewrite *Romeo and Juliet* as a comedy, a class might go on to investigate the ways in which Shakespeare's tragedy was read and revised during and after his lifetime. Such investigation might be performed individually, with students assigned to read and report on various ancillary texts. It might also be undertaken collectively; students might read and discuss a selected text or texts or passages from those texts in relation to *Romeo and Juliet*. Shakespeare texts that students might pursue individually include not only *A Midsummer Night's Dream* but also *Much Ado about Nothing* (which briefly flirts with the kind of tragedy one sees in *Romeo and Juliet* through Beatrice's "Kill Claudio" [4.1.289]) and the love tragedies *Troilus and Cressida*, *Othello*, and *Antony and Cleopatra*. The narrative poems *Venus and Adonis* and *The Rape of Lucrece*, which emphasize the tragic results of passion, might also prove useful in this regard.

Several plays by Shakespeare's contemporaries registered a deep engagement with *Romeo and Juliet* and can provide insight into questions of genre and cultural reception. Such plays include John Marston's *Antonio and Mellida* (in which Antonio rises from apparent death to wed Mellida); John Fletcher's *The Knight of Malta* (in which Zanthia administers a sleep potion and describes a plot to recover Oriana in "her family's monument" [138] 4.1); Henry Porter's *The Two Angry Women of Abington*; Thomas Dekker's *Blurt, Master Constable*; and Edward Sharpham's *Cupid's Whirligig*. Mary Bly has argued that these last three plays incorporate a character type new to the early modern stage, that of the "bawdy virgin," inaugurated by Shakespeare with Juliet.

Romeo and Juliet was also filtered into nondramatic forms that an instructor might bring into the classroom for general discussion. For instance, a profitable classroom exercise could result from examining the use to which Thomas Carew, the seventeenth-century poet, put *Romeo and Juliet*. Carew's "Pastoral Dialogue" ("This mossy bank they pressed"), a poem of thirty-five lines, is easily reproduced and distributed to students. Its amatory dialogue between a shepherd and a nymph (45–46) draws on Romeo and Juliet's sunrise farewell (3.5.1–36). Students might also benefit from a relevant part of Thomas

Prujean's *Aurorata: Love's Looking Glass Divine and Humane* (1644), which offers two poetic epistles exchanged by Romeo and Juliet during Romeo's banishment from Verona. These texts can help extend students' study of form to include letters and lyric poetry.

For students interested in pursuing questions of genre and form, an instructor might suggest various critical readings. Students could begin with Heather Dubrow's *Genre*, a useful introductory text on the topic. Advanced students might be directed toward Alastair Fowler's *Kinds of Literature: An Introduction to the Theory of Genre and Modes*, which deals with genre across various traditions and eras. The workings of genre in the early modern era are the focus of Rosalie Colie's foundational text *The Resources of Kind: Genre-Theory in the Renaissance*. Those interested in criticism relating to genre in *Romeo and Juliet* might consult J. M. Nosworthy's "The Two Angry Families of Verona," Franklin Dickey's *Not Wisely but Too Well* (esp. 63–88), and Harry Levin's "Form and Formality in *Romeo and Juliet*" before reading Susan Snyder's account of the play in *The Comic Matrix of Shakespeare's Tragedies*. Snyder's chapter on *Romeo and Juliet* consolidates and expands much of the earlier commentary on the play's comedic basis (56–90). Ranier Lengeler examines the tragicomic nature of *Romeo and Juliet* alongside what he sees as similar generic blending in *The Spanish Tragedy*. Likewise, James Forse has described *Romeo and Juliet* in the context of *Arden of Feversham*, arguing that both texts belong to a genre of "comedy-suspense" plays. The relation of *Romeo and Juliet* to *A Midsummer Night's Dream* is the subject of a densely argued note by Amy Riess and George Williams, who hold *Romeo and Juliet* to be the prior of the two plays. Although Riess and Williams's argument is ultimately unconvincing, it succeeds in setting out some of the critical questions that spring from the relation of these two dramas and the assumptions we make based on our ideas about this relation. Finally, a useful collection of essays on *Romeo and Juliet* (including the essay by Mary Bly, mentioned earlier) appears in *Shakespeare Survey* 49, Romeo and Juliet *and Its Afterlife*, edited by Stanley Wells.

Teaching *Romeo and Juliet* in an Introduction to Drama Course

Jennifer Low

While I teach *Romeo and Juliet* in several different courses, I find that the context of an introduction to drama course offers special rewards because it permits an extensive discussion of genre issues, which I consider crucial to an understanding of the play. The syllabus for my Introduction to Drama course includes several very different plays as well as readings about tragedy from Aristotle's *Poetics*, Northop Frye's *Fools of Time*, and John Willett's edition of *Brecht on Theatre*. Given the limits of the course and the lack of sophistication of the students (most of whom are not English majors), I find that an emphasis on a single genre helps students gain a sense of historical change. Throughout the semester students see how elements of tragedy are first defined and then stretched by theatrical developments.

I select texts that ensure certain consistencies: all the plays can be read as tragedies and all present women in heroic or antiheroic roles. Yet the plays range geographically from Greece to England, Sweden, and France and in time from the fifth century BC to the 1980s. Before *Romeo and Juliet*, the class reads Sophocles's *Antigone* and selections from Aristotle's *Poetics* (secs. 6–18). I begin with a lecture on dramatic practice in Athens and the importance of music and spectacle in ancient Greek drama. We discuss each element of Aristotle's well-known definition of tragedy: dramatic action, a coherent plot, grandeur ("of a certain magnitude" [61]), lyrical language, and the ability to call forth pity and fear. I also emphasize the role of the spectator and the religious function of drama, which will contrast later on with the social role of theater in early modern England. This initial information provides a context not only for *Antigone* the play but also for Antigone the heroine, whose actions cannot be fully understood without knowing the significance of the community in Greek life. In the interest of explaining Antigone's actions, I also give some background on the status of women in Sophocles's time.

In class discussion, we look at the different hierarchies of responsibility that various characters perceive and acknowledge. Antigone explains, "Not for a husband, you understand, / Not even for a son would I have done this," prizing her siblings above those relatives who can be replaced (170). But Haemon kills himself for love of his fiancée, Antigone, and Euridice commits suicide at the news of her son's death. Creon places the state's concerns above the concerns of kinship; yet he is broken by the deaths of his wife and son.

Assessing the reason for Creon's harsh fate takes some time; students too easily condemn the king's apparent hard-heartedness. Looking for a tragic flaw, or hamartia, we can see how his initial desire to lead Thebes soon hardens into a refusal to consider the possibility of his own error. Creon shows himself both proud and obstinate. Yet it is equally important to recognize Creon's suffering at the end. Later in the course, students read in Frye that "in Greek tragedy especially, we can see how death is both the punishment of the aggressor and the reward of his victim" (5); when we read that line, we can revert to Creon to consider the meaning of Frye's statement. *Antigone* prepares us for the other plays in the course: the issues I raise include public versus private life, love as defined by the recipient's relation to the lover, love as defined by behavior, the contrast between masculine and feminine heroics, and women's potential stature in drama. All these themes recur later in the semester.

We spend four eighty-minute sessions on *Romeo and Juliet* plus a session on early modern English stage practice and a session discussing Frye's chapter "My Father As He Slept: The Tragedy of Order" (*Fools* 3–39). We examine Frye's main points (which I ask the class to mark in advance) by working carefully through the chapter. While Aristotle explains the elements of tragedy, Frye shows how recurrent themes underlie most tragic plots. Many of Frye's ideas provoke discussion—for example, Frye suggests that there are three types of tragedy, each dealing with a different kind of identity: social identity, erotic identity, or individual identity. He offers several systems for understanding the types of tragedy, among them this one: "In terms closer to Christianity, [these types] might be called the tragedy of the killing of the father [. . .] the sacrifice of the son, and [. . .] the isolation of the spirit" (16). Thinking about plays they know, students may offer other correspondences between tragic themes and types of identity; when I ask them to categorize commonly read plays according to Frye's terms, a useful debate about central and subordinate plots frequently results. As is obvious, the biblically derived terms address only issues of male identity, and since we consider female heroes, some students want to find stories that represent women's circumstances. In discussing *An-*

tigone, we can see the heroine as a princess, a sister, or a lover; each of these roles suggests a different kind of tragedy. This discussion can spill into the next session.

Once we have come to understand Frye, we move to *Romeo and Juliet.* Discussion of the play begins with the question of whether act 1 seems like the opening of an Aristotelian tragedy. Does the plot have the magnitude Aristotle refers to? Do we see language appropriately "embellished with each kind of artistic ornament" (Aristotle 61)? The latter question leads to a discussion of different kinds of diction and highlights the status of the main characters in the stratified society of Verona. In class I ask why Shakespeare might have decided to begin the play with Sampson and Gregory. What do we learn from them? The servants in *Antigone* provide perspectives that contrast strikingly with those of the ruling class, and students see Shakespeare using Sampson and Gregory similarly.

No matter what edition of the play one uses, students need a teacher to explain the opening scene—to clarify the jokes, to make the puns as funny as possible (given the need for explanations), and to point out the misogyny and objectification implied by the humor. (I tend to focus the results of our close reading on the points made by Coppélia Kahn in her essay "Coming of Age in Verona.") I ask how tragedy can originate in such earthy material and whether any elements in the first act foreshadow the tragedy that follows. Students are quick to cite the prologue, and they argue that such a violent society could easily bring tragedy to the community. But with a reminder about the issues of magnitude and embellished language, students often dig deeper. Prince Escalus often comes across as a figure fit for tragedy: his authority and his diction contribute to a sense of *his* magnitude.

Romeo, in contrast, seems to be unpromising material for a tragedy, especially when compared with the rational but passionate Haemon, who is torn between respect for the father he loves and devotion to his bride. The Renaissance cult of melancholy needs a lot of explaining, so at the next session I introduce melancholy as one of the conventions of courtly love. We talk about precedents for Romeo's behavior and the possibility that Romeo is playing a role he enjoys rather than suffering genuine pain. This discussion leaves the class free to think of Romeo as immature, even effete, and exploring this negative view of Romeo can lead to a consideration of the dichotomous roles of men in the play: if male aristocrats are not prepared for a brawl at any moment, the only alternative for them seems to be an irritating passivity. I end the session here, as this point makes it possible to see Romeo's immediate response to Juliet as a moment of awakening—a decision to choose reality over fantasy.

I also try to present love melancholy as an aspect of adolescent alienation, however anachronistic that view may be. Certainly, an examination of the role of the Montague parents suggests that Romeo is alienated from them. His chosen confidant is Friar Lawrence, Romeo's "ghostly father" (2.3.45). As Romeo's spiritual adviser, Friar Lawrence has clearly lent a sympathetic ear to Romeo's love troubles in the past, but the Friar may be no more able to comprehend the magnitude of the lovers' feelings than are the lovers' parents. The Friar is the first to see the potential benefit of the lovers' match for the feuding families (2.3.91–92), but his consistent advocacy of moderation belies the value Shakespeare places on the lovers' private passions that, from the first, transcend the feud. The Friar's wish to use the match to reconcile Capulets and Montagues shows by contrast the degree to which Romeo and Juliet's love, unlike Antigone's for her brother, is not public, not a political statement (Calderwood 95). The lovers first disregard and then reject their family ties, seeking instead a world in each other. The play balances individualistic desires against the order and continuity of family and the state. While *Antigone* argues that the private and the public cannot be separated, *Romeo and Juliet* shows that the two spheres can be separated—but only at terrible cost to both.

When the class has read act 3, with its striking reversal of the lovers' fortunes (peripeteia, in Aristotle's terms), I revert to Frye's notion of time and tragedy. Frye begins with this statement:

> The basis of the tragic vision is being in time, the sense of the one-
> directional quality of life, where everything happens once and for all,
> where every act brings unavoidable and fateful consequences.   (3)

Perhaps understandably, students of traditional college age have great difficulty in paraphrasing this statement. Frye's point is that tragedy comes from the realization that time only moves forward and that deeds performed cannot be undone. This idea may be more easily understood by older students. I don't belabor Frye's point because I know that the lovers' "misadventured piteous overthrows" (prologue 7) will give us ample opportunity to see that, in *Romeo and Juliet,* actions can never be reversed but lead to ever broader and less controllable circumstances.

The following writing assignment starts off our discussion of time in the play:

> Read from the beginning of the play through act 3 and mark all refer
> ences to the passage of time, including references to morning and
> evening, day and night, hours and minutes, passing years and passing sea
> sons, early and late, speed or haste and delay, clocks striking. Select three
> speeches referring to time. Write a sentence or two on each reference,
> explaining the significance of time—how it passes quickly or slowly, how
> its passage is positive or negative, how it indicates maturity or any other
> trait associated with time passing.

I point out that while the parents in the play respond to time's inevitable pressure by planning marriages and births intended to defeat time, the young characters can only submit to subjective experience. Students often note the play's stress on continuing the family name. During his initial talk with Paris, Capulet expresses equal concern at Juliet's physical immaturity and at her possible incapacity to carry a pregnancy to term and thus ensure the continuation of the Capulet bloodline (1.2.7–15). This scene needs to be discussed even if students do not mention it, because they often assume erroneously that it was customary during the Renaissance period for girls to marry at Juliet's age.

The stages of the life cycle are memorably presented in 1.3 when the Nurse interrupts Lady Capulet's discussion of Juliet's readiness for marriage with a recollection of the girl's weaning. The joke about Juliet's fall as a toddler foreshadows her entrance into sexuality and adulthood. Many editions do not gloss the line "Thou wilt fall backward when thou hast more wit" (1.3.42), so I explain that it refers to falling backward to receive a sexual embrace. The class generally enjoys the joke when it is clarified, and students make the connection between past bawdry and the imminent future of Juliet's romance. Though Juliet appears as one link in her family's dynastic chain ("I was your mother much upon these years / That you are now a maid," says Lady Capulet [1.3.72–73]), as an individual she must leave behind an infancy to which she cannot return.

The metaphor opening the chorus of act 2 ("Now old desire doth in his death-bed lie, / And young affection gapes to be his heir" [1–2]) continues the concern with inheritance and bloodlines, while the tenor of the metaphor reminds us of the swift changeability of young people's affections and implies that we should question whether Romeo truly loves Juliet. The images of time in the balcony scene, however, lay this question to rest. Juliet expresses her concern about Romeo's constancy by alluding to the changeable moon and the sudden appearance and disappearance of lightning (2.2.109–20). Like Antigone, she sees proof of love in actions, not words, and asks Romeo to show his sincerity by engaging in an unbreakable bond, since he cannot give evidence of a long-standing affection.

When the lovers bid each other good-bye (2.2.164–76), time seems to slow almost to a stop. When Juliet regrets the time that will pass before they meet again, Romeo pledges to stand beneath her window indefinitely, and does so until Juliet sees the coming of dawn, the promise of their imminent meeting. Although the adults in the play perceive time dynastically, moving through years or generations, the lovers see time subjectively—it slows or quickens according to their feelings. Moments of togetherness seem timeless and separation seems endless. Juliet's later impatience with her nurse (2.5.1–17) shows Juliet's sense of time's slowness, of her desire to hasten toward love's fulfillment. But in the middle of act 3, time speeds up, pressing the lovers toward the moment of separation (see 3.5.1–53). As Susan Snyder points out, "Time is the villain. Time in comedy generally works for regeneration and reconciliation, but in tragedy it propels the protagonists to destruction; there is not enough of it, or it goes wrong somehow" ("*Romeo*," in Andrews 80).[1] As the class will find when they read the last two acts, time repeatedly works against the lovers: the Capulets press Juliet for a hasty marriage to Paris; Friar John fails to leave Verona before being confined because of the plague; Friar Lawrence reaches the Capulet tomb too late to prevent Romeo's suicide.

Although *Romeo and Juliet* does not conform to the neo-Aristotelian notion of the unity of time (as *Antigone* does), this play, of all Shakespeare's major tragedies, is by far the most compressed in time. The entire action occurs in less than a week: Tybalt dies on Monday, the day after the Capulets' feast, and one day later Juliet takes the potion that produces signs of death for forty-two hours. The compression of events is emphasized by the tightness of the plot (quite unlike the episodic plots that Aristotle decries). Tybalt's animus toward Romeo derives from Romeo's attendance at the Capulets' feast; Juliet's engagement to Paris had already been planned by her parents, and her marriage is hurried on specifically to dissipate the girl's supposed grief over Tybalt's death.

I have the class consider how time structures characters' expectations and how events restructure characters' perceptions of time. Snyder, to whom I refer the class, points out that both the Nurse and the Friar are functionaries of a comic world that initially "endorses opportunistic shifts and realistic accommodations as means to an end of new social health" ("*Romeo*," in Andrews 73). I ask students to identify events that cause time in the play to speed up, that create a sense of urgency and inevitability. The most obvious events are the deaths of Tybalt and Mercutio, but students may also point to the consummation of the marriage, symbolic of entrance into adulthood, or to the proclamation of Romeo's exile, which makes the lovers anticipate the pain of extended absence.

When the class has finished reading the play, I recontextualize the lovers in the world of Verona, the world that the choruses force us to confront. (Significantly, film versions often eliminate the choruses, although Baz Luhrmann in his 1996 film retains them as evening news reports about the lovers' shocking double suicide.) I ask the class to consider the prologue's depiction of Verona as a sick society and then to examine the following lines: 2.3.1–22; 3.5.65–242; and 5.3.101–310. I ask students to give thought to how marriage, the passage of time, or the death of the lovers might be perceived as a *pharmakon* (both poison and cure) for a sick society.

Romeo and Juliet's construction of private versus public differs from that of *Antigone*. In both plays, lovers are torn apart by the intrusion of civic concerns into their private world, but Shakespeare's Verona lacks the strong civic structure evident in *Antigone*. Escalus never holds the moral force of the senators of Thebes, and ultimately his attempts at maintaining law fail to prevent disorder and bloodshed. In *Antigone*, the public arena is obviously the more significant one: tragedy results from the heroine's determination to enter that arena and to demonstrate that the private and the public spheres are one. But in *Romeo and Juliet* the public order appears to be subordinated to the lovers' private concerns. Frye comments (and students sometimes recall the idea) that "tragedy often ends with the survivors forming [. . .] a secondary or social contract, a relation among more ordinary men which will achieve enough working justice or equity to minimize further tragedy" (*Fools* 5–6). The deaths of Romeo and Juliet achieve what Escalus cannot: a lasting bond between the warring households and the promise of peace. It is *because* Verona lacks a strong civic component that the tragedy occurs, but as each patriarch promises to erect a golden statue representing the other family's child (5.3.298–304), the words of the patriarchs evoke the possibility that they will begin to act again as elders should, strengthening the order of their community.

Asking students to consider Verona itself as a character moves them away from the lovers and less productive questions about love at first sight. The final image of the two golden statues promises an apotheosis of the lovers, making Romeo and Juliet's love less important than their attempt to rise above family feuds. The statues are public icons of a private, hitherto secret feeling; the tragic deaths of Romeo and Juliet become at once an illustration of the evils of feuding and a way of resolving the Capulet-Montague feud (see Calderwood 108–09). My students easily see how the deaths of the lovers entail the reconciliation of the families, and students' diagnoses of Verona's illness offer many valuable ideas—especially when nonmajors attempt to apply what they have learned in psychology or sociology courses. Bringing the class to recognize the salutary effects of time is more difficult, since time is an obstacle in the play's second half. But students' "Why didn't they . . . ?" questions can be reconstructed as comments that less precipitate action at some points might have preserved the lives of the lovers and enabled marriage rather than death to end the feud. That observation returns us to the Aristotelian concept of hamartia, which we discussed in the context of *Antigone*. We can consider whether a tendency toward haste or a desire for finality may indeed be the tragic flaw of the lovers. Naive readers frequently hold the view that the play is a moralistic production about what ensues when children fail to obey their parents. The concept of hamartia allows us to integrate elements of that view without reducing the play's complexity to a simplistic parable for errant children.

The class reads several other plays after *Romeo and Juliet*. As we move toward more contemporary dramas, I spend less time on historical context; instead, I increasingly emphasize the interplay of class and gender issues in the construction of tragedy. I usually teach Strindberg's *Miss Julie* (but Ibsen's *A Doll's House* or *Hedda Gabler* would also work well), Genet's *The Maids*, and Caryl Churchill's *Fen*. Whether or not these plays are indeed tragedies is irrelevant—the generic uncertainty gives us the opportunity to consider just what we mean by the word *tragedy*. Strindberg's play contrasts starkly with *Romeo and Juliet*: the sexual attraction between Julie and her father's manservant, Jean, makes the love relationship between Romeo and Juliet appear more plausible by virtue of its differences. The innocence and comparative naïveté of Shakespeare's lovers become more apparent when compared with the self-gratification of Strindberg's couple. Julie's views on sex, alternately cynical and overly romantic, contrast with Juliet's spiritual understanding of love. But elements of heroism remain in Julie. While her lover lives on, she commits suicide, presumably to erase and to atone for her descent into a sordid liaison; her death echoes those of mythical figures such as the Roman Lucretia and reaffirms Julie's position as an aristocrat. The students' definition of tragedy is refined by considering the suicides of Julie and Juliet and whether such self-destruction increases the magnitude of the dramatic action. These questions lead to a valuable discussion of Aristotle's implication that social rank determines heroic stature. Although Julie and Juliet seem to come from similar milieus, Julie's heroism often seems lesser. Asking the class why that should be so provokes a worthwhile discussion. Even when conservative students argue that Julie demeans herself by her liaison (a view that simplifies the play considerably), they are helping the class develop its ideas about heroism and the relation between heroism and tragedy.

Questions about social rank offer a wonderful lead-in to discussion of Genet's play *The Maids*, the story of two servant girls who, dressed as their mistress, engage in repeated ritual humiliations that culminate eventually in the suicide of one of the maids. I ask students to compare the ritualism in *The Maids* with the emphasis on ceremony and proper forms in *Romeo and Juliet*. Students often point out that time is important in *The Maids*, as it is in Shakespeare's play, though for different reasons. Genet's play enables us to reconsider Shakespeare's mingling of kings and clowns. No one finds the death of Claire tragic in the sense that one is moved to pity or to regret the wasted life, but the maids' desire for greatness helps the class think about legitimate and illegitimate notions of grandeur and the magnitude necessary to create a classical tragedy.

During the unit on *The Maids*, we read excerpts from John Willett's *Brecht on Theatre: The Development of an Aesthetic*, and Brecht's Marxism offers yet another way to consider tragedy. Brecht condemns dramas that privilege a single character's point of view. He objects to plays like *Romeo and Juliet*, which encourage audiences to accept misfortune as inevitable and even, perhaps, attractive because it is "poetic." Brecht offers a number of techniques to alienate the watcher from the performance and remind the audience that the play is only a dramatized fiction. We discuss the different messages a director could send by using these techniques in productions of the plays in the course.

The final play, Caryl Churchill's *Fen*, is heavily influenced by Brecht; it presents a series of episodes in the lives of twentieth-century women in the isolated fen country of England, where economics and geography severely limit women's options. To construe *Fen* as a tragedy is to rewrite it, but the play does represent an interesting intersection between art and politics. Class discussion tends to focus on one character, a young woman with the abbreviated name of Val. Like Miss Julie, Val attempts to run away and fails. Like many of the female protagonists in the other plays, Val gains a much-desired respite from pain by committing suicide. But Val's story is only one of many in the play. The dramatic construction of *Fen* contrasts with that of Shakespeare's play, which offers an easily recognizable hierarchy of dramatic importance among the characters.

While *Romeo and Juliet* stresses the individuality of the lovers in a way that is decidedly antithetical to Brechtian epic theater, *Fen* suggests that the identities of Val and her lover Frank hardly matter—thus rendering the play antithetical to the values of tragedy. It is this Marxist aspect of *Fen* that makes the play useful for crystallizing students' understanding of the construction—and even the ethics—of tragic drama.

Romeo and Juliet differs from many classic tragedies in that it focuses on two characters rather than one. That emphasis enables the class to question Aristotle's implication that a tragedy should be about one person. On the one hand, *Romeo and Juliet* is about the two lovers and their dual fall; on the other, the play is about the community of Verona as a whole, its sickness and recovery —just as *Fen* is about the fen country. Such comparisons help the class consider tragedies as reflections of social problems, while a critical reading of Brecht prevents students from understanding plays solely as social critique or polemic. Brecht helps the class recognize and avoid simplistic analyses of the plays; Frye helps students to develop complex analyses based on familiar models such as those of the Bible. By the end of the semester, students recognize not only the beauty of *Romeo and Juliet* but also the fact that its valorization of beauty and timelessness can be interpreted and evaluated as a statement about what Shakespeare considers of enduring importance.

NOTE

[1] My discussion of time in *Romeo and Juliet* draws extensively on Snyder's ideas and on those of James Calderwood in "*Romeo and Juliet*: A Formal Dwelling."

Teaching *Romeo and Juliet* Historically

Dorothea Kehler

"Some shall be pardon'd, and some punished," states Prince Escalus at the close of *Romeo and Juliet* (5.3.308). I like to ask students, Whom would *you* pardon or punish? On the one hand, I want them to realize that the Shakespearean text does not foreclose interpretive possibilities but rather speaks to our values; *Romeo and Juliet* "means" something different to each of us. On the other hand, since my question invariably elicits some harsh judgments, it gives me the opportunity to play defense attorney. I have a few favorite clients—Friar Lawrence, the Nurse, the Apothecary—on whose behalf I situate the play historically so that students can develop a more complex understanding of why these characters act as they do.

By locating *Romeo and Juliet* in early modern Europe, I encourage students to rethink the play's social dimension. My hope is that the class will come to perceive *Romeo and Juliet*, long regarded as a tragedy of fate, as no less a social tragedy. To assert that in a better world than Shakespeare's—or ours—parents would not teach hatred, boys would not murder their way to manhood, and girls would not be made mothers at puberty is perhaps to belabor the obvious. Less obvious to students, however, is the extent to which Veronese society determines behaviors and events that drive the play toward its tragic conclusion. My lesson for students, then, is that while the play allows for plural interpretations, it speaks with greater subtlety to those who have some familiarity with the early modern world.

After Friar Lawrence relates the occurrences leading to the protagonists' deaths, the Prince seems to exonerate him, saying, "We still have known thee for a holy man" (5.3.270). My students are often less lenient, primarily because of the Friar's flight from the tomb. I have also found that a significant number of students share Juliet's contempt for the Nurse when she advises a bigamous second marriage. And whereas some students overlook the scene with the Apothecary (as did Franco Zeffirelli in the 1968 film), perhaps because they don't find it relevant to the main action, others are quick to condemn the Apothecary as an archetypal drug dealer, seeing him as the character most worthy of punishment. These students trust that in a retributive act 6 the Prince will track him down.

I begin my defense by explaining that although time out of mind well-meaning men have lost their nerve, the older generation has urged the younger to regard marriage opportunistically, and the wealthy have tempted the impoverished to commit crimes, societal conditions generating such responses can be historically specific. To take the class a step further, I point out that conditions portrayed in *Romeo and Juliet's* Italy existed in corresponding forms in Elizabethan England, the only milieu we can be sure Shakespeare knew and therefore the one inevitably reflected in his plays. Moreover, the English had a predilection for displacing what they regretted about their own society onto the Italians. Thus in many respects we can read these settings interchangeably, aware that Shakespeare, working under an absolutist government given to censorship and brutal methods of correction, put a premium on caution and distanced his plays, at least nominally in time or place, from England.

Once students appreciate the blurring between Shakespeare's English experience, set against the background of the Reformation, and the play's Catholic Veronese setting, Friar Lawrence's abandonment of Juliet in act 5 appears less callous. That is to say, in Verona the Friar represents the established religion; his actions, not his faith, are in question. But if he is as much an English as an Italian friar—which the name Lawrence could suggest to English ears—the situation is radically different. An English Lawrence would have faced the sectarian hatred that gains prominence during hard times. The English version of the mendicant orders represented by Friar Lawrence consisted of between three and four hundred priests who were participants in the Catholic mission (Meyer 163n1). After Protestant Elizabeth's excommunication by Pius V (published in 1570, following the unsuccessful Catholic-led Northern Rebellion of the previous year), those priests faced increasing peril. By the mid 1580s they faced death. After the defeat of the Armada in 1588, a renewed attack by Catholic Spain was thought imminent, most particularly between 1592 and 1597 (Outhwaite 24–25). In England fear of war exacerbated the anxieties of economic hardship. The much remarked-on "crisis of the 1590s" afflicted all of Europe, perhaps the Continent more severely than Shakespeare's London, but historians describe the 1590s in England as a time of "plague, repeated harvest failure, massive price inflation, heavy taxation, depression [. . .], large-scale unemployment, and escalating crime and vagrancy" (Archer 9). Such conditions intensified paranoia and scapegoating. Catholic clergy, commonly regarded as spies, were hounded all the more fiercely.

Young English priests, trained at Continental seminaries and newly returned to their homeland, served Catholic recusants. They were instructed by their superiors to assume secular disguises; they slept in fields until they could find cramped quarters in safe houses and were ready to flee at a moment's notice. Arnold Oskar Meyer, a Catholic historian and apologist, quotes a mission priest who in 1581 depicted conditions that were only to worsen:

> Sometimes when we were sitting merrily at table, conversing familiarly on matters of faith and devotion (for our talk is generally of such things), there comes a hurried knock at the door, like that of a pursuivant. All start up and listen—like deer when they hear the huntsman; we leave our food and commend ourselves to God in a brief ejaculation; nor is word or sound heard till the servants come to say what the matter is. If it is nothing, we laugh at our fright. (209)

But capture was no laughing matter, for priests were subject to excruciating torture and savage deaths. Meyer estimates that during Elizabeth's reign a third to a half of them were executed, while others died in prison (163, 184).

For Elizabethan playgoers, a friar whose first response to danger is to bolt must have appeared the height of realism: "Stay not to question, for the watch is coming. / Come go, good Juliet *[noise again]*, I dare no longer stay" (5.3.158–59). Thanks to the publicity accorded our military's "don't ask, don't tell" policy on homosexuality, publicity that draws attention to so-called status crimes, students are quick to understand that in Protestant England a friar's crime was his status as a Catholic clergyman. Whereas in historical Verona a friar might flee because he had exceeded his authority, that is, because of what he had *done,* in Shakespeare's Verona (to the extent that it draws on Protestant England), he flees because of what he is.

While a friar ministering to Catholics in turn-of-the-century England was almost certain to lose his life, a servant who betrayed a master's trust was liable to face less severe punishment. The Nurse, apt to be dismissed from her position, since she loses both her charge and her good name with Juliet's death, had already lost Juliet's respect. By advising bigamy—"I think it best you married with the County"—the Nurse transforms herself into an "Ancient damnation" in Juliet's eyes (3.5.217, 235). Why bigamy? The Nurse advises:

> Beshrow my very heart,
> I think you are happy in this second match,
> For it excels your first; or if it did not,
> Your first is dead, or 'twere as good he were
> As living here and you no use of him.   (3.5.221–25)

In Protestant England, as in Catholic Italy, divorce was not an option. Consequently, in the Nurse's socioeconomic class, a group whose members were sufficiently unimportant to be unknown outside their immediate locality, informal separations and desertions often ended dismal unions. Bigamous marriages were one corollary of these escapes. Geographic distance—even of slight extent by modern standards—lent anonymity, making bigamous marriages difficult to detect. (Some culprits, of course, were apprehended; Bridewell Hospital—actually a house of correction—counted detected bigamists among such other sexual offenders as prostitutes, bawds and pimps, clients of prostitutes, adulterers, rapists, and child molesters [Archer 239].)

The social historian Susan Dwyer Amussen offers enlightening stories from the late-sixteenth and early-seventeenth centuries (124–26). A country rector, asked if a parishioner (one Henry Farthing) about to wed already had a wife, replied that it was impossible to tell, Farthing having come from a town all of sixteen miles away. Women abandoned their spouses less often than did men, but some wives deserted too. Richard Rockley's wife left him; he later remarried, claiming that she was dead, but his neighbors doubted his assumption and thought the marriage bigamous. John Lebie bigamously married Margaret Peach, then left her, whereupon Margaret, too, attempted to make a bigamous marriage. Another Margaret, Margaret Least, maintained that her first husband, who had abandoned her, was dead, but he reappeared six years after her bigamous remarriage. When the Nurse urges Juliet to accept Paris on the grounds that Juliet's "first [husband] is dead, or 'twere as good he were," Renaissance playgoers might have recalled the claims of spousal death, frequently but sometimes dubiously made to justify remarriage. In a society where public records were few, communication was limited, and distance was momentous, bigamy was an option, albeit a radical one.

Or rather, bigamy was an option for the less fortunate. "This was no way out, however," observes Keith Wrightson, "for those whose property and obligations kept them tied to a particular locality. If their marriages were unsuccessful, then they had to be endured" (100). Members of prominent families could not walk away and remarry. That Juliet finds the Nurse's counsel—which is congruent with the behavior of ordinary folk—outrageous and vicious not only testifies to Juliet's innocence, ethics, and love for Romeo but also serves as a class marker. Shakespeare sharpens the characterization of the Nurse through her flexible conscience regarding matters domestic and sexual. Class codes divide Juliet from her nurse, who may have been self-protective but who nevertheless, like Romeo, "thought all for the best" (3.1.104). When alerted to the social factors that shape the Nurse and her moral values, students are less inclined to condemn her.

What future awaits the Nurse if she is discharged? In London some widows were offered relief by their parishes; in fact, in the 1590s widows were the most common beneficiaries of what today we would call welfare (Archer 190). If, however, the Nurse is punished as a disorderly servant—a standard category drawing a routine sentence—she would be imprisoned for a month, be forced to perform hard labor, and be whipped regularly (Archer 218). The middle-aged widow of a poor man (poor, else why would she have become a wet nurse?), kept on as a servant and nanny, she cannot expect to remarry as might a younger and better-off woman (Brodsky 122–24). She will have to support herself, albeit servants in England of the 1590s, lacking skills and references, had a hard time. Positions were scarce and in high demand; many workers were forced to travel in search of them:

> Servants turned out of service [. . .] would mingle on the road with migrant workers, harvest workers, and youngsters in search of service or apprenticeships. To such people, begging, stealing, or working might well have been equally attractive methods of getting by, each of them to be employed when appropriate.   (Sharpe 100–01)

In the 1590s crime was a means of survival for people who might have been law-abiding, given a choice. And even vagrancy—read homelessness, a plight that afflicted servants more than it did any other occupational group and that swelled over twelvefold between the 1560s and 1620s—was a punishable offense (Beier 204, 212).

Shakespeare instantiates the relation between poverty and crime in his portrayal of the starving Apothecary: "meagre were his looks, / Sharp misery had worn him to the bones" (5.1.40–41). Romeo, "[n]oting this penury," remarks to himself:

> An' if a man did need a poison now,
> Whose sale is present death in Mantua,
> Here lives a caitiff wretch would sell it him. (5.1.49–52)

This representation of social injustice may have had a source in the wide gap between rich and poor Elizabethans: poverty rapidly increased in the last quarter of the sixteenth century because of failed harvests, stagflation, and the enclosure of large tracts of grain-growing land for sheep grazing. Romeo, a mere adolescent leading a privileged life, has already perceived enough about his society to persuade a poor man to crime:

> APOTHECARY.   Such mortal drugs I have, but Mantua's law
>   Is death to any he that utters them.
> ROMEO.   Art thou so bare and full of wretchedness,
>   And fearest to die? Famine is in thy cheeks,
>   Need and oppression starveth in thy eyes,
>   Contempt and beggary hangs upon thy back;
>   The world is not thy friend, nor the world's law,
>   The world affords no law to make thee rich;
>   Then be not poor, but break it, and take this.
>   (5.1.66–74)

The crisis of the 1590s is reflected in the Apothecary's predicament. To survive, the Apothecary, like many famished Englishmen, reluctantly agrees to break the law: "My poverty, but not my will, consents" (5.1.75).

An apothecary in Elizabethan England ranked at the low end of the medical profession, itself inferior in status to the military, the church, and the law. William Harrison, who in 1557 described the structure of English society, would probably have placed well-to-do apothecaries directly below the nobility and gentry, among those urban commoners of sufficient wealth to hold financially demanding political offices. But how easy in a period of economic stress for the wealthy to experience downward mobility, slipping into the lower strata of itinerant workers, poor farmers, artisans, and servants—those who were altogether without "voice nor authoritie [. . .] to be ruled and not to rule other"— and from thence into pauperism, vagrancy—and disproportionate susceptibility to plague (Harrison qtd. in Wrightson 19).

As famine weakened the poor, overcrowding and substandard health habits formed a matrix of vulnerability to death from "infectious pestilence" (5.2.10), the worst being bubonic plague. A disease of rodents, spread first by fleas and then by its human victims, plague claimed as many as four out of five of those taken ill, usually within a week of infection (Slack 7). The practice of quarantine, while an important public health measure, could aggravate misery and create new predicaments. Quarantine frustrates Friar John's attempt to deliver the crucial letter to Romeo. Friar John reports that because the fellow Franciscan with whom he intended to travel to Mantua was comforting the sick,

> the searchers of the town,
> Suspecting that we both were in a house
> Where the infectious pestilence did reign,
> Seal'd up the doors and would not let us forth,
> So that my speed to Mantua there was stay'd.

"Who bare my letter then to Romeo?" asks Friar Lawrence. Friar John answers, "I could not send it—here it is again— / Nor get a messenger to bring it thee, / So fearful were they of infection" (5.2.8–16). The practice of quarantine was common in England. In fact, *Romeo and Juliet* was presumably composed in 1595, shortly after the reopening of the theaters, which had been closed— "Seal'd up"—for two years because of the plague. Thomas Dekker, a contemporary of Shakespeare's, describes the 1603 visitation of bubonic plague to London, "the diseased Citie":

> For he that durst (in the dead houre of gloomy midnight) haue bene so valiant, as to haue walkt through the still and melancholy streets, what thinke you should haue bene his musicke? Surely the loude grones of rauing sicke men; the strugling panges of soules departing: In euery house griefe striking vp an Allarum: Seruants crying out for maisters: wiues for husbands, parents for children, children for their mothers: here he should haue met some frantickly running to knock vp Sextons; there, others fear- / fully sweating [C₃ᵛ] with Coffins, to steale forth dead bodies, least the fatall hand-writing of death should seale vp their doores.   (38–39)

Friar John's aborted mission is grounded in the dread of plague, a disease that made victims even of survivors. In 1590s London, plague so burdened the city's economy and minimal safety net that it was easier for inhabitants to elude death than to avoid penury (Archer 9, 13). The Apothecary may represent bottom-rung professionals and small-business owners impoverished by plague. Some students suggest that in a time of sickness an apothecary would thrive. But most agree with Romeo that nothing can make a wealthy man of the Apothecary; he has fallen too low: "The world is not thy friend."

Awareness of *Romeo and Juliet*'s analogues in Elizabethan social conditions

tends to soften how students judge the characters some had initially condemned. As for the Prince, if he keeps his word, more likely than not it is the
poor who will be punished. The sentences meted out in Arthur Brooke's *The
Tragicall Historye of Romeus and Juliet,* Shakespeare's "main and perhaps sole
source" (Bullough 274), are always of interest to students and generate considerable discussion. In Brooke's poem, the Friar is "discharged quyte, and no
marke of defame / Did seeme to blot, or touch at all, the honor of his name"
(lines 2999–3000), yet he chooses to spend the remaining five years of his life as
a hermit; the Nurse "is banisht in her age" (2987); and the Apothecary is
hanged.

Most students also qualify their opinions about the nature of tragedy in the
play. For the protagonists, it is a tragedy of fate; Romeo and Juliet are fortune's
fools, born to die young in a world they never made. But for the play's original
audiences—and for us, given some slight historical prompting—Shakespeare's
perception of human responsibility for destructive social formations is not far
submerged in the text. That perception surfaces in Romeo's speech to the
Apothecary and anticipates King Lear's condemnation of justice for sale:

> Thorough tatter'd clothes [small] vices do appear;
> Robes and furr'd gowns hide all. [Plate sin] with
>   gold,
> And the strong lance of justice hurtless breaks;
> Arm it in rags, a pigmy's straw does pierce it.
>   (4.6.164–67, brackets in original)

A historicist approach, then, can lead students to readings that include but
reach beyond thwarted love or bad luck and that value *Romeo and Juliet* as a
richly allusive, politically progressive social tragedy.

Teaching *Romeo and Juliet* with *Troilus and Cressida* and *Antony and Cleopatra*

Thomas H. Blackburn

The pedagogical setting in which I assign the trio of *Romeo and Juliet* (*Rom.*) *Troilus and Cressida* (*Tro.*), and *Antony and Cleopatra* (*Ant.*) uniquely enables so demanding an intertextual exercise. This group of plays comes roughly at the midpoint of the fourteen meetings of an honors seminar in Shakespeare in which we read twenty-three plays of the canon. The ten or fewer students in the seminar meet with me for one weekly session lasting up to five hours. Since the seminar counts for half of each student's class load for the semester, it becomes reasonable for me to assign the three plays over two weeks and require a five- or six-page essay as well. In the first meeting on the plays, students read aloud scenes they have selected to open up issues that interested them in their first reading of the plays. The students' essays, made available through the campus computer network before the second session, provide the focus for discussion in that session. Though the experience would not be so concentrated, one could work with these plays through three or four weeks of class sessions or read *Romeo and Juliet* in conjunction with only one of the other two plays.

When we come to this group of plays, my seminar students have already worked intertextually with plays from different points in Shakespeare's career in a one-week assignment that paired *The Taming of the Shrew* with *Measure for Measure*. They will also have covered *Love's Labours Lost*, *Two Gentlemen of Verona*, *As You Like It*, *Twelfth Night*, and *Much Ado about Nothing*. This earlier work in comedy provides students with contexts for viewing the blocking action of Old Capulet as he demands that Juliet marry Paris, for recognizing the Petrarchan excesses of some of Romeo's love discourse, and for seeing how his obligations to his young Montague kinsman and to friends such as Mercutio lead to conflicts with his maturing love for Juliet.

In addition to choosing and preparing scenes for the first session on the plays, the students receive an assignment I have devised to ground their reading in particular attention to the texts. The first part of the assignment asks students to go through the plays and list the adjectives, images, and other descriptive terms or actions defining each of the sides in the central oppositions in the plays: Montague and Capulet in *Romeo and Juliet,* Greek and Trojan in *Troilus and Cressida,* and Rome and Egypt in *Antony and Cleopatra.* Working from those lists and from the close reading of the plays necessary to formulate them, students then draft a conclusion about the nature, scope, and origins of each opposition. Through this part of the assignment the students also become aware of the extent to which scenes associated with each side of the opposition alternate to constitute a distinctive structural feature of the plays.

The second part of the exercise turns attention to the pairs of lovers by asking the students to pay close attention to the language in a series of comparable scenes in which the nature and basis of the evolving love relationships may be discovered. The list of scenes to be examined usually includes three in which the man describes his beloved and reveals something of the nature of his feelings (*Rom.* 1.5.46–55; *Tro.* 1.1.49–64; *Ant.* 1.1.35–42, 50–57); three in which the woman reflects on the man's strategies of wooing (*Rom.* 2.2.85–106; *Tro.* 1.2.284–97; *Ant.* 4.13.1–10); three in which the lovers face the dawn after a night together (*Rom.* 3.5.1–64; *Tro.* 4.2; *Ant.* 4.4); and three in which the lovers declare their response to the certainty that they shall not live happily ever after (Romeo and Juliet and Antony and Cleopatra on their resolve to commit suicide, Troilus and Cressida on revenge or resignation to change). The essay assignment for the second week asks the students to use the evidence and definitions they have gathered to address issues such as the relation of the lovers' society to the nature of their love, the extent to which the conditions of the society determine the fate of the lovers, and the sense in which the fate of each pair is or is not tragic.

Summarizing the discoveries to which this assignment has led in the course of several seminars may suggest the potential of this intertextual reading to illuminate aspects of the earliest play of the trio. Study of the conflict between Capulet and Montague in *Romeo and Juliet* reveals, for example, that the feud is never more fully defined than as an "ancient grudge" (prologue 3) giving rise to "civil brawls, bred of an airy word" (1.1.89).[1] No cause for the families' rooted hatred of each other is adduced, and, until Tybalt slays Mercutio and Romeo kills Tybalt in revenge, no substantial reason appears for the continuance of the quarrel. The feud threatens the peace of Verona and is criticized by the other citizens, who cry "Down with the Capulets! Down with the Montagues!" (1.1.74) in a manner that foreshadows Mercutio's dying curse, "A plague o' both your houses!" (3.1.98–99, 105). But the feud has no influence beyond Verona's city walls. It is merely a matter of "mad blood" (3.1.5), stirred by a difference that seems no more than "What's in a name" (2.2.44). Set against the epic events of the Trojan war announced in the prologue to *Troilus and Cressida* or against the multifaceted political and cultural differences between Egypt and Rome in *Antony and Cleopatra,* the real—if deadly—meaninglessness and fundamental simplicity of the quarrel between the Capulets and Montagues are highlighted. Greek and Trojan in *Troilus and Cressida* are not merely family names but opposing states; the strife between them has its origin and explicit cause in "[t]he ravished Helen, Menelaus' queen, / With [whom] the wanton Paris sleeps" (prologue 9–10). No local civil brawl, the war has lasted seven weary years, seems no nearer resolution than when it began, and, as Hector notes, has literally decimated the Trojan forces (2.2.19).

The prize at stake in the contests between Mark Antony, Octavius Caesar, and Cleopatra in *Antony and Cleopatra* is discovered to be nothing less than empire. The opposition arises in part from the politics of the failed triumvirate of Caesar, Antony, and Ptolemy, which was destabilized by Caesar's drive for singular hegemony. The strife, however, is not only a political rivalry between two Romans but also a clash of cultures between Rome and Egypt. Rome is cold, its frigidity mirrored in Octavia's "holy, cold and still conversation" (2.6.124–25); Egypt is hot, the land of Cleopatra, "with Phoebus' amorous pinches black" (1.5.29). Rome is duty and the masculine culture of the warrior who would "drink / The stale of horses and the gilded puddle / Which beasts would cough at" (1.5.62–64); Egypt is the site of pleasure where Antony "fishes, drinks, and wastes / The lamps of night in revel" (1.4.4–5) and where a "triple pillar of the world" (1.1.12) may, from the Roman point of view, become "the bellows and the fan / to cool a gipsy's lust" (1.1.9–10) and be "transformed / Into a strumpet's fool" (1.1.12–13).

Students discover in analyzing these oppositions that all three male protagonists must deal with the threat of effemination as they try to negotiate between their love and the demands of the masculine cultures that perpetuate the conflicts. Romeo is taunted by Mercutio in 2.4 for having abandoned the bawdy wit of his adolescent fellows in favor of "driveling love" (2.4.90), and, when Romeo acknowledges that Mercutio has got his "mortal hurt / In my behalf" (3.1.109–10), he laments that Juliet's beauty "hath made me effeminate, / And in my temper softened valor's steel" (3.1.113–14). Choosing to honor the masculine obligations defined by the feud fatally compromises Romeo's chances of living happily ever after with Juliet.

Triolus early in the play acknowledges that his desire for Cressida has made him "weaker than a woman's tear" (1.1.9) and, when faced with the necessity of turning Cressida over to the Greeks in exchange for Antenor, accepts the loss rather than forfeit his status among his warrior brethren (4.4). Antony, when he is in his own Roman mood, recognizes that his passion for Cleopatra has deprived him of the masculine warrior prowess that made him great. As he complains to Cleopatra after he has followed her fleeing ships in the first battle against Caesar,

> Now I must
> To the young man send humble treaties, dodge
> And palter in the shifts of lowness, who
> With half the bulk of the world played as I pleased,
> Making and marring fortunes. You did know
> How much you were my conqueror, and that
> My sword, made weak by my affection, would
> Obey it on all cause.   (3.11.60–67)

Finding similarities among the lovers' choices may occasion students to reflect on the pervasive conflict in Shakespeare's plays between patriarchal ideologies of honor, which call for sacrifice of life and reduce women to objects of exchange, and the life-affirming potential of heterosexual love. Recognizing the stakes involved in the lovers' choices may lead to the further recognition that Romeo's choice is much closer to the comic dilemmas faced by characters like

Valentine or Benedict than it is to the choices faced by Antony and Troilus—though its outcome is far from comic.

Close reading of the assigned scenes both for themselves and in the context of the plays' central oppositions may lead finally to an understanding of the different modes of loving that the plays represent. To take just one example from the four sets of passages I assign for analysis, the language of the speeches in which each of the men first describes the object of his love establishes a mode that students may trace into the other scenes.

Romeo's first glimpse of Juliet calls forth the hyperbolic fervor of his sudden passion, a passion springing, like the family feud, from no cause but itself:

> O, she doth teach the torches to burn bright!
> It seems she hangs upon the cheek of night
> As a rich jewel in an Ethiop's ear—
> Beauty too rich for use, for earth too dear!
> So shows a snowy dove trooping with crows
> As yonder lady o'er her fellows shows.   (1.5.45–50)

Embedded in the praise is the dramatic irony that Juliet's beauty will indeed turn out to be "for earth too dear" and will eventually be preserved from otherwise inevitable corruption only in the timeless gold of her funeral monument.

When in a speech to Pandarus Troilus first reveals to the reader his passion for Cressida, the contrast between Troilus's words and Romeo's innocent hyperboles is striking. Troilus describes himself as "mad / In Cressid's love" (1.1.53–54). The vestiges of Romeo's Petrarchan comparatives in Troilus's speech are surrounded by images of love as disease or wound:

> Thou answer'st she is fair;
> Pour'st in the open ulcer of my heart
> Her eyes, her hair, her cheek, her gait, her voice;
> Handlest in thy discourse—O!—that her hand,
> In whose comparison all whites are ink
> Writing in their own reproach, to whose soft seizure
> The cygnet's down is harsh, and spirit of sense
> Hard as the palm of plowman. This thou tell'st me,
> As true thou tell'st me, when I say I love her;
> But, saying thus, instead of oil and balm
> Thou lay'st in every gash that love hath given me
> The knife that made it.   (1.1.54–65)

The language here is of a piece with the perfervid anticipation Troilus recounts as he awaits the consummation of his passion. He is "giddy" (3.2.17), he fears "swooning destruction" (3.2.22), and his "heart beats thicker than a feverous pulse" (3.2.35). In response to Paris's genealogy of love—"hot blood begets hot thoughts, and hot thoughts beget hot deeds, and hot deeds is love" (3.1.129–30) —Pandarus proposes that love is a "generation of vipers" (3.1.133). In this play, because the adulterous Helen is at its center, love is not "too rich [. . .] for earth." Based only on desire that depends on presence and can never be satiated, the relationship between Troilus and Cressida cannot survive change or achieve even a posthumous transcendence. Just as the honor of battle heroes is corrupted by Ulysses's petty schemings and Hector's overriding of the "moral laws / Of nature and of nations" (2.2.184–85), love is tainted by futile lust in an overall vision that reduces epic matter to a bitter and nihilistic satire on human folly.

The first description of Cleopatra voiced by Antony emphasizes not her transcendent beauty or his feverous desire but her changefulness, what Enobarbus later calls her "infinite variety," which "custom" cannot "stale" (2.2.245–46). Diverting Cleopatra from her insistence that he give audience to the Roman ambassadors who will eventually call him back to confront Caesar, Antony replies:

> Fie, wrangling Queen!
> Whom everything becomes—to chide, to laugh,
> To weep; whose every passion fully strives
> To make itself in thee, fair and admired!   (1.1.50–53).

For the "love of Love and her soft hours" (1.1.46), Antony is content to deny the claims of empire. Antony consciously measures the strength of his love against what that love may cost him; even though his experience tells him that his beloved is "cunning past man's thought" (1.2.153), he will wish that "Rome in Tiber melt, and the wide arch / Of the ranged empire fall!" (1.1.35–36). The very changefulness that Romeo and Juliet and, with different anxieties, Troilus and Cressida must vow to resist is the essence of Cleopatra's power to transcend the inevitable death of desire in desire's fulfillment. Romeo and Juliet escape the diminution of love by dying early; Troilus and Cressida enjoy no such release. In lines that notably echo Antony's earlier formulation, Enobarbus defines the queen's power over the satiety that makes Cressida so fearful of submitting to Troilus and makes Juliet regret for a moment her frankness to Romeo in the balcony scene:

> Other women cloy
> The appetites they feed, but she makes hungry
> Where most she satisfies, for vilest things
> Become themselves in her, that the holy priests
> Bless her when she is riggish.   (2.2.246–50)

For Antony and Cleopatra, long experienced in love and sensuality, love is neither a matter of simple absolutes, as it is for Romeo and Juliet, nor a fantasy of constancy based on ephemeral passion, as it is for Troilus and Cressida. Antony and Cleopatra do not come to a swift suicidal end, dying on a single kiss, as do Romeo and Juliet. Nor are they left to linger in unheroic disillusion, as are Troilus and Cressida. Their protracted and complicated suicides reflect the ambiguities of role and relationship that both doom and glorify the choices they make for themselves and for each other. The Roman sword with which Antony fails to end life briefly and the "pretty worm of Nilus" (5.2.243), which is Cleopatra's still erotic but "easy [way] to die" (5.2.356), lack the romantic simplicity of the poison and dagger in *Romeo and Juliet*. The grand scale of the older lovers' passion and sacrifice, however, is summed in Cleopatra's lament that with Antony's passing,

> withered is the garland of the war;
> The soldier's pole is fall'n! Young boys and girls
> Are level now with men. The odds is gone,
> And there is nothing left remarkable
> Beneath the visiting moon.   (4.15.65–69)

Students may finish this comparative study with the conclusion that *Romeo and Juliet* either is or is not more tragic than *Antony and Cleopatra* or *Troilus and Cressida*. The naive idealism of the young lovers set against the meaninglessness of the feud that envelops them evokes deep sympathy in some students. Others see in Romeo and Juliet's naïveté and helplessness a lack of self-knowledge and of conscious choice that renders the young lovers' suicides less tragic than Antony and Cleopatra's complex sacrifice in the name of love. The world of *Troilus and Cressida* is discovered to be tragic only in the sense that there is no escape from the taint of excessive and adulterous passion or from the futile folly of a war fought for a worthless prize. Reading these ampersand plays together, students find that *Romeo and Juliet* emerges as a romantic tragedy; *Troilus and Cressida*, as a love story for cynics; and *Antony and Cleopatra*, as a tragic romance, a *Romeo and Juliet* for grown-ups.

NOTE

[1] Citations in this essay are from *The Complete Works of Shakespeare*, edited by David Bevington.

Queer Romeo and Juliet:
Teaching Early Modern "Sexuality" in Shakespeare's "Heterosexual" Tragedy
Nicholas F. Radel

Despite what seems to be *Romeo and Juliet*'s wholly unapologetic celebration of heterosexuality, the play serves as an excellent point of departure for discussing early modern sexuality in England as well as the uses—or, more to the point, misuses—of Shakespeare's plays in the history of sexuality. As Jonathan Goldberg's recent article "Romeo and Juliet's *Open Rs*" makes clear, it is possible to read this play without reproducing modern biases about sexuality. Goldberg deconstructs the text to show that modern binaries around homosexuality and heterosexuality simply do not function in the play. What is more, he argues that the modern construction of sexuality as the place of the private individual (as the space of subjectivity) distinguished from the space of the social is not germane to the discussion of this early modern text. Goldberg's essay, then, is an indispensable guide to the process that we might call queering *Romeo and Juliet*, the attempt to read the play within its historically specific context in order to understand early modern erotic desire and behavior. But rather than emphasize the fungibility of gender constructions in *Romeo and Juliet*, as Goldberg does, I focus on male-male relationships and the implications of these relationships for reading the social contexts of the love story.

To begin, I like to introduce some basic ideas about early modern sexuality by discussing one of two later plays, the comedies *Twelfth Night* and *As You Like It*. Most students, like most teachers, are prone to think of male-female erotic attraction as the ground on which other eroticisms should be adjudicated and, at best, tolerated as marginal. Students and teachers also tend to think that the closure of Shakespeare's plays in marriage (or proposed marriage) contains erotic desire within an institutional structure, a structure that legitimizes heterosexuality even if it does not ensure monogamy. Most of us simply do not consider that the marriages in Shakespeare's plays are primarily social and economic structures that tell us only so much about erotic desire. But as Valerie Traub has shown, both *As You Like It* and *Twelfth Night* provide multiple examples of desire crossing and recrossing boundaries of gender (chs. 4 and 5). So, even though there are methodological problems in using a literary text as historical evidence, I have students read one of these two plays to forestall some common historical errors. For either play illustrates in a specific context two fundamental facts about early modern sexuality: erotic desire and sexual-object choice were not determinants of individual identity as they are for us, and desire was not necessarily delimited by the sex or gender of the person desired.

Rather than rely on literary evidence alone, however, I ask my students to read portions of Alan Bray's social histories. I try to help students understand Bray's point that specifically homosexual actions in the period would have failed to signify, would have remained unseen or unrecognized as a special category of sexual sin, unless they were otherwise disruptive of the social order, at which point they would have been identified as sodomy. The early modern period simply would not have made the distinction between behaviors that, for us, demarcate homosexual and heterosexual identity (*Homosexuality*, ch. 3). Equally important, Bray argues that eroticism itself may have been fully part of social institutions that we carefully distinguish from the erotic, a point clarified in a later essay, "Homosexuality and the Signs of Male Friendship in Elizabethan England." In this essay Bray shows that the discourses of male friendship in the period were often rendered in significantly erotic terms and that they could and did overlap with the discourses of sodomy. This overlap meant that anyone aware of the social and discursive codes could manipulate them, transforming what was usually seen as friendship into sodomy. Under the right conditions, anyone could reveal the presence of disruptive social factors in a relationship between two men, bringing the men's potential for real erotic involvements into focus as sodomitical.

Armed with some fundamental historical knowledge about erotic discourses and desire, students are more fully prepared to discuss *Romeo and Juliet*. The obvious place to start is with the erotics of male bonding that are so much a part of this play. Students who have seen the Zeffirelli movie or the newer Baz Luhrmann production will be inclined to locate the play's homoeroticism exclusively in Mercutio, whose phallic energy and erotic interest in Romeo are (arguably) obvious. A reading of the play that attempts to decenter heterosexuality cannot afford to ignore Mercutio, and I spend a great deal of time looking at the language of his exchanges with Romeo. In particular, I like to study the gendered and sexual ironies of 1.4.25–28,[1] when Mercutio and Romeo joke about love "pricking" Romeo. In this famous passage, Mercutio plays with the idea that Romeo has been penetrated by love in the form of the boy Cupid and invites Romeo to use his own "prick" likewise. I then take up where Mercutio "conjure[s]" (2.1.7) Romeo in the likeness of Rosaline in order to "raise" him up (2.1.30). Students also need to be made aware of the bawdy sexual innuendo of the textual crux at 2.1.38–39: "O, Romeo, that she were, O, that she were / An open-arse, and thou a poppering pear!" As Goldberg makes clear, only some modern editions supply "open-arse"; no early editions do. While including these words seems more sexually enlightened, their inclusion actually tends to suppress some of the erotic implications of the passage, in particular that Romeo's "arse" may be as open to penetration as Rosaline's (Goldberg, "*Open Rs*" 229–30, 233–34nn10–11).

Such exchanges seem to sum up Mercutio's intensely erotic image of Romeo, as does much of the sparring between the men in 2.4, when they wait for the Nurse to bring news from Juliet. But in case the potential erotics of the young men's "switch and spurs" (2.4.68) are in doubt, I ask the students to consider Tybalt's words to Mercutio when Tybalt comes to challenge Romeo after the Capulet ball: "Mercutio, thou consortest with Romeo" (3.1.44). I have the students consult the *Oxford English Dictionary,* where they discover that the primary meaning of the verb *consort* is "to accompany, keep company with." But they also find a secondary, sexual meaning that bears directly on Romeo and Mercutio's friendship. I then argue that Tybalt employs the second sense of the term in an effort to turn the normally erotic discourse of friendship into a discourse of sodomy. As Bray suggests was possible, Tybalt manipulates linguistic codes to imply that the relationship between Romeo and Mercutio is disorderly. It is not, of course, so Tybalt's insult carries little illocutionary force. But Mercutio's attempt to deflect the word toward a third definition, one with a musical valence (" 'Consort'? What, dost thou make us minstrels?" [3.1.45–6]), betrays a sense of affront that perhaps confirms the erotic undercurrent Tybalt maliciously reveals.

While remaining focused on Mercutio's relationship with Romeo, I make clear that the homoerotic energies between the two men cannot be located exclusively in Mercutio. Such a reading is not historically adequate because it imagines Mercutio as a marginal figure, disappointed in his unrequited love for Romeo, whose seemingly heterosexual identity demands that his own erotic interest will always be elsewhere than in Mercutio. As the students should realize by this point, the binary divide between homo- and heterosexuality is largely a figment of our imaginations. We have little reason to believe that Mercutio is solely interested in men or that Romeo is solely interested in women. The witty banter between the two men, like the verbal sparring and actual physical violence that occur throughout the play, stands for male-male eroticism just as surely as witty exchanges between men and women stand for male-female eroticism in other plays (in, for example, *Much Ado about Nothing*). So long as the wit and violence constitute the status quo of male homosocial relations, the implicit eroticism is neither threatening nor apparent as sodomy.

I develop this point by having students analyze the (homo)erotics of the opening scene. Although the first eighteen or so lines of Sampson's and Gregory's speech quite obviously focus on the women of the house of Montague, the scene actually plays out the men's powerful interests in each other and in the Montague men. I do not overlook the baldly phallic aggression against women that is fully inscribed in Sampson's and Gregory's bragging about the skillful use of their weapons. But I try to help students see that Gregory and Sampson objectify the women of the house of Montague in order to identify themselves as men of the house of Capulet. In other words, Sampson and Gregory take their identities not from their sexual interest in women but from their masculine identification with each other and with their masters:

GREGORY.   The quarrel is between our masters and us their men.
SAMPSON.   'Tis all one.   (1.1.19–21)

The scene illustrates what Eve Sedgwick identifies as the homosocial bonds between men and indicates how women are used to secure these bonds. If in the first scene the phallus is a tool of erotic aggression, it is also the symbol of men's powerful (and eroticized) bonds. This symbolism becomes explicit with the appearance of the Montague men: "Draw thy tool," Gregory says, "Here comes of the house of Montagues." "My naked weapon is out," Sampson returns (1.1.31–33). The scene clearly shows that the erotic interest Sampson and Gregory have in women (they imagine thrusting maids against the wall) can be easily deflected onto the men of the house of Montague, who move Sampson at least "to stand" (1.1.11). The eroticized discourse of violence here is not related in any simple way to what we call heterosexuality (nor perhaps is erotic desire itself). It is, instead, connected to the men's brawling interest in other men, both those with whom the men identify and those whom they wish to engage.

Once again, my point is reinforced by Tybalt, who here, too, conflates the discourses of orderly (erotic) male fraternity with those of disorderly sodomy. When Tybalt enters, he says to Benvolio, "What, art thou drawn among these heartless hinds?" (1.1.66). Again, sending students to the dictionary helps them understand some of the multiple valences of Tybalt's language. Literally, of course, a hind is a laborer or servant, and Tybalt's calling the Montague and Capulet men "heartless" suggests that they lack heat or passion, presumably in battle. But a hind is also a female deer, and a hart, a male one. Tybalt thus insults the brawling men's masculinity by suggesting that the men are female deer without their male mates. They are effeminate, he implies, both because they are unable to secure mates and because they lack the spirit to act boldly and effectively in battle—at this point Benvolio appears to have halted the fray. Tybalt may also energize a more long-standing poetic use of the word *hart* to signify the hunted object of erotic desire. If so, he implies that the "heartless hinds" have failed to attain their desire by failing to thrust their enemies to the wall. His words encode a discourse of sexual failure and imply that the men's hesitancy (in the face of Benvolio's opposition) is effeminate, even sodomitic. But Tybalt's transformation of this moment into a sodomitic one is also directed at Benvolio, who is "drawn" among hinds, that is, who reveals his naked weapon to his social inferiors, the servants, and who fails to master them in the only way that counts in an economy of eroticized male violence: by thrusting them to the wall. It is an extraordinarily complex moment, one that brings together the discourses of phallic aggression, erotic desire, and sodomy and one that implies that eroticized violence is normal in this world. The scene repays careful attention, then, as a paradigm for reading the play as a whole.

It is not worthwhile to dispute the self-evident ways in which *Romeo and Juliet* constructs the love of its eponymous characters as a transcendent moment seemingly outside the larger social world. But it is important to emphasize that the attractive rhetoric of withdrawal and individual self-determination that provides the tragic impetus of the play is largely the lovers' own. A historical awareness of the place of romantic love in the period suggests that the lovers are held accountable, through the logic of the play, for their rebellions against the social order. Who Romeo and Juliet are is determined not simply by their romantic desires for each other but also by the clash of conflicting social forces. The lovers are not above the fray but part of it; they are a function of their social world and represent the very terms in which that world will be reordered.

But if there is little doubt that *Romeo and Juliet* rehearses a Petrarchan-based ideology of love as withdrawal from the world, an ideology made memorable in the period by Donne's "The Good-Morrow" ("For love, all love of other sights controules, / And makes one little roome, an every where" [lines 10–11]), this view of love must be understood as a convention and not merely as a natural expression of heterosexuality. There is a relevant distinction to be made between, on the one hand, a passionate desire that seems to reflect, and indeed constitute, the lovers' identities in contrast to the world around them (and in so doing seems to rehearse the fundamental terms of modern heterosexuality: desire, identity, subjectivity) and, on the other hand, an ideology of love that imagines love distinctly within the social body. Despite the indulgences of romantic or Petrarchan poetry, love that was not in the service of orderly marriage or other social and economic institutions would have been seen as disruptive. To make this point, I ask students to look at evidence from the period that romantic love could be seen as disorderly. Robert Burton's *Anatomy of Melancholy*, for example, seems clearly to suggest that love melancholy, that is, love that causes a person to withdraw from the social world and from social responsibilities, is indeed a sickness. Because this was so, Goldberg reminds us that it may be Romeo and Juliet themselves who, in fact, commit sodomy, who violate the social order ("*Open Rs*" 225).

There are other ways to demonstrate that the lovers never escape the defining and constitutive pressures of the social world. First, Romeo and Juliet's attempt to withdraw from the world is undercut by the Friar, who, as we all know, manipulates their love in an attempt to end the feud (see 2.3.89–92). Second, even Juliet's nurse participates in returning the lovers to the social world, for she construes their relationship as an acceptable alternative to Juliet's match with the County Paris. She thus rationalizes Juliet's disorderly love for Romeo as a simple exchange within a patriarchal economy of bodies. Although commentators are frequently dismayed by the Nurse's cynical advice to Juliet to marry Paris after Romeo's banishment, that advice actually represents the second time the Nurse has authorized an exchange of men within marriage, for she knows, while negotiating with Romeo for Juliet, that Old Capulet intends for his daughter to marry Paris. The Nurse's subsequent change of heart suggests that she knows she has failed and, in fact, highlights the disorderliness that she hoped to circumvent. Her manipulations reveal how love may conflict with the social order but not stand above social laws and institutions. Finally, as Goldberg points out, the Prince, Old Capulet, and Montague construe the lovers as sacrificial victims to their own reconciliation ("*Open Rs*" 220). At the end of the play, the lovers are returned to the social world they hoped to escape, returned as evidence of that world's failures and as symbols of its future. Although the play ends with the seemingly verisimilar responses of Capulet and Montague to the deaths of their two children—the two men acting as real men responding to a family tragedy—in truth, the tragic tale of love has been conceived throughout as a way of making a point about the desirability of Montague and Capulet's reconciliation. Romeo's and Juliet's deaths, like those of all Shakespeare's tragic heroes and heroines, become the basis for the proper functioning of society.

To cement my students' sense that the lovers' identities and destinies are secured within the social world, not outside it, I have the class explore characterization, particularly Romeo's. If anything distinguishes Romeo from the other men in this play, if anything sets him apart from his social environment, it is not his supposedly sexually exclusive interest in Juliet but rather his studied refusal to participate in the world of eroticized masculine violence that defines his fellows. I build this point, first, by having students explore Romeo's character in the early scenes with Benvolio, the Friar, and Mercutio. Here, his romantic posturings make Romeo a figure of fun, subject to ridicule. He is seen as such not only by his friends but also by writers throughout the critical tradition, who persistently belittle him, comparing him unfavorably to the more mature and sophisticated Juliet. But I stress that his stepping aside from the world of his male friends does not truly take him outside Verona and its feud, for it has significant consequences for him within that world: it renders him effeminate. As is by now well known, effeminacy in the early modern period resulted not from one's too close association with men but from one's doting on women. Romeo does not live in the modern world, where his love for Juliet would be presumed to define his masculinity. He lives in the early modern world, where his masculinity is defined by his relation to other men. He himself reveals his effeminacy when Mercutio is fatally wounded by Tybalt:

> O sweet Juliet,
> Thy beauty hath made me effeminate,
> And in my temper softened valor's steel. (3.1.112–14)

Romeo responds to Mercutio's death by seeking Tybalt to exact revenge—a response that plunges him back into the world of male violence (makes a man of him, as it were). Unfortunately, this response also precipitates Romeo's tragedy and clarifies his relation to the other men in the play. He is not separate from them but fully part of their world of bravado, banter, and violence.

What is finally clear about *Romeo and Juliet* is that our modern language of sexuality seriously distorts our understanding of the play's unique historical contexts. Seeing the two young lovers as heterosexual and Mercutio as a homosexual or seeing the men in this play as safely removed from an erotic world defined primarily in terms of male-female sexual interest prevents us from fully understanding the social dynamics that make *Romeo and Juliet* a document in late-sixteenth-century discursive histories. "Queering" the play in the classroom helps return it to its contexts and, ironically, in doing so, shifts the emphasis of investigation away from sexual behavior toward the social institutions that authorized or condemned that behavior.

NOTE

[1] Citations to *Romeo and Juliet* in this essay are from *The Complete Works of Shakespeare*, edited by David Bevington.

"Who Wrote the Book of Love?"
Teaching *Romeo and Juliet* with Early Rock Music

Cynthia Marshall

Many moments in Shakespearean drama play themselves out in my mind to the accompaniment of popular music. Some of these moments I freely share with students in my classes: students seem to gain an indelible understanding of Richard of Gloucester's wooing of Lady Anne when they hear me humming the Stones' "Under My Thumb." But my associations are often too dated, eccentric, or lowbrow for many students to follow. (Othello's anguished skepticism plays for me to Springsteen's "Brilliant Disguise"; *Antony and Cleopatra* has bizarrely gaudy similarities to Hank Williams Jr.'s "Queen of My Heart" and, more raucously, "All My Rowdy Friends Are Coming Over Tonight.") Recently, however, I have realized how my inner rock and roll soundtrack to *Romeo and Juliet* proves useful in tackling a major problem of teaching this play: negotiating cynicism.

Romeo and Juliet holds the distinction of being the one play by Shakespeare that virtually every student has read before college. This acquaintance presents definite advantages to college teachers constructing a pedagogy. The characters and plot are already familiar, so attention can turn more quickly to matters such as language and thematic interpretation. More important, students can be counted on to register their sense that the play seems different now from the way it seemed when they encountered it four or five years before. It seems more bawdy, for one thing: since high school anthologies usually feature versions of the play with bawdy passages edited out, students now have an opportunity to realize not only the range of Shakespeare's humor but also the importance of editorial choices. The other, more pervasive difference students report is that the play, which seemed so compelling when they were fourteen or fifteen, now strikes them as overblown and unrealistic. In experience and maturity they have surpassed the characters with whom they previously identified. They notice the unlikely details of plot and some irritating insufficiencies of character and find it difficult to treat the play seriously as a tragedy.

For several years, pleased to see my students exercising critical judgment of any sort, I championed their cynicism. By pointing out competing discourses of affectional bonds and sexuality, I encouraged them to see the play's presentation of love as strictly rhetorical. But, perhaps because twenty-year-old students seem way too young to disbelieve utterly in the possibility of love, I began to realize that my students were missing the most important thing about the play, namely, how *Romeo and Juliet* presents at once an intensely sweet romance and a corrosively realistic perspective and expects viewers to believe, somehow, in the rightness of both. The movement from youth to age—a favorite theme of the play's formalist critics—reflects this duality, which is why my students feel smarter and more mature when they take the disbelievers' view of romance. Yet even though a crucial lesson afforded by the study of drama is the possibility of growth and change, in *Romeo and Juliet* the developmental passage does not explain enough. Mercutio, after all, is more cynical than any of the older characters are. The play challenges viewers to feel the pathos of young love and to observe love's follies. I wondered how I could help my students understand this curious mixture of effects, which corresponds closely to that of theatrical presence, in which one may weep for Romeo and Juliet even while knowing that the characters are merely actors playing dead.

What my students needed was an expanded sense of context. Judging *Romeo and Juliet* by the single criterion of mimetic realism, they deemed the play a failure because the characters' actions often seem foolish by modern standards. Given a firmer understanding of early modern courtship norms, family structure, and church influence, students are better prepared to sympathize with the young lovers' plight. But the historical grounding maintains a realistic status for a play that has acquired the status of myth, so I turned to the conscious artifice of early rock and roll music as a way to tutor my students in the construction of romantic experience. Like the play, rock music of the 1950s and 1960s mystifies heterosexual coupling: teenagers idolize members of the opposite sex; they embark on a rapid journey through a prescribed course of attraction, profession of affection, and marriage; and they understand themselves as rebels against a social structure that their romantic union in fact largely recapitulates (see Goldberg, "*Open Rs*" 220). *Romeo and Juliet*'s cultural status seems to compel belief in its central social tenets, recently defined by Robert Appelbaum as "love, heterosexual love [. . .] and the regimes of masculinity and femininity required by such a value" (253). Similar ideological constructions of gender identity and sexual experience appear in the rock songs, and there students are better able to recognize them as ideologies, perhaps because the songs are an alien intrusion into a classroom devoted to the study of high culture.

One could register the sort of verbal and thematic similarity I am concerned with as evidence of Shakespeare's immense cultural influence, though I suspect it would be difficult to establish a link between rock groups like the Monotones or the Crystals and the bard. A somewhat more viable explanation for the similarities would admit the recurrence of certain situations, emotions, and terms of expression through several centuries (or longer) of cultural tradition, perhaps with an interest in establishing the superiority of Shakespeare's version as the most universal. I am arguing, however, for a more radical form of intertextuality, whereby Shakespeare's play is understood not only to exist alongside other forms of romantic utterance but in some ways also to intersect with them. Julia Kristeva describes this interpenetrative model as one in which "in the space of a given text, several utterances, taken from other texts, intersect and neutralize one another" ("Bounded Text" 36). The model disputes the notion of clearly demarcated textual boundaries and, as Roland Barthes makes clear, confirms multiplicity of discourse and meaning:

> Every text, being itself the intertext of another text, belongs to the intertextual, which must not be confused with a text's origins: to search for the "sources of" and "influences upon" a work is to satisfy the myth of filiation. The quotations from which a text is constructed are anonymous, irrecoverable, and yet *already read*: they are quotations without quotation marks. [T]he text might well take as its motto the words of the man possessed by devils: "My name is legion, for we are many" (Mark 5:9). (77)

A professor's reading experience of *Romeo and Juliet* is intersected by many phenomena: Renaissance plays and poems, theoretical paradigms, critical essays, memorable theatrical performances, prior teaching experiences. Why choose to share with students the particular intertextual relation between the play and rock songs from the 1950s and 1960s? The material has pedagogical value because the songs are old enough to be recognized as stylized. Whereas students view the music of their own era as conforming to experience, an earlier era's songs are revealed by time to be conventional period pieces that are anything but simple expressions of truth. The distancing effect of time exposes a song's emotionality as constructed and its words as rhetorical, alerting students to how cultural norms construct or package the experiences of youthful passion and rebellion. This awareness can take students from pondering whether the lovers' story is believable to analyzing the social forms that produce the story.

We might begin with a moment in *Romeo and Juliet* that strikes many students as indicative of the play's hackneyed imagery, or at least of the utter insincerity of Juliet's mother and nurse: the first attempt to interest Juliet in Paris's courtship. The Nurse calls Paris "a man of wax," and Lady Capulet says he is "a flower" (1.3.78, 79).[1] Then the mother launches into a conceit describing Paris as "[t]his precious book of love" (89). It is appropriate to register the artificiality of the mother's rhetoric as evidence of her emotional unavailability and to note the Nurse's quick relapse into bawdy innuendo ("Women grow by men" [97]). But comparing this scene to the Monotones' 1958 hit "Book of Love" can help students move beyond reading the scene solely in terms of character. The Monotones' song can provoke conversation about the paradox of learning about love, or even about love's language, given that cultural tradition supposes the experience of love to be unique. The lyrics delineate the "chapters" of pre-scribed courtship, while the refrain questions the authorship of love's mystery: "Who wrote the book of love?" As in all the songs I discuss, jingly rhythms and unemotional delivery undercut any pretension to seriousness. Students can hear the song's trope as a trope because they are outside the range of the song's romantic rhetoric. They can start to see that "it is culture that enables love to make sense" (Belsey, "Name" 127 [*Yearbook*]); love is not natural or inevitable. Love's textbook begins to be deconstructed. Indeed, with a little prompting students recognize that the play itself calls into question the idea of loving by the book. The Friar diagnoses Romeo's attachment to Rosaline as a love seeking to "read by rote, that could not spell" (2.2.88); and Juliet, in an apparently teasing criticism, tells her new lover "you kiss by th' book" (1.5.107). In both scenes, creative and original love are contrasted with loving "by th' book"; the play ex-poses ideology in order to contrast ideology with truth and sincerity. Yet until students recognize the extent to which romantic constructions organize the story of Romeo and Juliet, they are unlikely to notice when ideology is punc-tured or exposed or is separated from authentic experience.

To understand Romeo's gloomy self-indulgences at the beginning of the play, students need background information about Petrarchanism as a form of ex-pression and about love melancholy as a subjective stance and experience. Yet the explanations can often seem as baffling as the behaviors they would explain. Why should it be fashionable to prolong one's unhappiness? to remain distant from the object of one's affection? Roy Orbison's rockabilly lyrics provide a re-vealing gloss to the early glimpses of Romeo. His song "Crying" (1961) features the paradigmatic self-pity and unusual vocal range that made Orbison memo-rable. Like Romeo "mak[ing] himself an artificial night" (1.1.133), Orbison had a stereotypically melancholy stance; yet, rather more successfully than Romeo, he made his style his own. Orbison's example suggests how a predetermined style or mode—even a style or mode of emotional experience—can afford sat-isfactory self-expression. One needn't be entirely original to be engagingly ex-pressive; it can even be preferable—as poets writing any established mode realize—to accept strictures in order to channel creative possibilities into cer-tain directions.

Students are likely to recognize that Orbison's stance does not conform to prescribed norms of masculinity. The persona of "Crying," instead of defining himself through phallic aggression, cultivates disintegrative emotion. This recog-nition opens the door to discussion of Romeo's masculine identity. Students are likely to see Romeo as proceeding through the play on a course toward firmer attainment of masculinity, along the lines of critical readings by feminist object relations critics (see Adelman; Kahn). He becomes more manly as he abandons his male companions and his devotion to the unattainable Rosaline in favor of the more vividly sexual Juliet and as he drops his pacifist stance and slays Tybalt, lamenting that his affection for Juliet's charms "hath made me effeminate" (3.1.109). The crisis Romeo suffers after killing Tybalt is specifically one of masculinity: he is enjoined by the Nurse—"stand an you be a man" (3.3.88)—and questioned by the Friar: "Art thou a man?" (3.3.108). Romeo's "comfort is revived" (3.3.164) by the promise of sexual union with Juliet. But students might be urged to question the supposition that possession of a female object and ability to deliver aggressive sword thrusts guarantee masculinity. The two figures in *Romeo and Juliet* most often seen as masculine are Prince Escalus, because of his undisputed authority, and Mercutio, because of his quick wit and ready defense of the challenge to Romeo's honor. Neither character has a female attachment, and neither uses a weapon successfully. On closer inspection, the masculinity limned in the play looks like a more complicated identity concept than students initially assume masculinity to be (see Appelbaum).

Along these lines, it can be helpful to point out the relatively effete stance of many white male rockers of the late fifties. Before Elvis Presley's sexual charge redirected the genre's energies, extremes of macho posturing were countered by safely polite expressions of devotion such as Sonny James's "Young Love" of 1957 or Dion and the Belmonts' "Teenager in Love" of 1959. In both songs, the course of love is understood to be completely out of the control of the male persona. Love engulfs him, leaving him awash in confusing and often painful emotions. The popularity of songs about the death of the beloved is evidence of this sense of an encompassing fate that ordains the course of affairs for "star-crossed lovers" (prologue 6). One can compare these songs of devotion with the desperate words Romeo speaks just before the wedding vows:

> But come what sorrow can,
> It cannot countervail the exchange of joy
> That one short minute gives me in her sight.
> Do thou but close our hands with holy words,
> Then love-devouring death do what he dare—
> It is enough I may but call her mine.   (2.5.3–8)

One might also compare Romeo's words on slaying Tybalt—"O, I am fortune's fool!" (3.1.131)—and on hearing the false news of Juliet's death—"Then I defy you, stars!" (5.1.24). In each instance, Romeo is unable to imagine alternative scenarios, unable to position himself as an author of his experience. The script of tragic young love is already written. Romeo's fatalism is understood by some readers as a character flaw, by others as an inevitable quality of youth. But the comparison of the fatalistic rockers shows that the ingrained assumptions about love and sexuality contribute to the sense of vulnerability and even impotence. When a first attachment is purported to be the truest sort of love—as it is in the romantic songs of the 1950s and in Shakespeare's play—first-time lovers are required to view their relationship with deadly seriousness, however false to their experience such a view may be. When young lovers are required to disavow the sexuality that impels them toward a relationship—as they were in the polite society of 1950s America and in the marriage market of Elizabethan England—a sense of loss and anxiety marks the attachment. And when a society's proffered scripts for sexual relations are limited to heterosexual love and early monogamous marriage, it's no surprise that young lovers are baffled by the prospect of imagining alternative stories for themselves. Where a traditional reading of the play understands the lovers to be punished for violating their society's norms, Susan Snyder has argued that "the norms themselves bring about the tragedy" and, further, that "the tragic predicament—possibilities for human development narrowed down and cut off—is built into the operations of ideology" ("Ideology" 95). An ideological reading such as Snyder's, brought into focus through the rock parallel, helps students move past an emphasis on character or plot to an understanding of how cultural norms determine perceived reality.

Where the emotions of the white male rockers of the late 1950s and early 1960s seem limited to extremes of defiance or anxious self-pity, the female singers of this period energetically proclaim the romantic script. The Crystals spell it out in "Then He Kissed Me" (1963): meeting the special person, kissing, introduction to parents, and then marriage. The same sense of wedlock as the hastily pursued teleology of an affectional bond is expressed in two other recordings from 1963, "(Today I Met) The Boy I'm Gonna Marry," by Darlene Love, and "Not Too Young (To Get Married)," by Bob B. Soxx and the Blue Jeans. The male songwriters and producers behind these songs were selling a definite romantic ideology, one that the sexual politics of the day strongly enforced. Today's college students are likely to find it peculiar that Juliet proposes marriage to Romeo on the night they first meet: "If that thy bent of love be honorable, / Thy purpose marriage, send me word tomorrow" (2.1.185–86). Many students, however, will have been led by the play's romantic mythology to see the speedy marriage proposal as evidence of the couple's true love. Understanding that marriage functioned as a financial arrangement in the early modern era and recognizing the value of female virginity in the transaction will deepen students' appreciation of Juliet's forwardness. But hearing Darlene Love's greedy jubilation can further reveal the societal structures that would lead a woman to this haste and can demonstrate to students that such structures are not remote from students' own social reality.

Another song by a girl group with revealing parallels to the play is the Dixie Cups' 1964 hit "Chapel of Love." It celebrates the culmination of the course plotted by Darlene Love and the Crystals: the wedding. The focus on the ceremony in the chapel may strike students in our more sexually knowing age as a peculiar form of displaced emotion. Indeed, the song offers a good contrast to

Juliet's erotic anticipation in the epithalamium of 3.2. Footnotes in new editions bring to students' attention the sexual innuendos of this speech. A surprisingly forthright declaration of desire, the speech catapults Juliet past the coy persona she presented earlier in the play (to her mother in 1.3; to Romeo in the introductory sonnet of 1.5.90–107; and, rather less consistently, in the scene at her window); she moves past even her early–1960s counterparts, into a stance of sincere individuality. The sheer beauty and density of the language in 3.2 bestows originality on Juliet, but her originality is also the result of two ideologies colliding. On the one hand, Juliet is represented as a shy and virginal daughter and her youth is emphasized throughout the play; on the other, the play celebrates erotic passion. The two discourses meet in the epithalamium, as Juliet is transformed from innocent object to knowing subject. The moment is typical of what Alan Sinfield describes as the ideological construction of character depth: "interiority is projected by an audience or reader as the place where discourses intersect" (64).

"Chapel of Love" also brings into focus the peculiarity and importance of Friar Lawrence's cell. Juliet's two visits to the cell—for the marriage in 2.5 and for the sleeping potion in 4.1—mark her only appearances outside the confines of her family home or family tomb. These escapes to the Friar's cell represent Juliet's two attempts to plot a course for herself that differs from those envisioned by her father (marriage to Paris) and the playwright (marriage to Romeo with its tragic outcome). Of course, the Friar offers Juliet only an escape to another construction of reality, not a route to freedom; moreover, his Christian agenda for approving the marriage and his plans for protecting that agenda turn out to have consequences as deadly as the feud he attempts to heal. Yet the very fact that Romeo and Juliet can come together in marriage in the Friar's cell— their only meeting outside the Capulet space—indicates, as Snyder shows, that the cell figures as an "aporia," or gap, "created by ideological contestation" ("Ideology" 93). Where the competitive forces structuring the feud that separates the lovers collide with the religious belief system represented by the Friar, ideological space is cleared for the lovers to meet, if only briefly. As in Juliet's epithalamium, the collision of belief systems creates a momentary deepening of possibility and choice. These instances of ideological conflict in *Romeo and Juliet* create a range of character, language, and thematic possibilities that the intact ideologies of the rock songs do not.

In general terms, the play differs from the songs in its tragic conclusion: early rock typically sounds bouncy even when the lyrics are sad. The Crystals' 1962 hit "He's a Rebel" nominally laments a teenage girl's unfortunate attraction to an outsider who "never ever ever does what he should"; but the song's idolatrous focus ("Look at the way [. . .] he shuffles his feet") and catchy refrain actually celebrate the rebel's stance. The inconsistency is comparable to Juliet's. Students are usually quick to realize that Juliet protests too much that Romeo's name is insignificant; they hear in her focus on "Montague" an indication that she is attracted to the forbidden object:

Deny thy father and refuse thy name.
[. . . .]
'Tis but thy name that is my enemy.
Thou art thyself, though not a Montague.
What's Montague? It is nor hand, nor foot,
Nor arm, nor face, nor any other part
Belonging to a man. O, be some other name!
What's in a name? That which we call a rose
By any other word would smell as sweet.   (2.1.76, 80–86)

Beyond the universal appeal of what is denied and the developmental urge of a teenager to react against parental requirements, the particular motivation here has to do with gender positions: virtually the only choice Juliet has even a chance of exercising in her life is the one concerning marriage partners. Similarly, the music historian Reebee Garofalo points out that "because gender roles had not yet been challenged," girl groups of the early 1960s "were confined to singing about their relationships with men who were 'rebels' or 'leaders of the pack' rather than singing about themselves" (189–90).

Debate can no doubt be waged on whether fictions of death offer a titillating intensity to young people or whether stifling romantic ideologies produce in teenagers a sense of hopelessness leading to images of death. What's clear is that students tend to see the deaths of Romeo and Juliet as the tragic proof of their love. To help students contextualize the play's conclusion—to encourage them to see the two suicides in either the developmental or the ideological view —one can use "Last Kiss," by J. Frank Wilson (1964), and "Teen Angel," by Mark Dinning (1960). Both are car crash songs in which the singer's persona disavows any sense of responsibility or survivor's guilt. Instead, the sudden eruption of death into the normal course of existence provokes feelings of disbelief. The suddenness may also inspire the sense of metaphysical continuity: although there are no specifically religious images or sentiments in these songs, both posit the beloved's existence in heaven. "She's gone to heaven so I've got to be good, so I can get to heaven when I leave this world," goes the refrain of "Last Kiss." Both songs are extraordinary for their utterly unrealistic memorials to the departed "angel" and for their upbeat rhythms. They are songs about death in which death seems unreal, no more than a lyrical opportunity or a site of displaced eroticism. These songs can productively expose the rashness of Romeo's and Juliet's suicides and forestall the easy confidence expressed by some students that "at least they will be together in the afterlife," since this confidence typically has less to do with the religious faith to which it is attributed than with indoctrination into romantic myth.

In the middle of the twentieth century, rock and roll was the voice of youth culture; indeed, the genre and the culture emerged simultaneously (Garofalo 4). Studying early rock music reveals striking congruencies with Shakespeare's play about teenage love. This similarity, in turn, suggests certain recurring motifs in the experience of adolescents: extreme emotion, idolatry of the beloved, the appeal of violence and rebellion, the eroticization of death. The familiarity of these themes is due, however, less to their developmental inevitability than to the cultural tropes in which they are packaged. It is helpful to learn how to read the "book of love," since Shakespeare's play, like early rock music, presents love not as an archetypal experience but as an experience organized by ideological and rhetorical norms.

NOTES

Thanks to Shaila Mehra, John Traverse, and especially Marina Pacini for their suggestions and assistance.

[1] Citations to *Romeo and Juliet* in this essay are from *The Norton Shakespeare.*

APPENDIX: NOTE ON LOCATING SOURCES

Because all the songs I discuss were hits in their day, they appear on numerous LP recordings and should be fairly easy to locate in any circulating collection. Less than an hour of searching in my local public library yielded the following recordings:

"Book of Love." The Monotones. Argo, 1958. *The Best of Chess Rock 'N' Roll*. MCA, CH2-6024, 1987.

"Chapel of Love." The Dixie Cups. Trio, 1964. *Oldies but Goodies: Vol. 8*. Original Sound, LPS 8858, n.d.

"Crying." Roy Orbison. Acuff-Rose, 1961. *In Dreams: The Greatest Hits*. Virgin, 90604-1, 1987.

"He's a Rebel." The Crystals. Spector, 1962. *Phil Spector's Greatest Hits*. PSLP 1, 1983.

"Last Kiss." J. Frank Wilson. Boblo, 1964. *Oldies but Goodies: Vol. 9*. Original Sound, LPS 8859, n.d.

"Not Too Young (to Get Married)." Bob B. Soxx and the Blue Jeans. Spector, 1963. *Phil Spector's Greatest Hits*. PSLP 1, 1983.

"Teenager in Love." Dion and the Belmonts. Laurie, 1959. *Dion's Greatest Hits*. Laurie, C 31942, 1973.

"Teen Angel." Mark Dinning. Acuff-Rose, 1960. *Oldies but Goodies: Vol. 7*. Original Sound, LPS 8857, n.d.

"Then He Kissed Me." The Crystals. Spector, 1963. *Phil Spector's Greatest Hits*. PSLP 1, 1983.

"(Today I Met) The Boy I'm Gonna Marry." Darlene Love. Spector, 1963. *Phil Spector's Greatest Hits*. PSLP 1, 1983.

"Young Love." Sonny James. Capitol, 1957. *The Great Stars and Their Greatest Songs*. RCA, R86-067-1/1, RDK-5551/F, 1984.

Teaching *Romeo and Juliet* as a Tragedy of the Generation Gap and of Teenage Suicide

Sara Munson Deats

In Tampa, Florida, in 1986, a high school teacher contacted the local suicide crisis center before teaching *Romeo and Juliet* and asked for advice in treating the play's delicate subject matter with her students. The crisis center referred the teacher to a university professor who had recently presented a paper on *Romeo and Juliet* at a local conference. In the same year, a psychologist at a Tampa high school where a young man had recently committed suicide in the classroom contacted a university English professor and requested guidance in teaching *Romeo and Juliet* for the English faculty (Lenker 2–3). That year in Washington, DC, the Shakespeare Theatre at the Folger Shakespeare Library and the Youth Suicide National Center collaborated to create a program intended to "enable teenagers to experience the high drama of Shakespeare's classic, and, at the same time, to understand its relevance to their lives" (Holmer, "Pedagogical Practices" 192).

These three incidents, of which I experienced two personally and one vicariously, reinforce my conviction that *Romeo and Juliet,* one of our culture's most cherished love stories and the culture's most celebrated dramatization of teenage suicide, has a special resonance for young people today. I find this play significant not because Shakespeare is a writer for all times or because this tragedy embodies essential, universal insights but because in this drama, as in many of his works, Shakespeare brilliantly synthesizes the traditions and customs from which our contemporary mores have evolved. Thus, despite the enormous technological advances and monumental social changes that have occurred during the past four hundred years, the problems confronting Romeo and Juliet—the tensions between parents and children in the nuclear patriarchal family, the pressures within masculine peer groups, and the failure of authority figures to mediate between young people and the establishment—are still a part of our culture. I stress the relation of these factors to the lovers' suicides in my teaching of *Romeo and Juliet.*

Throughout the centuries, this popular and provocative play has evoked a multitude of interpretations. Commentators have read the play as a tragedy of fate and the stars (Charlton; Smidt; Waters), a tragedy of haste (Stirling), a tragedy of excessive passion (Dickey), a tragedy of unawareness (B. Evans, "Brevity"; Cole, Introduction), a tragedy of violated ritual (Liebler), and the locus classicus of the *Liebestod* myth (Mahood). Other critics have focused on the conflicts of the individual versus the patriarchy (Kahn), love versus friendship (Holmer, "Tragic Effects"), and subversion versus tradition (Laroque). Several intriguing interpretations of the play present *Romeo and Juliet* as a dramatic oxymoron, a study in contrarieties—love and death, age and youth, high and low spheres, authority and rebellion, love and hate, comedy and tragedy

(Levin, "Form"; Slater; Cartwright; Laroque; Goddard; Lucking, "Metaphysics"). To this list of antinomies, I would add the frequently overlooked polarities of communication and alienation, since this play showcases some of Shakespeare's most dazzling rhetoric while dramatizing a radical breakdown in communication on all levels of Verona society. This aspect of the play, enacting a dilemma as old as a cuneiform chronicle yet as current as the six o'clock news, is particularly relevant to the contemporary epidemic of teenage suicide.

The collapse of communication pervades the society of the play. First, and most crucially, parents and children cannot relate to each other; as most of us are aware, *Romeo and Juliet* is one of the definitive treatments in literature of the generation gap (Goddard 118; Griffin). Second, and not so frequently recognized, Veronese society's masculine peer group cannot establish a frank and open dialogue. Lastly, societal institutions—the state and the church—are unable to maintain order or mediate between the estranged parents and their children. Ultimately, Romeo and Juliet, alienated from both family and peers, make a total, exclusive commitment to each other while appealing to the church for solace and aid. When the church, in the persona of the bumbling, pusillanimous Friar Laurence, fails them, they cling desperately to each other. Even this support collapses, and each lover, believing the other to be dead, feels isolated and abandoned and sees no recourse but suicide.

The introductions of both teenagers stress the psychic gulf separating parents and children in Verona. Although Juliet makes her debut flanked by her mother and her nurse, Lady Capulet's reluctance to discuss intimate matters of sex and marriage with her virgin daughter without the moral support of the Nurse suggests the strained relationship between mother and child, a relationship foiled by the warm, convivial rapport between Juliet and the earthy Nurse. Lord Capulet initially seems a fonder, more solicitous parent than his rather frigid wife, although he does not engage Juliet in onstage conversation until much later in the play, during a scene in which he violently rejects his daughter. A similar lack of communication typifies Romeo's relationship with his anxious father, who must seek out Romeo's friend Benvolio to inquire about Romeo's bizarre behavior. Romeo's failure ever to appear on stage with his parents highlights this alienation (Kahn 182 [Lenz, Greene, and Neely]). Not surprisingly, therefore, when the two adolescents, each an heir of the other's enemy clan, fall head over heels in love, they fail to confide their transcendent passions to their parents. Instead, the lovers marry secretly, embarking on a course that leads to catastrophe.

Although Romeo shares his self-indulgent infatuation for Rosaline with two friends, the skeptical Benvolio and the scoffing Mercutio, he is unwilling to divulge his rapturous love for Juliet to either of his comrades. Mercutio, part phallogocentric icon (Moisan, "Gender" 116), part lord of misrule (Laroque 18), equates love with sex and makes women the object of bawdy jeers; whereas romantic Romeo elevates women to a pedestal, macho Mercutio shoves them into the ditch. Marjorie Cox, employing the lexicon of Freudian psychoanalysis, explains Romeo and Mercutio as representing familiar antithetical responses to the sexual stresses occurring during adolescence. Romeo responds to the revival of libidinal energy by seeking an appropriate non-Oedipal love object to satisfy his desires, whereas Mercutio channels this upsurge of libido into mocking and avoiding women while seeking the exclusive company of his own sex (381–82, 385). The difference in psychological response erects a barrier that renders meaningful dialogue between the two friends virtually impossible. Understandably, therefore, Romeo hesitates to subject his ecstatic, private passion for Juliet to the ribald locker-room jests of his cynical sidekick Mercutio or even to the remonstrations of the more sympathetic but still skeptical Benvolio. However, Romeo's reluctance to confide in his friends proves fatal.

During acts 2 and 3 a great deal of action occurs of which both the lovers' parents and Romeo's friends are unaware. In search of youthful mischief and romance, Romeo and his cohorts crash the Capulet party, and Romeo predictably forgets the less attractive girl (Rosaline) when he spies the prettier one (Juliet). Whereas Romeo's former crush was cold and inaccessible, Juliet responds warmly to Romeo's overtures. Romeo and Juliet have no trouble communicating, and the balance and harmony of their initial repartee, couched in the form of a perfect sonnet, may reflect the mutuality of their desire. As many critics have argued, the trite oxymora and shopworn Petrarchan conceits studding Romeo's initial amorous laments indicate the superficiality of his feelings for Rosaline, and even after his first exchange with Juliet, Romeo continues to woo "by the book" (1.5.111).[1] However, in the later exchange of vows in the enclosed Capulet garden—the secluded setting mirroring the privacy of the lovers' passion—Juliet, proclaiming "farewell compliment" (2.2.89), teaches Romeo to jettison the book of social and amorous etiquette. In a series of remarkable colloquies, Juliet seeks to level the barriers that society has erected to occlude communication between individuals—conventional labels, conventional gender roles, conventional language. As Harry Levin memorably observes, Juliet first "calls into question not merely Romeo's name but—by implication—all names, forms, conventions, sophistications, and arbitrary dictates of society" ("Form" 4). Later Romeo and Juliet momentarily exchange gender roles: Juliet blazons Romeo and compares him to the standard courtly symbol for feminine beauty, the rose (Whittier 34–35), while also wooing him and proposing to him. During this secret tryst, Juliet, eschewing cliché, tutors Romeo in a new, spontaneous language of love. Romeo and Juliet attempt not only to discard names and gender roles but also to reject their parents and adopt the garrulous Nurse and the platitudinous Friar as their surrogate mother and father. Equipped with the Nurse as covert go-between and the Friar as spiritual mentor, the two lovers engineer a clandestine marriage. Ultimately, however, the lovers learn that no matter how heroic the attempt, individuals can never escape the limitations of patriarchal naming, culture, and language (Belsey, "Name" 67–71 [Porter]; Lucking, "Balcony Scene").

Returning from his secret wedding to Juliet, Romeo encounters Benvolio, Mercutio, and Romeo's nemesis, Tybalt, in the sweltering town square, and impeded communication again serves as a catalyst to calamity. Furious that the scion of the enemy clan crashed the Capulet family's celebration and still smarting from Lord Capulet's stern rebuke, Tybalt has sent Romeo a written challenge, a missive obviously not received, because Romeo has not been home since the night of the ball (Holmer, "Tragic Effects" 349). Romeo, knowing nothing of Tybalt's challenge, hopes for reconciliation (had he known of the challenge, he might have been more cautious); Mercutio and Tybalt, knowing nothing of Romeo's private nuptials, misconstrue Romeo's attempts at peacemaking as cowardice. The result is a melee of misrecognition that leaves Mercutio and Tybalt dead and Romeo banished. The racking scene dramatizes the deleterious effect of masculine peer pressure on a sensitive adolescent, as Romeo allows his concern for masculine honor to overwhelm his love for Juliet and, unmanned by folly, kills his newly made cousin Tybalt. Escalus, the prince of Verona, arrives—as always, too late—and the state, which is unable throughout the play to maintain order, can only inflict punishment. The death of Tybalt unleashes the heretofore precariously restrained hostility between the two warring houses and combines with the demise of the far from "grave man," Mercutio, to signal the play's reversal from comedy to tragedy (3.1.97).

The climax for Romeo occurs in the duel scene with Mercutio and Tybalt; the turning point for Juliet arrives shortly after the fatal duel, following the consummation of her marriage to Romeo. Adhering to the pattern of noncommunication controlling the action of the play, Capulet has contracted a precipitous union between Juliet and Paris without even consulting his daughter. When Juliet is informed by her mother that her "careful" father has prepared for her "a sudden day of joy," her surprise wedding to Paris within two days, she panics (3.5.107, 109). Desperately, she begs her father, "Good father, I beseech you on my knees, / Hear me with patience but to speak a word" (3.5.158–59). But the angry Capulet, enraged that his daughter has defied him and fearing a loss of face if he relents, refuses to hear. The same vulnerable masculine pride that goaded the pacific Romeo to kill Tybalt—and probably also sparked the violence of Mercutio and Tybalt—now spurs Capulet's heated vituperations, as Capulet threatens to disown Juliet and cast her into the street if she fails to obey. In despair, Juliet turns to her mother, pleading for delay, but Lady Capulet also rejects communication. Juliet's poignant plea to her father, "Hear me with patience but to speak a word," and her mother's later stony declaration, "Talk not to me, for I'll not speak a word" (3.5.204), together provide a motto for the dialectic of the play, in which crucial words cannot be spoken and many appeals go unheard or unanswered. After her parents' departure, Juliet turns to her confidant, the Nurse, but again communication breaks down. Unable to comprehend the depth of Juliet's commitment to Romeo, the Nurse counsels marriage to Paris (3.5.223–27). For the pragmatic Nurse, the two attractive young men are interchangeable, objects to be enjoyed and used. Juliet, failed by her surrogate mother and biological parents alike, resorts to seeking aid from the Friar. But neither the too worldly Nurse nor the too otherworldly Friar has the courage or wisdom to save the two adolescents.

Commentators have traditionally interpreted Romeo and Juliet as either the *pharmakos* of Verona society or the victims of fate, chance, or even providence. Yet despite the monumentally bad luck suffered by the lovers, almost every circumstance leading to the tragedy can also be traced to an instance of impaired communication. Like the refrain of a poem linking stanza to stanza, the motif of occluded communication pervades the play, linking episode to episode. Had Romeo confided in Mercutio the details of his secret nuptials, his friend would certainly not have intervened in the altercation between Romeo and Tybalt. If either of the surrogate parents, the Friar or the Nurse, had possessed the nerve to confront the biological parents to confess their complicity in the concealed marriage, tragedy would doubtlessly have been averted. Had the eminently eligible Paris been told of Juliet's clandestine wedding, he would certainly not have pursued a married woman. Even the most salient example of fortune's animus, the quarantined messenger and the undelivered letter, results from failure to suit action to word and to provide necessary information. In a crucial epistle to Romeo, Friar Laurence outlines his harebrained scheme to give Juliet a potion that will simulate her death. This plan goes awry because Friar Laurence makes two major errors. First, he forgets his promise to entrust the letter to Romeo's servant Balthasar; and, second, he neglects to explain the importance of the missive to his surrogate messenger, Friar John. Thus Friar John meanders to a plague-ridden area in search of a companion for his journey, becomes quarantined, and never delivers the letter, whereas Balthasar, the expected messenger, rushes to Mantua with false information concerning Juliet's death. Through these many episodes of short-circuited communication, the play consistently reminds the audience that the calamitous deaths of five young people—Tybalt, Mercutio, Paris, Romeo, and Juliet—could all have been prevented had the citizens of Verona been able to talk candidly to one another. But the five youths and their bereaved parents, friends, and confidants all become victims of a conspiracy of silence.

The question has frequently been asked, Why do Romeo and Juliet commit suicide? Rowland Wymer associates the double suicide with the sin of despair, citing the frequent references in the play to this destructive emotion and commenting on the suicidal tendencies of both lovers (116–18). More relevant to my approach is that of M. D. Faber, who locates the suicides of the two lovers within a complex web of emotions commonly represented in clinical studies of youth suicide. These emotions include rage and hostility toward a cruel world and the world's authorities as well as hopelessness and frustration. Combined with these emotions is the desire to find surcease from unendurable pain ("Shakespeare's Suicides" 39–40; see also Breed; Farberow and Shneidman 153–289; Shneidman, *Nature* 8, *Definition* 126–35). Although generally agreeing with Faber's analysis, I would discriminate more precisely between the suicides of the two adolescents, just as contemporary critics have carefully differentiated between the language and maturation of the two lovers (Kahn; Dash 67–100; Snow; Cartwright). Hostility toward both society and fortune, guilt over Tybalt's death, thwarted dreams and hope, and the loss of Juliet—all these contribute to Romeo's final hopelessness. Conversely, Juliet's self-murder lacks the anger, guilt, or even frustration characteristic of Romeo's last desperate hours. Rather, her suicide is rendered virtually inevitable by her progressive isolation resulting from the series of physical and psychological bereavements Juliet suffers in the last days of her life: the death of a cherished cousin; alienation from her father, mother, and nurse; desertion by the Friar; and, finally, the devastating loss of her beloved Romeo. Edwin Shneidman, a leading authority on suicide, insists that psychological pain, no matter how severe, "is endurable *if* the individual feels that he is truly not alone and can evoke some response in a significant other" (*Definition* 215; see also Farberow 391–92). But Juliet is ultimately stripped of all significant others, her total isolation symbolized by the hermetically sealed tomb in which, abandoned and alone, the adolescent girl takes her life.

Jerry Jacobs, in his analysis of adolescent suicide, follows Shneidman in speculating that persons commit suicide primarily because they encounter nonshareable problems. Jacobs further hypothesizes that adolescent suicide attempts result from "a chain reaction dissolution of any remaining meaningful social relationships in the days and weeks preceding the [suicide] attempt which leads to the adolescent's feeling that he has reached the 'end of hope'" (28). As I have tried to demonstrate, Shakespeare, that shrewd recorder of human behavior, anticipates in *Romeo and Juliet* the very factors identified by Jacobs and other prominent authorities on youth suicide (Farberow; Shneidman, *Definition, Essays, Nature*), factors that appear over and over again in clinical case studies on the subject: confused teenagers who seek to resolve conflicting psychosexual instincts; cold and authoritarian parents who impede the turbulent drives of adolescents toward individuation and fulfillment; impotent counselors; insensitive, often belligerent, peers; aggravating circumstances, particularly the loss of a loved one; frustration of primary needs; rage and defiance toward an environment perceived as hostile; helplessness and hopelessness; and, most agonizing of all, progressive isolation of the adolescents from meaningful social relationships. To a large degree, both in contemporary case studies of youth suicide and in *Romeo and Juliet,* this isolation results from the total severance of communication between the desperate teenagers and the narcissistic society that fails to heed their cry for help.

David Lucking remarks that not a single one of the written messages sent in the play arrives directly at its intended destination ("Balcony Scene" 6; see also Whittier 30–31n8). I further suggest that the letters that never arrive provide poignant emblems for the ubiquitous failed communication dramatized by the play—the spoken words that cannot be delivered, at least partially because the characters have quarantined their affections. This issue of quarantined affection has aroused one of the most heated debates in early modern studies. Lawrence Stone postulates that several factors combined to produce a lack of affection in the early modern family: the increased authority of the father in the emerging nuclear patriarchal family; the high adult and child mortality rates; and prevalent childrearing practices, such as the farming out of newborn infants to wet nurses by the upper classes and of young children to foster homes by all classes (*Family* 22–145). Other scholars have challenged these conclusions, denying the widespread practice of wet nursing and the general lack of affect that Stone posits as characteristic of the family at this period (Wrightson 70–71, 90–119). If, despite *Romeo and Juliet*'s obvious debt to dramatic and poetic conventions, we view the play as a mimetic document reflecting the tensions and conflicts of Shakespeare's society, we could argue that the drama provides ammunition for both camps. On the one hand, despite the blatant commodification of Juliet by her authoritarian parents, Capulet eloquently expresses his deep affection for Juliet (1.2.14–15), and both parents respond to their daughter's death with hyperbolic lamentations (4.5). Furthermore, although Romeo never appears in a domestic setting with his parents, his perplexed father seems genuinely concerned over his son's behavior, and Lady Montague dies of grief as a result of her son's banishment. On the other hand, the play clearly dramatizes a society plagued by alienation on all levels—the family, peer groups, the church, the state. Since the complex relation between Shakespeare's great love story and the society that produced it remains outside the purview of this essay, I will simply conclude by observing that the newspaper headlines daily assaulting and shocking even the most desensitized twentieth-century reader indicate that a similar alienation infects our contemporary society. No cure has yet been found for this dread disease, and this may be one of the reasons that, despite the gap of four hundred years, *Romeo and Juliet* speaks so urgently today to both young and old.

NOTE

[1] Citations to *Romeo and Juliet* in this essay are from *The Complete Works of Shakespeare*, edited by David Bevington.

Teaching Shakespeare's Bawdry: Orality, Literacy, and Censorship in *Romeo and Juliet*

James R. Andreas, Sr.

It is a curious phenomenon that we introduce Shakespeare to eighth- and ninth-grade students across the United States with a play like *Romeo and Juliet,* arguably one of Shakespeare's bloodiest tragedies and certainly his bawdiest. The violence of the play—the vendetta of the parents, the dueling of the young men, the clan-condoned murder, the suicides of the young lovers—particularly insofar as it is directed at and perpetrated by youths, has not much offended contemporary audiences. But the bawdry has. I am writing, of course, about the sexually charged exchange between Gregory and Samson in the opening scene; the Nurse's reminiscences about the weaning of Juliet; Mercutio's Queen Mab speech; and virtually every scene in which Mercutio, the Nurse, and servants appear—all scenes that are touchy to teach at whatever level. There was a time when *A Midsummer Night's Dream* was the introductory play for junior high and high school students around the country, but that was before the unilateral decision to eliminate comedy from the national Shakespeare curriculum.[1] Dangerous sexual sentiments and innuendos permeate comedy, as they should, but merely punctuate tragedy, as Michael Bristol, Susan Snyder (*Comic Matrix*), and others have shown. And tragic bawdry, the kind indulged in by Hamlet, for instance, is more easily explained away in introductions to the text as comic relief or qualified by being glossed as something else or strategically excised from the text altogether as extraneous and even dangerous to public morals.[2] The decision to introduce students to Shakespeare with *Romeo and Juliet* was followed by systematic expurgation of the texts of the play and selective approaches to sexuality in filmed and live productions that would be viewed by students.[3]

My classes afford a synoptic view of how *Romeo and Juliet* is taught in middle school and high school as well as in college and graduate courses. I teach a Shakespeare telecourse that includes twenty-five undergraduate students in the television studio on campus and twenty-five middle and high school teachers across the state of South Carolina, who receive the class by satellite at their home schools, usually in groups of two or three teachers. The course is live and fully interactive; teachers call in their responses to questions, discussion, and film clips and even recite or perform over the phone. The course is tied in directly with the Clemson Shakespeare Festival, which features five or six live productions of plays we study in class. *Romeo and Juliet* is the perennial favorite during the festival, having been featured recently in productions by Shenandoah Shakespeare Express and the Warehouse Theater of Greenville, South Carolina. The play was also performed by the Acting Company of New York along with a production of *West Side Story* presented by the Booking Group, also of New York.

Discussion of *Romeo and Juliet* in the telecourse invariably tiptoes around sensitive curricular issues. Teachers want to know how their colleagues approach the play, and the college students are interested in discussing how the play was presented in middle or high school. The touchiest subject in these discussions is Shakespeare's bawdry. Teachers worry about introducing sexually sensitive material to fourteen-year-olds, students precisely the same age as the play's young protagonists. The telecourse format provides us with the means to study the play and the play's pervasive sensuality in three forms: as a printed text (an easily censored medium), including the early quarto editions, the Folio, and modern editions of the play; in film versions that recontextualize the play in terms of historical preoccupations with sexuality; and in live stage productions that approximate conditions of Elizabethan staging while reflecting contemporary issues, including bawdry, in the play. The representation of the play's vibrant sexuality is conditioned by the medium of expression, a fact that would not have been lost on Shakespeare, who deals in the play with themes of literacy and orality and their impact on sexual freedom and choice.[4]

In *Romeo and Juliet*, Shakespeare seems preoccupied with orality and suspicious of literacy, which is, in a sense, deconstructed in the play by the persistent deprecation of letters, books, and reading. The servants in *Romeo and Juliet*, agents of both orality and vulgarity, are illiterate. Romeo and Juliet meet because the servant-clown of Lord Capulet cannot read the list of invitations he is sent to deliver to assemble the Capulets at the home of Juliet's father for a ball. Students find the following exchange interesting, because they themselves are often accused of a sort of lazy illiteracy in their persistent and understandable preferences for visual media:

> SERVANT.   God gi' god-den. I pray, sir, can you read?
> ROMEO.   Ay, mine own fortune in my misery.
> SERVANT.   Perhaps you have learn'd it without book.
>   But I pray, can you read any thing you see?
> ROMEO.   Ay, if I know the letters and the language.
> SERVANT.   Ye say honestly, rest you merry!
> ROMEO.   Stay, fellow, I can read.   (1.2.57–63)

Romeo proceeds to read the list aloud, and after some banter with the servant, Romeo and Benvolio make plans to crash the party. The improvisational nature of speech is apparent here: because the servant cannot read, the Montagues and Capulets are allowed to mix in social and ritual ways that throw Romeo and Juliet together into a coupling that eventually will reconcile the two families. The servant, even before he meets Romeo in the street, demonstrates the happy accidents that result from oral exchange in his consternation over the list his master has handed him.

Find them out whose names are written here! It is written that the shoe-maker should meddle with his yard and the tailor with his last, the fisher with his pencil and the painter with his nets; but I am sent to find those persons whose names are here writ, and can never find what names the writing person hath here writ. I must to the learned. In good time!

(1.2.38–44)

The servant already has the words out of sequence here in his prose rendition of his master's poetic instructions: in reality, the tailor has his yard, the shoe-maker his pencil, and the fisherman his nets. Lists are often a problem in European culture, which since the sixteenth century has mapped and demar-cated the world in order to partition, administer, and dominate it. The Montagues and Capulets have each other on their lists of enemies. Moreover, in the quotation above, Romeo suggests that his melancholy, no doubt condi-tioned by a bookish, Petrarchan attitude toward his affection for Rosaline, has been "read" as his "fortune" of "misery." Literary texts, like lists, are fixed and—once written or printed—do not evolve into solutions to the difficulties the texts project. The plot of the play, of course, hinges on the fate of the young lovers being fixed or "star-crossed" (prologue 6) by Friar Lawrence's letter, which ar-rives too late to inform Romeo of the confessor's harebrained plan to reunite the lovers. As if to remind us of this antibookish theme, Benvolio, the normative character in the play, announces that the Montague entrance to the Capulet ball will not be anticipated by any bookish prologue, "Nor no without-book pro-logue, faintly spoke / After the prompter, for our entrance" (1.4.7–8). The en-trance of the Montagues will be unprompted, spontaneous, and unrehearsed. They will crash the party.

Other passages in the play reveal a suspicion of literacy and reading like that advanced by Shakespeare's contemporary Miguel de Cervantes in the narrative of a knight beguiled by his readings in chivalric romance. Paris, Juliet's un-wanted suitor, is praised by Lady Capulet as a weighty tome and "golden story" (1.3.92), a book just waiting to be opened and read by Juliet. As if recommend-ing a good book, Lady Capulet urges Juliet to accept Paris on her parents' rec-ommendation, sight unseen:

> Read o'er the volume of young Paris' face,
> And find delight writ there with beauty's pen;
> Examine every married lineament,
> And see how one another lends content;
> And what obscured in this fair volume lies
> Find written in the margent of his eyes.
> This precious book of love, this unbound lover,
> To beautify him, only lacks a cover.
> The fish lives in the sea, and 'tis much pride
> For fair without the fair within to hide.

That book in many's eyes doth share the glory,
That in gold clasps locks in the golden story.   (1.3.81–92)

What an anatomy of reading we have here at the end of the century that produced the first printed book: reading, volume, pens, lineaments, content, mar-
gent, books, unbound papers, covers, clasps, golden stories—all enumerated by
the mother who is a sworn enemy to the Montagues and to her own daughter's
love interests and choices. The book is the text that eliminates free choices and
fixes outcomes according to the dictates of propriety and the canons of authority. The Latin word for "read," *lego*, is the root of the word *lex*, or "law." In this
play, the spirit of the lovers is literally defeated by the letter—the letter that
doesn't arrive in time to allow Romeo and Juliet's safe reunion.

I am always quick to point out to students that early in the play the servants,
Mercutio, and the Nurse are free to undercut the authority and predictable, le-
galistic morality of their superiors. When Lady Capulet praises Paris, the
Nurse, who has already delivered her paean to nursing—and oral activity—and
sexual pratfalls, is there to undercut her lady's literary conceit:

LADY CAPULET.   So shall you [Juliet] share all that he doth possess,
                 By having him, making yourself no less.
NURSE.   No less! nay, bigger; women grow by men.   (1.3.93–95)

In the Nurse's back talk, Juliet is represented as a natural woman who will not
be made "less," or reduced, to a cover beautifying the book of Paris. She will
"grow" beyond the limits of the book in pregnancy. She will be inspirited,
"blown up," as Shakespeare says of pregnancy in other contexts (see *All's Well*
1.1.118–19).

Romeo's affections for Rosaline early in the play—archaically bookish and
Petrarchan—are undercut initially by Mercutio in the Queen Mab speech and
then again in the first, chance encounter of Romeo and Juliet at the masked
ball. I like to show filmed versions of that meeting beginning with the line "If I
profane with my unworthiest hand" (1.5.93), where the lovers construct one of
the most ingenious sonnets in all English literature, a collaborative, recitative
poetic improvisation that is so spontaneous, students rarely recognize the sonnet form. Yet, with the kiss that concludes the sonnet, Juliet reminds Romeo
that he, under the influence of his amatory reading, still "kisses by the book"
(1.5.110). By the second act, Romeo himself is suspicious of names that fix
character and reputation, names that are inscribed permanently on lists of enemies. Speaking of his name, he confesses, "Because it is an enemy to thee; /
Had I it written, I would tear the word" (2.2.56–57). Romeo looks for something (like a book) to "swear by" as testimony to his love for Juliet, but his mate
is smarter than that. She replies:

Do not swear at all;
Or if thou wilt, swear by thy gracious self,

> Which is the god of my idolatry,
> And I'll believe thee.   (2.2.112–15)

By this time Romeo has apparently unlearned his bookish approach to love-making. Love teaches its own lessons and has no need of books or schoolrooms: "Love goes toward love as schoolboys from their books, / But love from love, toward school with heavy looks" (2.2.156–57).

Mercutio, perhaps the bawdiest and most mercurial of Shakespeare's characters and therefore a favorite of young students, also undercuts the rhetoric of Petrarchan sentiment, particularly when it comes to Romeo's manufactured feelings for Rosaline. Undoubtedly all teachers linger over the improvised stand-up of Mercutio, whose Queen Mab speech mocks the bookish pretensions of lovers, lawyers, parsons, and soldiers alike. Mercutio has his own pet peeves against literacy and bookishness, particularly when it comes to Tybalt, the robot soldier who fences by the worst of all kinds of manuals, the mathematical textbook:

> No, 'tis not so deep as a well, nor so wide as a church-door, but 'tis enough, 'twill serve. Ask for me to-morrow, and you shall find me a grave man. I am pepper'd, I warrant, for this world. A plague a' both your houses! 'Zounds, a dog, a rat, a mouse, a cat, to scratch a man to death! a braggart, a rogue, a villain, that fights by the book of arithmetic!
>
> (3.1.96–102)

Even as Mercutio is dying, he challenges the ability of scripted language to render puns humorously. Mercutio the trickster will become a "grave man" tomorrow, for like Tybalt he is grave bound. He is also engraved, his body marked like a text by the predictable fencing passes of Tybalt, who "fights by the book of arithmetic." As Susan Snyder has argued (*Matrix*), the yuck stops here, with the death of Mercutio at the play's heart. The grace of the "comic matrix" has given way to the gravity of a tragic "patrix," if I may coin a term. The open-endedness of the plot represented by fun and games; the flaunting of love's conventions; and the shameless, bawdy punning of the first half of the action have been short-circuited. Mercutio is dead, the Nurse is silenced, and the servants are in retreat for most of the rest of the play. Destiny is fixed; the lovers are at this point "star-crossed."

It is no wonder Shakespeare so frequently celebrates orality and excoriates literacy in his plays. The language of his stage is ear candy. Audiences, not spectators, attend Shakespeare's plays. With the reconstruction of the Globe Theatre in London, we have rediscovered what theater architects in Shakespeare's era knew implicitly: the Elizabethan stage is a huge sounding board like the case of a grand piano or the rounded body of a cello. With airplanes booming overhead and buses accelerating all around the theater, the lines of the actors resound and reverberate in the arena, surpassing all acoustic expectations. To be sure, scholars contemporary with Shakespeare must have complained about the threat to reading as a principal pedagogical mode represented by an upstart playwright and his fellow actors and writers in this new, unruly, folk or vulgar theater. Schoolmasters probably said something like, "My students aren't reading Homer or Sophocles anymore, not to mention Plutarch and Ovid. They congregate down in Southwark near the brothels and bearbaiting pits to watch *Troilus and Cressida,* which desecrates Homer, and *A Midsummer Night's Dream,* which turns Ovid on his head. What a pity! What a waste! They need to be reading Cicero, not watching *Sejanus.*" We, of course, advance the same sorts of arguments to defend literature against film, television, and most recently the computer with its multimedia and Internet capacities. But Shakespeare made a conscious career choice to turn away from the sonnet and from poetic narratives like *Hero and Leander* to devote himself to a more direct and unmediated form of literary expression—live popular theater. I like to tell my students that theater was reinvented by Shakespeare and his dramatic colleagues as a technology with a new shape, space, and form, a technology developed to deliver the riches of a rapidly evolving language apparently at the peak of its powers. And Shakespeare, I point out, obviously preferred to deliver that language in its purest form—orally—rather than in print. Otherwise he certainly would have shown signs that he would one day authorize the publication of his plays, as did his contemporary Ben Jonson in composing his *Works.*

Oral language is, of course, the medium of bawdy exchange because it is open and relatively immune to the censorship, excision, expurgation, abridgment, and prosecution to which written or literate texts are subject. Print may well have been encouraged and developed as the major medium of exchange in European culture because it was so easily controlled through licensing, selective expurgation, and listing on various indexes. Shakespeare certainly exercised his bawdy sense of humor on the stage to secure and sustain interest and to extend dramatic language into new and popular registers with jargon, slang, and billingsgate derived from the scurrilous profanity of fishmongers and pickpockets. How else do we explain the sheer abundance of vulgar slang in the tirades of Petruchio, Pompey, Thersites, Autolycus, and even Hamlet, not to mention the insults on stage that teachers the world over use to inspire interest in the oral Shakespeare. The comments of the servants, the Nurse, and Mercutio all sustain dramatic interest on the stage, if not the page, through the sexual innuendo that is an important theme in the play—at least according to Friar Lawrence, who announces, "The earth that's nature's mother is her tomb; / What is her burying grave, that is her womb" (2.3.9–10). Tomb and womb are locked in a cycle in which each is linked to and generated out of the other. The sexuality of the womb is a crucial motif in the opening scene and throughout the first three acts of the play.

The editors of the standard school texts—sometimes professionals with no educational experience hired by the publishing conglomerates but often Shakespearean scholars—have, for all practical purposes, neutered these texts of

Romeo and Juliet by undermining the play's comic core, sexual allure, satiric thrust, and ironic ambiguity. Some four hundred lines of the play are customarily eliminated, including virtually all the comic and satiric as well as the bawdy lines of the Nurse, Mercutio, and the servants. The following passages are typically excised: the sexual braggadocio of the servants in 1.1, the discussion of the weaning and the sexual "fall" of infant Juliet in 1.3, the scatological elements of the Queen Mab speech and of the comic exchanges in the death scene of Mercutio in 1.4 and 3.1, and the raucous entrance of the musicians after the apparent death of Juliet in 4.5.

Cuts in the first scene of *Romeo and Juliet,* a scene that I always encourage students to act out in both expurgated and full-text versions, illustrate how the censorship process works. As Northrop Frye suggests about this scene, "The macho jokes, 'draw thy tool' and the like, are the right way to introduce the theme that dominates this play: the theme of love bound up with, and part of, violent death. Weapons and fighting suggest sex as well as death, and are still doing so later in the play, when the imagery shifts to gunpowder" (*"Romeo"* 16).

The Montague and Capulet servants exchange off-color jokes about maidenheads and dried-up codpieces that delay the violence which erupts when the servants' social betters rush in to start fighting for real, with swords instead of words (see Andreas, "Wordplay"). Gone in the student texts I examined is the boast of Samson, who says, "Me [the maids] shall feel while I am able to stand, and 'tis known I am a pretty piece of flesh" (1.1.28–29). Gone as well are all the Aristophanic jokes about naked tools and naked weapons. References to thrusting women against the wall, to taking maidenheads instead of real heads, and to Samson's "pretty piece of flesh," which hangs dry and dead like a cod (a sword at rest) rather than standing and drawn—all this bawdy fun is deleted. In the student texts, when Gregory commands Samson to draw his "tool" against the Montagues (31), there is no bawdy innuendo, no sexual ambiguity. The weapon is "naked" (34)—unsheathed—but it is not the "prick" (2.4.113) or the "fiddle-stick" (3.1.48) Mercutio will later allude to but the "naked weapon" itself, the sword (1.1.34). The high school texts pick up after Gregory's line with Samson's cry: "My naked weapon is out. Quarrel, I will back thee" (1.1.33–34). The oral resonance here is deadened: the phallic references to "tool" and "piece" all give way to one inescapable, literalized meaning: weapon. The naked weapon is an unsheathed sword. The humor of the passage is expurgated here to be sure, along with the bawdry, but so are the stated and associative meanings. The comic option that the reader of an unabridged edition enjoys until the muzzling of the Nurse and the murder of Mercutio is here canceled out immediately. The characters are cornered into a mean little street brawl with none of the capacities for comic chaos that are Shakespeare's design in the opening scene. For all the students know from their textbooks, real lethal weapons are drawn the moment the servants first appear onstage. And students, of course, are left uninformed about the reasons for the excisions. They think they are reading Shakespeare, and their suspicions about this stuffy dead white man whom they never expected to enjoy are confirmed. What students still (I bet) call "the good parts" are generally cut from student texts: references to tools, codpieces, nipples, maidenheads, and pricks all fall under the censor's knife. Whatever these texts of *Romeo and Juliet* are, they simply are not Shakespeare, not in form or spirit. Somebody has slipped a bra on the Venus de Milo and slapped a fig leaf on Michelangelo's David to protect our students from art as it was conceived and executed, and we are expected not to notice, or, worse yet, we are expected to approve. The artistic work has supposedly been improved. The considerable violence in the play—the stabbings and the poisoning—has not been touched, but the jokes are cut most unkindly, and the comedy is simply murdered.

Missing also from student texts are the spontaneous, meandering lines about the Nurse's weaning of baby Juliet, including these:

> When it did taste the wormwood on the nipple
> Of my dug and felt it bitter, pretty fool,
> To see it teachy and fall out wi' th' dug!   (1.3.30–32)

Gone are the lines about the "fall" of the baby Juliet anticipating her fall back on the marriage bed. More ominous, gone are all the typically teenage and often obnoxious jokes of Mercutio, the class wiseacre. To characterize these deletions generally, in language Shakespeare ascribed to Friar Lawrence, the imagery of the "tomb" is privileged, while allusions to the "womb" are excised. The version of the play the students read is one-dimensional, a neat illustration of Freud's concept of the death wish. Much of the human and humorous interest has been removed in order to sanitize the text and to displace some of the play's principal themes—the renewal of life through the pleasures of eros and the playfully illicit humor that verbalizes such pleasures. Derogatory comments about the church and the law in the Queen Mab speech are also removed. In the expurgated version *Romeo and Juliet* is reduced to a brutal, mechanistic tragedy with little humor, erotic appeal, grace, or depth. As in the eighteenth century, notorious for its comic amendments of tragic plays, the resulting text is offered by its editors as an improvement, the perfection of Shakespeare's abortive early attempt to re-create tragedy in the Renaissance mode.

To sum up the dramatic argument against what Elspeth Stuckey calls the "violence of literacy," I emphasize that literary texts, as Shakespeare seems to know, are easily manipulated and even transformed by authority. During the five hundred years since the invention of the printing press, states and communities have devised strategic ways to contain dangerous literary texts, particularly those that are faithful to their vulgar (from *vulgus*, meaning folk) oral roots: revocation of the license to publish, excision, abridgment, bowdlerization, selective translation, indexing, book banning, book burning, and, of course, systematic, strategic censorship.[5] With the advent of moving pictures a hundred years ago, censorship had to be reinvented: questionable films could be clipped and snipped—and often were, by local theater owners—but they could also be licensed, banned, burned, and, in a recent turn of events, theatrically rated, a process that, curiously, has never been applied to books.

What, then, of the filmed versions that we all use in teaching *Romeo and Juliet,* and what of the live productions that the lucky few among us are able to encourage our students to attend? How is the bawdry handled in these resources for teaching? To illustrate the importance of the Nurse in the first half of the play, I show students five versions of the "weaning scene," where she ruminates on and reminisces about the deaths, fourteen years ago, of her husband and her child, Susan. These tragic events—remembered in connection with an earthquake!—the Nurse conceives as evidence of a huge cosmic "jest" epitomized in the pratfall little Juliet takes the day she learns to walk. The Nurse remembers:

> And then my husband—God be with his soul!
> 'A was a merry man—took up the child.
> "Yea," quoth he, "dost thou fall upon thy face?
> Thou wilt fall backward when thou hast more wit,
> Wilt thou not, Jule?" and by my holidam,
> The pretty wretch left crying and said, "Ay."
> To see how a jest shall come about!   (1.3.39–45)

As I have pointed out, this passage and others like it are clipped from the textbooks, but what about the films? In the film productions I show students—by George Cukor (1936), Renato Castellani (1954), Franco Zeffirelli (1968), and Baz Luhrmann (1996)—this speech and the reference to wormwood on the nipple are cut, and no visual analogy is offered. In the Zeffirelli production Juliet's breast is exposed on the wedding night, but I know teachers who feel compelled to block out this scene lest students (or parents) be offended. Only the BBC production (1978) leaves the entire weaning scene intact, but the Nurse in that production is so cold and humorless, and Juliet so stiff, that the speech does not resonate the way it should as thematically central to the play.

In live productions, I am happy to report, the comic heart of the play—Mercutio—is alive and well. In the Mercutio of the BBC production or even in Baz Luhrmann's black Mercutio, students see a hothead, a carbon copy of the warlike Tybalt, who fuels the disastrous feud in Verona. On stage, however, Mercutio is usually portrayed as a wise guy, a smart-ass, who revels in displaying a vulgar wit he seems to lift right off the street. Even John Barrymore, in his only speaking role as a Shakespearean character (Cukor version), plays up this element of Mercutio's character. The Mercutios in recent productions of *Romeo and Juliet* at the Clemson Shakespeare Festival were real hams, reveling in intimate and bawdy contact with the young members of the audience and providing masturbatory and coital gestures to drive home the innuendos. One Mercutio was so scandalous that the festival got letters protesting the suitability of such lines and gestures in a play for young audiences of students. The students, in fact, were approximately the same age as the teen actors (playing teen characters) who delivered the jokes onstage in Shakespeare's day.

In conclusion, *Romeo and Juliet* is a play fully suspicious of the expectations about literacy and of the propriety literacy was to instill in young people of the new Europe that was about to take control of the world. To strip the play of its life-affirming erotic language of the womb is to eliminate the real source of the play's attraction to young people and to reconstitute the play as a mechanistic moral exemplum about disobedient children predestined for the tomb. *Romeo and Juliet* alternately moves in the direction of the womb or the tomb, or, as Freud put it, toward affirmation of Eros or the defeat of Thanatos. Some teachers and students do find the references to genitalia, intercourse, and nursing offensive or, at best, write them off as incidental comic relief. Worse yet, exposed to expurgated versions of the play, students think they are reading or watching Shakespeare and are later surprised to see deleted passages restored in unabridged versions on the page or stage or screen. To ensure that students appreciate Shakespeare fully, we need to teach the text, the whole text, and nothing but the text—at least in spirit, if not to the letter.

NOTES

[1] On the turbulent and well-documented history of Shakespearean pedagogy, see Frey, "Teaching"; Stephen Brown; and Levin, "Core."

[2] "As the situation now stands, students who wish to investigate the bawdry at the opening of *Julius Caesar* or at various points in *Twelfth Night* must resort to the less-than-impeccable scholarship of Partridge, Rubinstein, and others, which may serve only to reinforce the entirely reasonable suspicion that the Shakespeare of their collected editions has been 'set up' in objectionable ways" (Frey, "Teaching" 555).

[3] See Andreas ("Neutering" and "Silencing") for an extensive consideration of the topic. The high school teacher Maureen Logan outlines the frustrations of trying to teach a truncated text of *Romeo and Juliet.*

[4] For a study of Shakespeare's "kinesthetic" imagery—including the bawdry—and how to teach it, see Frey, "Making Sense."

[5] See Jansen for an invaluable study of these various methods of censorship.

Teaching Mothers in *Romeo and Juliet*: Lady Capulet, from Brooke to Luhrmann

Michael Basile

When teaching Shakespeare, I encourage my students' active and critical engagement of the play texts by introducing several written and performance versions of each play. Additionally, I give students opportunities to analyze, rehearse, and perform their own interpretations of selected scenes so that they will, in effect, gain initiation into the large and respected community of readers, directors, and actors who have themselves reshaped Shakespeare into meaningful new forms. I suspend judgment on all interpretations—both student and professional—and pass the responsibility for judging to the class instead, requiring only that students' evaluations be scrupulously defended by generous evidence from the plays.

This approach may be useful for many of Shakespeare's plays, but it is particularly suited to *Romeo and Juliet* for two reasons. Practically speaking, the play is available in several versions, both written and performed: two extant Renaissance texts and five or more films. Moreover, experience teaches me that two of those films—Franco Zeffirelli's production of 1968 and Baz Luhrmann's of 1996—have passionate devotees among undergraduates. Since I aim to encourage fresh, flexible approaches to Shakespeare's play texts, I find it more rewarding to begin an exploration of multiple versions using as a springboard my students' zealous and sometimes rigid dedication to the "one and only" *Romeo and Juliet*. I need kindle no fires. When we conclude our work, however, light has replaced heat, as students have transformed their somewhat blind championship of a single film version to a respectful appreciation of the vast interpretive range sustained by the play.

Examining the entire play in its many versions is impossible within the time constraints of the two, eighty-minute classes I allot for this task. Instead we focus on a single scene, 1.3., featuring Lady Capulet and Juliet. Inquisitive students often require a justification for this choice. Besides citing limitations on time, I inform them that 1.3 varies markedly from version to version, inviting the comparative analysis on which we are soon to embark. Further, in no other play does Shakespeare develop a relationship between a female protagonist and her mother. What was uniquely interesting to him may offer rare insights to us.

Students evaluate 1.3 in Zeffirelli's and Luhrmann's films and in the two earliest versions of *Romeo and Juliet*—quarto 1 (Q1), published in 1597, and quarto 2 (Q2), published in 1599. We also briefly discuss Arthur Brooke's interpretation of the mother-daughter relationship in his narrative poem *Romeus and Juliet,* Shakespeare's source. Since according to Robert Scholes "a text always echoes other texts" (16), it is important to consider not only where the tremors resound but where they originate as well.

I begin by providing a brief outline of the critical debate surrounding the two quarto texts. The development of rookie textual scholars is hardly my goal, but students should be apprised that the quarto versions of *Romeo and Juliet* inspire passionate debate, a debate that functions as an analogue to their own positions concerning the Zeffirelli and Luhrmann films. Far from alienating students, this critical overview makes them feel like members of an important and respected club.

Some scholars believe Q1 represents an early draft by Shakespeare that was later expanded and revised into Q2, but most hold that Q1 is a product of memorial reconstruction: actors who had performed the still unpublished play recited it from memory to a renegade publisher. And as the story goes, it is this process of transmission—memory—that accounts for what some consider bad, or un-Shakespearean, readings.

When I have finished this overview, students insist I reveal my own position. I steadfastly resist. But since my goal is to encourage flexibility in their interpretations, I ask them to accept, provisionally at least, that Q1 is a legitimate version if only because it may record changes made by actors in performance or may be what Stanley Wells and Gary Taylor call "a more finished, dramatic, socialized phase of the text" than the Q2 version (28). But we can eat our cake and have it too, I tell them, for if Q1 is instead Shakespeare's authorized draft, we are privileged to witness his earliest interpretation of the story.

Our comparative analysis usually proceeds chronologically, starting with Arthur Brooke's narrative poem (available in an appendix to the Arden Shakespeare, edited by Brian Gibbons), continuing with the Q1 and Q2 versions, and finishing with the Zeffirelli and Luhrmann films. This order allows us to evaluate any progressive reinterpretation of the mother-daughter relationship in 1.3. After presenting a version of the scene, I may ask students to discuss it in class or to stage the scene, demonstrating their interpretations through their choices of movement, facial expressions, vocal intonations and rudimentary props and other theatrical tools.

In the Brooke poem, the relationship between Lady Capulet and Juliet is shaped without dialogue, so we focus here on descriptions of the mother's feelings and actions with respect to her daughter. This task takes little time and engenders little or no debate. Lady Capulet, referred to as Mother throughout, is a minor figure, and half of what we learn of her comes from the Nurse's description. The Nurse says to Romeo that "the mother loves her [Juliet] well" (line 651) and will be sure to react favorably to the proposed marriage because "she will in no way say her nay" (649). Later, during the father's brutal confrontation with Juliet over her refusal to marry Paris, the poem's speaker describes how "ruthfully stood by the mayden's mother milde" (1947). Finally, the mother's reaction to Juliet's supposed death, while extreme, confirms the mother as a conventionally maternal and nurturing figure: "Alack dear child my tears for thee shall never cease; / Even as my dayes of life increase, so shall my plaint increase" (2436–37).

The instructor may here entertain discussion on this sketch of Juliet's mother, but my experience teaches me it is more provocative to introduce briefly the Shakespearean versions of the character and then perform a retrospective comparison to Brooke's "mother milde." So we next scan the Q1 and Q2 versions of 1.3. Lady Capulet first appears in this important scene during which she proposes that Juliet marry Paris. I provide my students with copies of the scene that have modern spellings but that are otherwise exactly transposed from facsimiles of the two extant texts available in *Shakespeare's Plays in Quarto* (Allen and Muir). Reflecting on Brooke's "mother milde," the students are immediately impressed by how drastically Shakespeare has reinterpreted the character —at least in the Q2 version.

Generally speaking, the Lady Capulet in the Q2 version is more aggressive, impatient, and preemptory than her counterpart in Q1. In Q2, Lady Capulet's apparent intention is to intimidate Juliet into accepting Paris's marriage proposal. But when Juliet hesitates—"It [the marriage] is an honour that I dream not of" (66)—Lady Capulet responds in the imperative—"Well, think of marriage now" (69). Unrelenting, Lady Capulet continues moments later in her attempt to secure Juliet's acquiescence: "What say you? can you love the gentleman" (79) and "Speak briefly, can you like of Paris' love?" (96). In contrast, Q1 presents a more empathetic mother who "delicately introduces the topic of marriage to her daughter" (Urkowitz, "Five Women" 298) with the line, "Tell me Juliet, how stand you affected / to be married?" To Juliet's subsequent hesitation this version of the character responds, "Well girl, the Noble County Paris seeks thee for his wife," and follows with a similarly mild question, "Well Juliet, how like you of Paris' love?" (C1r).

When I present these versions of 1.3, however, I do so without comment. The instructor's opinion holds disproportionate sway in the classroom, and my goal throughout the course is to encourage students' own interpretations. The following exercise gives students an opportunity to practice their interpretative skills.

I divide the class in half, giving copies of the Q1 version to one half and copies of the Q2 to the other. These halves are then subdivided into groups of three or four, and each group becomes an acting company. (With groups of four students, three take the roles of Juliet, Lady Capulet, and the Nurse, and one directs; with groups of three, the actors direct themselves, much as Shakespeare and his company probably did.) Now students retire to separate areas of the classroom to accomplish several related tasks: evaluate the general tone of the mother-daughter relationship in the assigned version and draw conclusions about each character's motivations and goals, agree on what theatrical means will be used to signify these conclusions, and, ultimately, stage the scenes. I advise students to use large, visible gestures and movements—in short, to overact —since our goal is not to train actors but to explicate theatrically two distinct versions of the play. I give students the rest of this first class to work on these tasks and advise them to rehearse on their own before our next meeting, when they will perform the scenes.

The practical value of performance day should never be underestimated. Performing Shakespeare offers students unique insights by forcing them to make clear, unambiguous decisions concerning character and action and to reach a kind of critical closure that traditional theoretically based pedagogies appropriately discourage. And to effect theatrical decisions, students must make a friend of the language, which, once a forbidding stranger, is now the key to their very survival on stage.

Interpretations of the Q1 and Q2 versions of 1.3 will vary widely, even among groups performing the same version. I delight in such diversity. It poignantly reconfirms the power of actors to significantly alter the linguistic material of the script and provides a modern analogue to the practices of Shakespeare, for, as Marvin Rosenberg says, "no other playwright obtained so much creative collaboration from the artists of the theatre" (33). In general, however, student performances of Q1 display a "mother milde" and, of Q2, a more impatient and domineering matriarch—much as clues found within the texts suggest.

Two performances I remember, given by students at a community college, represent (dare I say) typical interpretative approaches to the quarto versions. In the Q1 version, Lady Capulet was shown preparing Juliet for the Capulet ball, carefully combing and braiding Juliet's hair. Lavishing her daughter with loving attention only served to emphasize her apparently mild entreaties such as, "Tell me Juliet, how stand you affected / to be married?" She kindly tolerated the Nurse, even laughed gently at the servant's verbose intrusions into the conversation she yearned to have with Juliet. Not only stage business but also pace helped define the relationship. The student playing Lady Capulet established a slow and deliberate pace, which contrasted effectively with Juliet's effusive and youthful haste. For instance, the line indicating Juliet's hesitation to commit herself to the marriage to Paris, blurted out almost hysterically—"it is an honour that I dream not of"—was met with calm silence. The mother continued the conversation only after a sustained pause, during which she gently stroked Juliet's hair several times with the brush. In sum, action and pace demonstrated an empathetic mother who was aware of the pressures her daughter felt and who took pains to minimize them.

My students' performance of the Q2 script also showed a mother preparing her daughter for the banquet. In this staging, however, Lady Capulet increasingly tightened a corset around her daughter's waist as she aggressively sought Juliet's acquiescence to marrying Paris: "What say you? can you love the gentleman?" she barked through clenched teeth. "Speak briefly, can you like of Paris' love?" she continued, putting her foot on Juliet's back to brace herself for the most violent jolt. In all, this was a less-than-subtle interpretation (perhaps influenced by a famous scene in *Gone with the Wind*), but the students' theatrical choices nonetheless clearly signified their understanding of the mother-daughter relationship in the Q2 version of 1.3.

Following a postperformance discussion, begun with kudos for all, I use the remaining time in the second session to show the Zeffirelli and Luhrmann versions of 1.3. By this juncture everyone in the class is an expert on the scene. It is delightful to sit back and revel in students' strong, informed opinions on the cuts made by the directors and the performance choices made by the actors.

If Zeffirelli consulted the Q1 version of this scene, his film offers no such indication. But neither does his Lady Capulet intimidate Juliet into submission. Zeffirelli's chief contribution to the development of the mother-daughter relationship in *Romeo and Juliet* was to cast the mother as relatively young, decidedly attractive, and still in her sexual prime. Consequently, the character's primary motivation in this scene appears to be perfecting her toilette in preparation for the ball and not, as the lines strongly suggest, securing Juliet's pledge to marry Paris.

Lady Capulet is first seen having her makeup applied by a servant. Several times throughout the scene she primps before a mirror, adjusting her jewelry, straightening her garment, and smoothing her hair. She directs her impatience at the Nurse's verbose ramblings, not at Juliet's initial hesitation about marriage —"It is an honour I dream not of"—and appears focused on making a prompt entrance to the ball, not on securing Juliet's consent to marry Paris. When she delivers her final, most pointed imperative, she looks away from her daughter and gestures toward the door, saying, "Speak briefly. Can you like of Paris' love?" In sum, Zeffirelli recasts the mother as a still-attractive, possibly still-active sexual player in Veronese society. For students seeing the film for the first time, this characterization comes as a surprise, and the keenest among them cite Lady Capulet's line in the last scene of the play to argue against Zeffirelli's reinterpretation of the character: "Oh me! This sight of death is as a bell / That warns my old age to a sepulchre" (200). Nonetheless, suddenly the mother-daughter relationship seems further complicated by an implied competition for breeding rights.

Most of my students agree that Zeffirelli's influence can be clearly seen in Luhrmann's eccentric 1996 film, which develops the mother-daughter relationship further in this direction—too far for some tastes. Lady Capulet, shown first in her bustier and underwear, prancing about in full view of male and female servants, preoccupies herself throughout the scene with preparation for the ball, much as her Zeffirelli counterpart does. Luhrmann's version of the character, however, is off to a bacchanal. She pops pills (one guesses amphetamines) and spasmodically lights and extinguishes a fashionably thin cigar, all the while appearing wholly indifferent to Juliet. (Robotic gestures made by the actress playing Lady Capulet are accentuated by the flickering effect of Luhrmann's camera work, created by decreasing the camera's shutter speed while recording.) Moreover, the script has been severely edited, leaving intact only a single command by the mother—"Speak briefly. Can you like of Paris' love?" But she delivers it as if by rote. The mother obligatorily solicits her daughter to marry Paris, but her heart is not in it; she just can't wait to party. Zeffirelli's implied sexual competition between Lady Capulet and Juliet becomes, in Luhrmann's film, brazen and public, for near the conclusion of the Capulet orgy we see Lady Capulet dragging Paris, obviously earmarked for marriage to Juliet, toward her own bedroom for a late-night sexual tryst.

Interestingly, early in 1.3 Luhrmann's film depicts servants violently corseting Lady Capulet—an almost obverse image of my students' Q2 performance, during which Juliet endured corseting at her mother's hands. And the link between these two interpretations is as tentative as that. Yet students learn from a transtextual exploration such as the one I have outlined that a play as ably constructed as *Romeo and Juliet,* well wrought but not fragile, can sustain (or weather) a wide range of interpretations and not break to pieces. They also learn something important about themselves; invariably, they come to be protective of the play, more protective than they (or I) could have predicted they would be. Teaching a classic is fraught with perils, not the least of which is students' aversion to being told what is worthy of their time and appreciation. Following the process of analysis and staging outlined here, students often conclude by instructing me of my priorities. I happily risk being my students' student to hear such a joyful noise. Collaboration, after all, can prove as sweet and harmonious in the classroom as it is on stage.

"My Ghostly Father":
Teaching the Friar in *Romeo and Juliet*

Paul J. Voss

After teaching *Romeo and Juliet* at the high school, undergraduate, and graduate levels, I realized that students often focus primarily on the story of young love and warring families, generally overlooking or dismissing the character of Friar Laurence as they read the play. Friar Laurence, however, performs an essential function in *Romeo and Juliet*. His nearly 350 spoken lines are surpassed in number only by Romeo's 591 lines and Juliet's 509 lines. Moreover, since most high school and college students know the story of Romeo and Juliet, studying the relatively ignored character of Friar Laurence offers students an intriguing change of perspective and, I believe, a fresh insight into this frequently taught play. Additionally, the role of Laurence grows in complexity when discussed in conjunction with the English Reformation, Shakespeare's source material, and other Renaissance plays that employ friar characters, allowing both beginning and advanced students ample room for scholarly investigation.

Before students read the play, I ask them to take special note of the Friar's role in the drama. I ask them, among other things, to note the number of scenes Laurence appears in (seven), to examine his speeches carefully, and to heed what other characters say about him. During our subsequent discussions, we seek answers to the following questions: Is Friar Laurence a noble figure, a hypocrite, or a combination of the two? Could he be a well-meaning but ineffectual friend? a coward? a scapegoat? a male counterpart to the Nurse? Answering any of these questions requires close reading of specific passages. The students must read for content (i.e., for evidence to make a case for or against Laurence) while assessing and reassessing the character as new evidence appears. Focusing on character also requires the students to grapple with the intriguing question of perspective.

Laurence's first speech in 2.3, a passage replete with contradiction and paradox, nicely captures the importance of perspective. According to Friar Laurence, all things in nature can, at different times, appear to be good and evil, contingent on their use:

> For nought so vile that on the earth doth live
> But to the earth some special good doth give;
> Nor aught so good but, strain'd from that fair use,
> Revolts from true birth, stumbling on abuse.   (2.3.17–20)

By addressing the question of use, Laurence also introduces, implicitly, the concept of perspective. The soliloquy challenges students to contemplate, for example, the philosophical idea of intrinsic good and evil: can anything, contra

Laurence, be wholly good or wholly evil? Must all judgments consider context and perspective? By raising these issues, Friar Laurence himself becomes implicated in the investigation of perspective. He can, like the many herbs he collects, be seen as good or evil. He is saint or sinner, reliable friend or bad counselor, concerned man of the cloth or meddlesome outsider.

Friar Laurence also functions, literally and figuratively, as a father to both Romeo and Juliet. In addition to performing his priestly duties for the community, the Friar befriends, advises, confesses, and marries Romeo and Juliet. Romeo has a somewhat distant relationship with his parents; the Montagues, worried about their troubled son, seek Benvolio's help early in the play. Juliet's trust in Laurence stands in stark contrast to her relationship with her own father; Lord Capulet actually threatens her with bodily harm, yelling "Beg, starve, die in the streets" after she refuses to marry County Paris (3.5.192). In the absence of trusted parents, both Romeo and Juliet run to the Friar with problems. Shakespeare reveals Laurence's personality gradually, so asking students to assess his character at different times throughout the play leads to a variety of opinions. Perhaps Shakespeare intended this reassessment process to happen (with regard to playgoers, of course).

Laurence's lengthy speech in 5.3 (frequently cut from productions of the play) supports this possibility. Why, for example, does Shakespeare have Laurence recount, in detail, the entire action of the play? What various thematic or dramatic ends does the Friar's speech serve? One possible answer comes from Laurence himself. Significantly, the Friar's final words in the play ask for a character assessment:

> and if aught in this
> Miscarried by my fault, let my old life
> Be sacrific'd some hour before his time
> Unto the rigour of severest law.   (5.3.266–69)

Shakespeare, in effect, wants all readers and viewers of the play to pass judgment on the Friar. The Friar's offer, however, complicates the issue: while the Friar does not deserve execution for his involvement in the plot, he may not be wholly innocent either. The students must determine, at this moment, how they view Laurence's actions in the tragedy. The discussion at this point usually creates a simple division between those who say, "Let him go; it wasn't his fault," and those who say, "Get a rope." Equivocation rarely materializes if students play the role of judge. But, of course, countless interim judgments exist between execution and exoneration. The play asks, nonetheless, for an answer, an answer that can be given only after one consults the entire body of evidence. The class then considers the Prince's final verdict, "We still [always] have known thee for a holy man" (5.3.270), and the debate continues. Does the Prince judge wisely in exculpating Friar Laurence or is this judgment merely another example of the Prince's inability to govern Verona effectively?

The emphasis on character requires elaboration. Assessing a character, especially the Janus-like Friar Laurence, demands a continual process of reading and evaluation. Robert Alter notes this challenge when he states that "we read character developmentally, so that later discoveries compel a reconsideration of earlier views" (60). In other words, no single snapshot of Laurence suffices. The students must balance, for example, the manifest care and concern Laurence feels for Romeo and Juliet with his equally obvious deception of the Capulet family in 4.5. How are we to understand his willingness to allow the Capulet family to suffer unnecessarily? In evaluating Laurence, students are asked to consider the character as a whole; this approach provides a dynamic model for reading and understanding the play.

Yet an approach to Laurence's character need not be limited to a close reading of the play in isolation. I find that making even brief remarks about the English Reformation and religious difference adds complexity to students' understanding of the character. By the 1590s, the presence of a Catholic priest on English soil was a capital crime; any Catholic priest apprehended could be charged with treason and executed. Robert Southwell's famous public execution in 1595 occurred around the time that Shakespeare finished writing *Romeo and Juliet.* Yet Laurence surely practices his faith on the English stage. He performs at least two sacraments during the play—confession and marriage. This legal reenactment of the illegal often escapes notice. Moreover, since friars and monks were expelled from England by 1535, very few, if any, members of Shakespeare's audience would have seen an actual friar. How does Shakespeare represent the unrepresented? In this sense, one could easily compare Laurence with Shylock, the ostracized Jew in *The Merchant of Venice,* or with the title character in *Othello.* Jews and Moors often appeared as characters on the early modern stage but were, like friars, publicly absent from Elizabethan society. While the community of Verona welcomes and accepts the Friar, the English community watching the play would not have been allowed to do so. Elizabethans could not have any contact with a Catholic priest—except perhaps at the Globe theater. If Shakespeare presents a sympathetic Laurence, the implications are worth considering. Does the play subvert the established church or government? Was Shakespeare, as some suggest, a crypto-Catholic? Does the play advocate a religious toleration not observed in 1595?

In Shakespeare courses (as opposed to general surveys of English literature), I also ask the students to consider Laurence in relation to his antecedent, the Friar Lawrence found in Arthur Brooke's 3020-line poem *The Tragicall Historye of Romeus and Juliet,* first printed by Richard Tottel in 1562. Source studies, often dismissed by contemporary scholars, offer undergraduates a challenging avenue of exploration. Such studies provide an opportunity for students to engage in sophisticated comparisons and contrasts that often require careful reading and nuanced literary judgment. Brooke's poem allows for just that. In addition to exposing students to the archaic poulter's measure (a verse form they find very difficult to appreciate) and to the unpredictability of Elizabethan spelling, selected passages from the poem (supplied as a handout) reveal that Shakespeare considerably alters the actions and reputation of the friar he found in his source. Brooke's preface to his poem, for example, harshly condemns friars, blaming the misfortunes of Romeus and Juliet, a "coople of unfortunate lovers," on "superstitious friars (the naturally fitte instruments of unchastitie) attemtyng all adventures of peryll, for thattaynyng of their wished lust, usying auriculer confession (the key of whoredome, and treason) for furtheraunce of theyr purpose" (2, 3). Brooke emphasizes Friar Lawrence's status as a "doctor of divinity" and implies an adulterous past for the friar, complete with a "secret place" where "he was wont in youth, his fayre frends to bestowe" (1267, 1273). Hints of lechery and black magic make Brooke's Friar Lawrence a shadowy figure with a murky past. The ensuing narrative does not, strangely, completely support the sentiments of the preface. Lawrence is not found guilty of wrongdoing per se; after his final speech, he leaves Verona and dies alone in a hermitage. Nevertheless, Brooke's Friar Lawrence is a sometimes philandering cleric who engages in various forms of questionable behavior; most friars in Elizabethan literature were likewise unsavory. But Shakespeare makes Friar Laurence a much more complex figure than Brooke's Friar Lawrence. What do the changes signify? Perhaps Shakespeare wanted to emphasize fate over human actions. By creating a nonvillainous friar, Shakespeare forces the reader to look elsewhere for an efficient cause of the tragedy. This explanation, however, raises a host of further questions about the nature of tragedy. If fate indeed controls the events of the play and characters are not agents but merely witnesses, can the play still be considered a tragedy?

No play, of course, exists in a vacuum. Students can also compare Friar Laurence with Friar Francis in *Much Ado about Nothing*. The similarities are more than coincidental. Both friars devise a subterfuge to assist troubled lovers. Both friars assume the role of surrogate father to a young woman whose natural father abuses or abandons her in a time of need. Both friars enjoy the respect and admiration of the communities they serve. But Friar Francis immediately comes to the defense of the falsely accused Hero and stakes his vocation on her innocence:

> [T]rust not my age,
> My reverence, calling, nor divinity,
> If this sweet lady lie not guiltless here
> Under some biting error.   (4.1.167–70)

Hero, of course, is redeemed, and by extension so is Francis. His role in society —his reverence, his calling, his divinity—receives implicit endorsement in the play.

In more specialized survey classes on Elizabethan and Jacobean drama, the friar character can serve as an excellent point of departure for a wide range of discussions and research projects. Early modern dramatists repeatedly used friars as characters in their plays. In fact, over sixty extant plays from the period contain a friar in a major or minor role—a number higher than that for any other single religious figure (including Puritans, who appear in just fewer than sixty plays, and Anglican priests) and nearly as high as that for all other Catholic characters (e.g., popes, cardinals, bishops, monks, and Jesuits) combined. Obviously, the friar as character struck a chord with dramatists and audiences of the period. In almost every play except Shakespeare's, friars are lecherous villains, comic buffoons, or black magicians. Examining the nature of this simultaneous attraction and repulsion often proves of value.

Reading these friars, especially in the plays of Marlowe, Greene, and Chapman, further contextualizes the figure of Friar Laurence. Marlowe's evil friars, Barnardine and Jacomo from *The Jew of Malta* (1589), commit numerous crimes while wearing the friar's habit. Barnardine unabashedly reveals his sham piety and his violation of the confessional when he states to the innocent Abigail:

> Know that confession must not be reveal'd;
> That canon law forbids it, and the priest
> That makes it known, being degraded first,
> Shall be condemned and then set to fire.   (3.6.33–36)

Immediately after hearing Abigail's confession, Barnardine betrays her trust, setting off with the newly acquired information to further his own desires.

In Marlowe's *Dr. Faustus* (1592), the title character demands that Mephistophilis change appearance:

> I charge thee to return and change thy shape;
> Thou art too ugly to attend on me,
> Go, and return an old Franciscan friar
> That holy shape becomes the devil best.   (1.3.23–26)

For the rest of the play, presumably, Mephistophilis wears the hood of a friar, reinforcing the common stereotype associating the Catholic Church with the devil. While some students note a possible compliment in the words of Faustus (friars, they argue, are more attractive than Mephistophilis), it is difficult to read "That holy shape becomes the devil best" without registering the insulting sarcasm.

The pamphleteer and playwright Robert Greene offers a semicomedic look at friars in his *Friar Bacon and Friar Bungay* (1589). While clearly not the evil villains found in Marlowe, Friar Bacon and Friar Bungay also derive from the negative stereotype found in much antifraternal writing of the period. Friar Bacon, like his legendary namesake, engages in necromancy and black magic. His incantations are powerful, and he vainly boasts of his abilities to frighten even the devil: "The great arch-ruler, potentate of hell, / Trembles when Bacon bids him or his friends / Bow to the force of his pentageron" (2.48–50). Although Friar Bacon's ultimate defeat and humiliation soften his characterization, his potential for evil remains consistent with contemporary depictions.

George Chapman includes a sinister, necromantic friar in *Bussy D'Ambois* (1604). In the play, the corrupt Friar Comolet, a conjurer who later returns as a ghost, serves as a panderer between Bussy and Tamyra. Comolet leads Bussy on a magical elevator ride to Tamyra's room, facilitating the adulterous relationship. Some years later, Chapman himself provides a perceptive, accurate remark about friars on stage in his comedy *May Day* (c. 1611). When considering a disguise to wear in order to avoid recognition, the servant Angelo rejects the weeds of the friar costume: "Out uppon't, that disguise is worne thread bare upon every stage, and so much villany committed under that habit, that 'tis growne as suspicious as the vilest" (2.4.146–48). Indeed, as Chapman observes, friars in drama had become virtually synonymous with vice, appearing as villains in dozens of plays. Such a comment begs the question, why friars? Was it simply that they were a recognizable target, functioning as a metonym for the Church of Rome? Or did their ubiquity in the recent past account for the negative characterizations? Or had Friars become, from the time of Chaucer and his outrageous clerics, a character type associated with hypocrisy and lechery? Ambitious students, both undergraduates and graduates, may want to pursue similar questions involving other stock characters from Shakespeare's plays (e.g., the scholar, the courtier, the fool, the Moor).

Elsewhere I have argued that Shakespeare's friars "convey a sense of dignity, understanding, respect, and piety" (14). In comparison with the scores of other friars on the early modern stage, Friar Laurence indeed seems unusual and rather virtuous. Students reading the play may not agree with this assessment. They will, as a result, be forced to gather evidence in order to refute the argument. In short, they will be required to read carefully, think logically, and write intelligently. The purpose of this essay is not to restate the case for Laurence but to underscore the richness and complexity of using an often overlooked character to study a familiar play. Using Friar Laurence to present a new perspective on *Romeo and Juliet* allows for both analysis and synthesis, both close reading and broad comparisons. Most important, it offers students a new opportunity to experience the play from another point of view. After reading *Romeo and Juliet*, most students agree that Friar Laurence is essential to the play; few come away without an opinion. The focus on character allows the students to explore the complicated presence of "my ghostly father" (2.3.45) in *Romeo and Juliet*.

Loving Shakespeare's Lovers: Character Growth in *Romeo and Juliet*

Karl F. Zender

Some years ago, after a less-than-satisfactory first class session on *Romeo and Juliet,* I began the next period by wondering whether I was too old to teach the play and whether my students were too old to study it. I didn't intend these doubts seriously, of course—I hope never to be too old to teach *Romeo and Juliet!*—but I wanted to raise as dramatically as possible the question of what teachers and students need to bring to the play in order to engage fully with the play's emotional power. The problem, I said, was that I had started our first day's discussion at the wrong place, by asking how Romeo and Juliet are responsible for their own downfall. Beginning there begged the more important question of why we should care about Romeo and Juliet at all. Before we see the young lovers as flawed, I said, we need to see them as valuable. Until we empathize strongly (and unashamedly) with their hopes and tribulations, their deaths will strike us as merely regrettable, not tragic. In a word, I said, we need first of all to love Shakespeare's lovers.

But how to do this? Getting a class to empathize with Romeo and Juliet's romantic ardor and tragic downfall faces obstacles both psychological and cultural: the guardedness late adolescents display when asked to discuss directly issues of sentiment; the status as shopworn cliché of many of the play's lines and scenes; the tendency of some young (and not so young) people, reinforced by our consumer culture, to treat love as synonymous with fantasies of effortless fulfillment. Fortunately, in my course on Shakespeare's early plays—an upper-division lecture class of seventy-five students—*Romeo and Juliet* is the third play we study, after two romantic comedies (*A Midsummer Night's Dream* and *Much Ado about Nothing*). Studying the comedies first allows me to make some assertions about Shakespeare's representations of romantic love that prove valuable when discussing *Romeo and Juliet*—most notably that love in Shakespeare is both a state that one falls into and a skill that one learns. Using a variety of examples—Troilus's reflections on "the monstruosity in love" in *Troilus and Cressida* (3.2.78), the contrasting understandings of love displayed by Othello and Desdemona—I point toward the deficiencies that Shakespeare's romantic heroes and heroines must overcome if they are to grow into a mature understanding of love.

Focusing on the contrast between Othello's "If it were now to die, / 'Twere now to be most happy" and Desdemona's "The heavens forbid / But that our loves and comforts should increase / Even as our days do grow" (2.1.187–88, 191–93), I draw a distinction between a (usually male) understanding of love as passionate intensity, shading into eroticized thoughts of death, and a (usually female) understanding of love as conjugal affection. From here, it is an easy step to tracing patterns of affectional growth in the comedies. In *A Midsummer*

Night's Dream, for example, Northrop Frye's notion of a circular journey—out of a fallen world into an unfallen one, then back into the fallen world transformed—provides a way of connecting the four young lovers' (mis)understanding of love to the society in which they live ("Argument"). Linking the rationalist, patriarchal, daylit Athens of the opening of the play to Lysander's "The will of man is by his reason sway'd, / And reason says you are the worthier maid" (as well as to Helena's more troubling "I am your spaniel; and, Demetrius, / The more you beat me, I will fawn on you") helps students see that the young lovers' misadventures in the moonlit world of acts 2 and 3 arise from inward as well as situational causes (2.2.115–16, 2.1.203–04). And comparing the Athens of act 5 with the Athens of act 1 underlines how a more mature and generous understanding of romantic affection—a mingling of the values of Athens with the values of the woods—ultimately prevails over those misadventures.

Romeo and Juliet contains no circular journey of regeneration and return. But the notion of an opposition between two worlds and between the values associated with each nonetheless provides a convenient route to understanding Romeo's and Juliet's attractiveness as characters. The two worlds, as I construe them, are the world of the everyday, associated primarily with Juliet's parents and with the other adult characters, and the world of romance, associated exclusively with Romeo and Juliet. A useful exercise is to ask the class to list characteristics (both thematic and stylistic) of the two worlds. The list will vary considerably from one discussion of the play to another, but at its core will be oppositions of the following sort, with the first term characterizing the world of the everyday and the second the world of romance: age / youth, past / future, materiality / spirituality, day / night, earth / sky, public setting / private setting, prose / verse, stasis / change.

Considered merely by itself, without elaboration, such a list of polarities points toward the poignancy of Romeo's and Juliet's deaths, emphasizing that the lovers are both individual characters and representatives of more general, deeply cherished human aspirations and potentials. For me, as for many other teachers of the play, the central polarity is between stasis and change—between the adults' fixity of attitude, symbolized by their devotion to a feud whose origin can no longer be recalled, and Romeo's and Juliet's openness to growth and desire to be "new baptiz'd" (2.2.50) by love. I find it rewarding to devote a considerable amount of class time to tracing the characters' patterns of growth and change, first for Romeo, then for Juliet. Doing so not only enriches my students' appreciation of the tragic loss depicted in the play but also broaches important questions about Shakespearean representation and about how the playwright genders the experience of emotional and romantic maturation.

For both Romeo and Juliet, I explore changes in attitude and language in key pairs or sequences of scenes. As a prelude, I establish a pair of "bookends" for Romeo's development by asking students to compare the words other characters use as designations for Romeo in the early parts of the play with the words he uses to designate himself in act 5. Tybalt's contemptuous references to Romeo as "boy" and "wretched boy" (3.1.65, 32) are fully congruent with Romeo's age and with the impression created by Romeo's maudlin posturing in 1.1. Yet by 5.3, scarcely three days later by the literal chronology of the play, Romeo addresses County Paris as "youth" and refers to himself repeatedly as "man":

> Good gentle youth, tempt not a desperate man,
> [. . . . .]
>   I beseech thee, youth,
> Put not another sin upon my head,
> By urging me to fury: O, be gone.
> [. . . . .]
> Stay not, be gone; live, and hereafter say
> A madman's mercy bid thee run away.   (5.3.59–67)

And when this effort at mollification fails, Romeo confronts Paris in language directly echoing (but with reversed application) Tybalt's in 3.1. "Wilt thou provoke me?" he says, "Then have at thee, boy!" (5.3.70).

A question I pose at this point, without necessarily inviting or expecting an answer, is whether (or how) the movement from the one designation to the other is realistic. What keeps Romeo's act 5 references to himself as a man (and his slightly later mention of "this world-wearied flesh" [5.3.112]) from striking us as merely the ludicrous posturing of a sixteen-year-old? Similarly, how are we to respond to the mature eroticism of the not-yet-fourteen-year-old Juliet's soliloquy, which begins "Gallop apace, you fiery-footed steeds" and stunningly insists that "strange love grow bold, / Think true love acted simple modesty" (3.2.1, 15–16)? Looming behind these questions are larger issues about Shakespearean representation, and I am happy to take the discussion further in this direction if the class is so inclined. But my main purpose is to invite students to extend their understanding of realism beyond the term's primary meaning of verisimilitude. The realism of the play, I argue, does not lie in the play's depiction of the changes that a sixteen- or thirteen-year-old might plausibly be expected to undergo in the span of three or four days. Rather, the realism lies in the play's commitment to depicting a contour of development that may never exist in unalloyed form in real life. The play's primary allegiance, I say, is not to fact but to truth.

Once this premise has been established (or at least brought forward for consideration), the way is clear to illumine different facets of Romeo's and Juliet's development, first by comparing the attitudes expressed in 1.1 (the discussion of Rosaline), 1.5 (the ball scene), and 2.2 (the balcony scene), then by comparing Romeo's mock offer of suicide in 3.3 with his and Juliet's actual acts of self-destruction in 5.3. How much time I devote to these comparisons varies from class to class, but at a minimum I want my students to see how changes in

Romeo's and Juliet's understanding of love are reflected in changes in their language. Comparing the frozen Petrarchanism of 1.1 and the artificiality of the sonnet exchange in 1.5 with the beautiful speech beginning "O, speak again, bright angel" in the balcony scene (2.2.26), I argue, following Brian Gibbons in the Arden edition of the play, that from the balcony scene forward, "the emergence of deeper and finer feeling is expressed not in rhyme but in blank verse"; and I extend this observation, as does Gibbons, into a general distinction between Romeo and Juliet and the other characters. In Gibbons's words:

> The play progressively distinguishes between characters who contentedly express themselves through received verbal and rhetorical conventions, and the hero and heroine who learn that greater maturity and fulfilment require language true to their own particular selves. (48)

Similar considerations apply to the scenes of mock and actual suicide. In the former scene Romeo enacts (in my view) the febrile and self-dramatizing erotics of death of the Petrarchan tradition, while in the latter scene he reveals a tragic complexity of attitude. Romeo's first offers of suicide are merely gestural, protected against enactment by the presence onstage of Friar Lawrence and the Nurse. But when Romeo stands alone in the tomb, saying that "unsubstantial Death" keeps Juliet "in dark to be [Death's] paramour" (5.3.103–05) and that Romeo therefore must protect his bride against death's lovemaking by lying with her in death himself, he transforms utterly the *Liebestod* tradition. How, I ask my students, are we to respond to Romeo's speech and to his and Juliet's subsequent acts of suicide? Drawing on my experience as the husband of a woman who served for years as director of a suicide prevention agency, I set the discussion in the context of the actualities of suicide among the young, striving to distinguish between the meaning suicide bears in life and in art and seeking to identify the mingled strands of folly, eroticism, and heroic defiance that constitute Romeo's and Juliet's final moments of life.

Tracing patterns of development relative to views of love and death intermingles discussion of Romeo with discussion of Juliet but puts greater emphasis on Romeo. Whenever I teach the play, I make sure that I reserve ample time for a separate discussion of Juliet's growth, both because the topic is relevant to many of today's students and because Juliet's development is less immediately apparent than is Romeo's. A good way to start this discussion is to ask where Juliet's parents believe her to be when she and Romeo are being wed. The answer, of course, is at confession. "Bid her devise / Some means to come to shrift this afternoon," says Romeo (2.4.176–77). "Have you got leave to go to shrift today?" asks the Nurse (2.5.67). Calling students' attention to Juliet's need to engage in this deception leads to their awareness of the extent—often surprising to students—to which her physical mobility is constrained by her parents. It also leads to an awareness of the sharp contrast between her situation and that of Romeo, who at the beginning of the play is free to wander alone before dawn in a "grove of sycamore," then to return home and shut himself away in his chambers (1.1.119).

Emphasis on Juliet's lack of physical freedom links back through a familiar series of ironies to the earlier discussion of the development of a mature language of love. "And all my fortunes at thy foot I'll lay, / And follow thee my lord throughout the world," says Juliet, in the full flight of her romantic ardor (2.2.147–48). Yet she makes this statement while simultaneously fending off the Nurse's repeated insistence that she immediately come to bed. And as my students often observe, when Romeo is exiled and thereby forced to travel "throughout the world," no mention is made—by Juliet or anyone else—of Juliet's following him. These ironies suggest a need in Juliet, parallel to the need in Romeo, to work free of a Petrarchan love rhetoric that is abstracted from experience. From the outset, she displays a greater awareness than does Romeo of the dangers of such a rhetoric. It is she, not he, who says, "O, swear not by the moon, th' inconstant moon, / That monthly changes in her [circled] orb" (2.2.109–10). Juliet, no less than Romeo, needs to gain command of a love language fully responsive to the tang of actuality.

Equally significant, to my mind, are other ways in which Juliet's confinement links to her inward development. Crucial to my understanding of the play is a view of Juliet's initial confinement as psychic as well as physical. Comfortably ensconced inside a loving and protective family, Juliet is initially fully compliant with her parents' wishes, both in her willingness to entertain County Paris's suit only to the extent that her parents' "consent gives strength to make [it] fly" (1.3.99) and, more important, in her modesty. It is of course a commonplace of Shakespearean commentary to say that all of Shakespeare's romantic heroines are modest. I find it useful to challenge this notion as a way of exploring the inward, erotic dimension of Juliet's development.

Here as elsewhere, the good fortune of having studied some romantic comedies before studying *Romeo and Juliet* serves the course well, for I am able to use my earlier discussion of Hero's modesty in *Much Ado about Nothing* as a starting point for discussing Juliet's modesty. Arguing that Shakespeare invites criticism of Hero's combination of prudishness and shallowness—her inarticulateness on matters of love and sex, her delight in the fashionableness of her wedding dress—I develop a contrast with Juliet's growing willingness to speak forthrightly of her desires. Citing the many references to Juliet's blushes in the early parts of the play as evidence of her innate modesty, I return again to the eroticism of the "Gallop apace" speech, where Juliet demands that "civil night / [. . .] / Hood my unmann'd blood, bating in my cheeks," allowing her to "lose a winning match, / Play'd for a pair of stainless maidenhoods" (3.2.10–14). From here, class discussion usually evolves quite naturally into a consideration of the other forms of growth that Juliet exhibits—her developing courage and independence of spirit, for example, as the emotional support afforded her by various members of the older generation (father, mother, Nurse, Friar) falls away, leaving her alone in her room, preparing to drink the sleeping potion.

This discussion of Romeo's and Juliet's development, then, offers students a way of loving Shakespeare's lovers. From the outset of our consideration of the play, though, and intermittently throughout, I promise my students that we will discuss Romeo's and Juliet's complicity in their own downfall. I am very much aware of the partiality of a reading that emphasizes only Romeo's and Juliet's attractiveness—the danger it poses of converting the play into a proto–*Love Story* that elicits pity but not fear. An obvious way of avoiding this danger, of seeing the play as more than the "misadventur'd piteous overthrows" of "star-cross'd lovers" (prologue 7, 6), is by focusing on Romeo and Juliet's impetuosity, their commitment to a love "too rash, too unadvis'd, too sudden, / Too like the lightning, which doth cease to be / Ere one can say 'It lightens' " (2.2.118–20). Much can be made of the ironic interplay between this impetuosity and the rapid succession of events and emphasis on accident in the play—quarrels begin on sight, messages arrive a little too early or too late, Capulet suddenly decides to move forward the date of Juliet's marriage to County Paris. But my own inclination is to focus instead on the more intricate topic of naming and identity—on how Romeo and Juliet misunderstand the relation between identities and names and on how this misunderstanding influences the lovers' actions throughout the play.

The locus classicus for a discussion of names and identities in *Romeo and Juliet* is Juliet's balcony speech:

> What's in a name? That which we call a rose
> By any other word would smell as sweet;
> So Romeo would, were he not Romeo call'd,
> Retain that dear perfection which he owes
> Without that title. Romeo, doff thy name,
> And for thy name, which is no part of thee,
> Take all myself.   (2.2.43–49)

This speech—especially its opening lines—is so much a part of our common cultural heritage that it may occasion little more than a nod of acquaintance from readers. As a way of restoring the speech to its dramatic function, I engage in an exercise I call "renaming the rose." Asking students whether they agree with Juliet's claim that "a rose / By any other word would smell as sweet" (almost all do agree at first), I question what it means to say that a rose smells—whether smell is a property of the rose or a function of perceiving. Then I propose, as dramatically as possible, some alternative, noxious name for the rose—*phlegm*, perhaps—and I ask again whether the rose smells as sweet.

Depending on the inclination of the class, the renaming exercise may lead to a general discussion of the power of language to construct reality, as in our present-day awareness of the need to achieve gender neutrality in titles of address (*chair* rather than *chairman*, for example). But I soon direct the exercise back toward the action of the play by exploring both the power and the naïveté of Juliet's assumptions about names. Romantic love, so Freud and others tell us, serves the function of social differentiation; it frees individuals from the social unit of the parental family, so that a new social unit may be formed. Romeo's response to Juliet's "What's in a name" speech—"Call me but love, and I'll be new baptiz'd: / Henceforth I never will be Romeo" (2.2.50–51)—states this goal of differentiation in religious language. The romantic dream of the young lovers is to start afresh, newly baptized and freed from the burdens of the past—the feud, being a Montague or a Capulet.

Yet the ironies attendant on abandoning a name immediately thrust their way forward. "What man art thou that thus bescreen'd in night / So stumblest on my counsel?" asks Juliet. "By a name / I know not how to tell thee who I am," replies Romeo (2.2.52–54). In their naïveté, Romeo and Juliet assume that they possess identities independent of the ones designated by the names Montague and Capulet. In some sense, they must be right, or love and growth could not occur. But in a more profound sense, they are wrong—most tragically so in assuming that the identities designated by their family names are entirely hateful. Interpreting Montague as synonymous with enemy of Capulet, Romeo and Juliet fail to remember that Montague also designates other, more positive, identities—son, friend—a fact brought home to Romeo in the duel with Tybalt, when Romeo affirms one identity, friend of Mercutio, at the expense of another, husband of Juliet. Like many of Shakespeare's romantic heroes, Romeo and Juliet must learn that love does not exist simply in opposition to hatred and anger. If it did, the lovers' situation would be simple. Only because romantic love exists in tension with other positive values—with other forms of love—is their situation tragic. The grandeur of their dream of new baptism is of a piece with its impossibility.

I normally devote four or five fifty-minute periods to *Romeo and Juliet*—long enough to develop the reading described above but not long enough to do much more than treat allusively other important topics such as stagecraft; patterns of imagery; the characterization of Mercutio, Capulet, Lady Capulet, County Paris, the Nurse, and Friar Lawrence; and the significance of male-male and female-female relationships. In a more advanced and leisurely reading, I would hope to explore these topics as well as the cultural determinants and limits of my approach to the play. In a later course, perhaps at the graduate level, I would want to explore the historicity of the idea of romantic love and of the notion of the integral self, and I would encourage students to place under erasure the various social, gender, and cultural assumptions informing the play's action. But in a first reading, my goal is to foster appreciation this side of idolatry—to help students experience the pathos and the glory and the pain of Romeo and Juliet's struggle to love and to help them understand the relevance of that struggle to their own lives. "O, speak again, bright angel, for thou art / As glorious to this night, being o'er my head, / As is a winged messenger of heaven" (2.2.26–28).

The Wild Goose Chase:
Teaching Metaphor in *Romeo and Juliet*

Joseph A. Porter

When I teach fiction-writing seminars, early on we spend an hour or so playing a game in which each student thinks of a public figure and then writes a series of words or phrases answering questions like, If your person were an X (animal, bird, day of the week, musical instrument, disease, common household substance, etc.), what X would your person be? When each one has accumulated a dozen items, the students read their lists in turn, and the class tries to guess the figure who generated each list. A good icebreaker, the game, which might be called Metaphor, also serves more particular pedagogical ends. Since guessing identities from the leads nearly always proves much easier than new players had supposed, the game quickly demonstrates how metaphor can find northwest passages through the mind. It also builds confidence in unsuspected powers of the unconscious. "Don't deliberate," I say when students are specifying the Xs. "Write what first occurs to you. We can deliberate later."

I teach metaphor in *Romeo and Juliet* in much the same spirit, moving quickly beyond the kinds of figuration that many students have already been taught to notice in secondary school, and beyond the ways students have often been led to consider figurative language, that is, as part of a texture of iterative images such as light and dark, whose significance may be decoded in straight-forward ways. To students interested in figurative language, I recommend as a starting point Ann Thompson and John Thompson's *Shakespeare: Meaning and Metaphor.* I also suggest a sampling of book-length theoretical and general studies of metaphor from the past decade, studies informed by the recent marked increase in prominence of the subject of mind in cognitive science and in the philosophy of mind.

With *Romeo and Juliet,* I find it useful to dwell on a particular metaphor, asking many questions about it, a bit like Peter with his insistent "Why 'silver sound', why 'music with her silver sound'?" (4.4.151).[1] The tactic works well both in graduate seminars and in my undergraduate Shakespeare classes of forty students, where it provides a happy variation from lectures. Students see that Shakespeare's metaphorical language excites me and that it often puzzles me. They know that my knowledge about Shakespeare exceeds theirs, but with these forays into somewhat unchartered territory students see that we are fellow explorers.

In 5.3, when Romeo says that Juliet's "beauty makes / This vault a feasting presence full of light" (85–86), some of the metaphor's uncanny power communicates itself to students. The unfamiliar "feasting presence" leads some students to relish what they take to be a kind of ravishing vagueness in the figure. Others subsume this phrase into a familiar calculus of light-dark imagery. For still others the metaphor hardly registers at all. Having occupied all these positions myself in the course of my experience of the play, I feel qualified to negotiate among them and to help the entire class reach deepened and informed versions of the first position. I aim not to explain away the metaphor's power but rather to tease out (as we say) more of it. By saying the right words, I attempt to conjure this power into the classroom.

Making sure the students understand what a feasting presence is—"a festive royal chamber for receiving guests" in Stephen Greenblatt's Norton gloss—can lead to discussion of how and why Juliet's beauty accords sovereignty to her and makes state visitors of Paris and Romeo. We may discuss how these lines exhibit some of the forging of the metaphor—Juliet's beauty "makes" the vault a lighted presence. Similarly, looking back to 1.5, we may recall that with her beauty Juliet "teach[es] the torches to burn bright" (41–44), and we may consider whether in the next scene it is her beauty that makes her the sun (2.1.44–45). Still staying as it were on the page, with metaphor as local imaginative construct, I ask the class to consider what it means to be "full" of light. Without shadow? But could a chamber be entirely shadowless, even with Baz Luhrmann's ten thousand candles? And if we grant that it could, wouldn't it always be possible to add more light? Might a chamber be so luminous that no more light could be added? Physics majors can put their expertise to use here.

We then may entertain the possibility that this presence's light comes not from imagined candles or sconces nor from the actual torches of Paris and Romeo but rather from Juliet herself. And we may consider how the recumbent gold statues promised by Capulet and Montague recapitulate Romeo's effulgent figure. We may consider this metaphor as a culmination—apotheosis, even—not only of what G. Blakemore Evans in the New Cambridge edition calls "the light-in-darkness imagery associated with[, . . .] particularly, Juliet" (200) but also of the play's indoor-female and outdoor-male givens. Juliet, who has spent the play receiving her second-story husband in secret and scarcely daring to set foot out in the public haunt of men, now in this metaphor receives guests ceremonially and quite publicly.

Following our initial sally with the metaphor, we may proceed in any of several directions. Whatever paths we explore, I prepare the exploring party by observing that the feasting presence figure stands in the center of a portion of the text—5.3.12–120—that is extraordinarily rich in metaphor. Sometimes I hold up a copy of the play in which I have highlighted metaphors from beginning to end to show in flourescent orange how here and in a few other passages, metaphor moves the lines into a gear different from that of the adjoining text, which may run for a page or more without a touch of color. The markedly highlighted metaphoricalness of the immediate context, I suggest, contributes to the resonance of the feasting presence and deserves scrutiny itself. At this junction I may mention a certain uncanniness the feasting presence gains not simply from the tomb's Halloween setting but also from less obvious Shakespearean tricks and treats, many in the surrounding texture of metaphor. So provisioned, we set out.

According to the text, the darkness in the vault is so intense that Romeo does not recognize Paris until Romeo has killed him and can peer closely at Paris's face. The darkness, entirely fictional on the stage of the Theatre, has unsettling comic possibilities, which may augment the scene's strangeness. Even more than in previous day-for-night scenes, this fictional darkness would seem to destabilize the metaphorical continuum of light and dark and could be metaphorical itself, metaphorical for the limits of human understanding. Assuming that Shakespeare's stage projected from the eastern edge of the wooden O of the theater, so placed to catch afternoon sun, we have in the "feasting presence full of light" not only a recollection of the mental double take prompted by Romeo's earlier "It is the east, and Juliet is the sun" (2.1.45) but also a still more unsettling metadramatic realization of the metaphor. For, if here the female sun Juliet, having declined from the balcony to the main stage, lies under the upper stage and perhaps even back in the discovery space, she may actually be more illuminated now by the more horizontal beams of the real sun shining in on her than she was two hours before.

A similar vertiginous oscillation between the concrete and the metaphorical occurs when Romeo, building to the "feasting presence full of light," calls the Capulet tomb "a lantern" (5.3.84), that is, a lighthouse (Greenblatt) or a "turret full of windows, by means of which cathedrals, and sometimes halls, are illuminated" (George Steevens, qtd. in *Romeo and Juliet* [ed. Evans] 185)—a high structure built to let light either in *or* out. Juliet, having come down from her balcony, is in this figure elevated once again, and the exactly opposed directions of the light in the two glosses echo the opposed directions of illumination brought to mind when Juliet, lighted by the setting sun, is said to be herself the sun rising in the east. The optical contradiction partakes of the widespread early modern uncertainty about light's direction (cf. "eye-beams," common in the period; *OED* s.v. *beam* 21) and resonates in the play not only with Romeo's early puerile oxymora but also with the lark-nightingale seesaw in 3.5. This conceptual shimmer itself is problematized, students admit (sometimes a bit uncomfortably), by a prop when Friar Laurence enters moments later "*with lantern"* (120sd)—as though Romeo's death precipitated the transformation of a metaphorical object of thought into a merely physical object.

Along with his lantern, Laurence brings another object that similarly, and more strangely, concretizes what earlier was memorably metaphorical. Many commentators, including students, note that Romeo's "So shows a snowy dove trooping with crows" at the Capulet ball (1.5.45) is foreshadowed by Benvolio's promise to "make thee [Romeo] think thy swan [Rosaline] a crow" in comparison with other beauties at the ball (1.2.87). Fewer, however, remark the uncanny reification of these two metaphorical crows in 5.3, in Balthasar's *"crow of iron"* (20sd) and Friar Laurence's *"crow"* (120sd). Some students, having trooped so far with these crows, notice that when Laurence bolts from the tomb, he evidently leaves behind both his ex-metaphorical objects, which seem to have ensorcelled him: one of the watchmen hauling him back mentions that "We took this mattock and this spade from him" (5.3.184)—that is, Laurence has unaccountably exchanged his crow for Balthasar's mattock.

Once students have noted that their own decidedly alimentary coloring for "feast" is mostly imminent in Shakespeare's English, they may savor how that connotation stirs disconcertingly in Romeo's figure, as if brought to premature life by his earlier, more extended metaphor of the tomb as a rotting mouth gorged with Juliet as its dearest morsel (5.3.45–48). Something of that grisly figure persists in the feasting presence and darkens its glory, I suggest. We may hence turn to other ways in which Romeo's swan song belies appearances. For instance, many students, even fresh from reading or rereading the speech, are inclined to think of it as addressed to the "dead" Juliet. Some of it is, but more is directed at the two genuinely dead men present, and the direction of address has everything to do with how metaphors function in the speech.

Romeo begins his speech addressing the man he has just fought to the death and acceding, surprisingly, to the still-unknown man's dying request to be laid in the tomb with Juliet (5.3.73). When, on identifying Paris, Romeo describes him as "writ with me in sour misfortune's book" (82), the metaphor repays attention for, despite a certain conventionality, it amplifies what may be called the author function, the eerie virtuality of Shakespeare's writing hand behind the moment. Misfortune's book, after all, is written, not printed, a fact emphasized by "thy hand" in the immediately preceding line. Romeo, having recognized Paris's face, recalls uncertainly Balthasar's report of the proposed marriage of Juliet and Paris. The uncertainty of the memory makes Romeo wonder whether in fact he dreamed Balthasar's words and whether even now he is "mad [. . .] / To think it was so" (80–81). The hypothesized dream chimes with others in the play, one of the most remarkable being that which Balthasar himself describes moments later:

> As I did sleep under this yew tree here
> I dreamt my master and another fought,
> And that my master slew him.   (137–38)

Balthasar's words wonderfully blur the boundaries between sleep and wakefulness, reality and dream, subject and figure. I direct students to Marjorie Garber's *Dream in Shakespeare* and invite them to entertain the possibility that all dreaming is intrinsically metaphorical. At this point we may glance forward to *A Midsummer Night's Dream,* usually the next play I teach.

Discussion of dreams and of the heightened author function may segue into a discussion of another factor contributing to the power of the feasting presence metaphor. As I elaborate in *Shakespeare's Mercutio: His History and Drama,* the god Mercury looms large in Shakespeare's amalgam of Mercutio, and the Mercutio-Mercury figure is notably revenant here at the fulfillment of Mercutio's dying curse, the fulfillment itself metaphorical to be sure, unless we choose to take the "infectious pestilence" (5.2.10) that prevented the delivery of Laurence's letter to Romeo as the direct and sufficient cause of the concluding woe. The baleful Mercutio-Mercury figure is immanent by virtue of the gratuitous mention of Mercutio's name (5.3.75) and the upswell of terms from Mercury's peculiar domains: the oneiric, the scriptorial, and the liminal. Mercutio, furthermore, is virtual here because the Apothecary serves as his double, and this is because medicine is another of Mercury's domains (we recall the caduceus) and also because Romeo's recollection of the Apothecary's overwhelming brows (5.1.39) reprises Mercutio's earlier reference to his own (1.4.32). The roles of Mercutio and the Apothecary may have been played by one actor; the resonance in any case amplifies the subtextual presence of Mercutio-Mercury. Thus Romeo, having begun his dying aria with the reference to Mercutio, in a sense addresses him at its conclusion: "O true apothecary, / Thy drugs are quick! Thus with a kiss I die" (5.3.119–20).

I encourage classes to probe other stretches of heightened metaphoricalness in the play—Friar Laurence's morning soliloquy (2.2.1–12); the ribald punning of Romeo, Mercutio, and Benvolio (2.3.33–87); Juliet's impassioned soliloquy (beginning 3.2); and Mercutio's Queen Mab speech (1.4.55–95), which, although mostly unmetaphorical, might almost be called metametaphorical and which rewards careful consideration. Students sometimes cite this last speech in the course of discussing metaphor in the play, and, when they do not, I sometimes lead discussion into this mare's nest. The Queen Mab speech raises fundamental questions about the nature of metaphor because, for all its metaphorical feel and focus on dreams, one might argue that it contains almost nothing at all metaphorical following the nearly subtextual metaphor "She is the faries' midwife," reprised after Mercutio calls dreams "children of an idle brain" (1.5.55, 97). Not metaphorical, Mab's chariot is a real hazelnut shell. Ah, so then perhaps metaphor obtains in the opposite direction: the shell is a metaphorical chariot? Perhaps, and yet this chariot (itself by metaphor a wagon) is (unlike other hazelnut shells) a product of art, having been made either by a squirrel (a metaphorical joiner?) or by an old (and boring, it goes without saying) grub. So this hazelnut shell, however concrete, is perhaps rather a "hazelnut shell." And as for its concreteness, when Mab's "team of little atomi" (57; the "team" encapsulating a metaphor) draws the shell over knees or a neck, the shell seems solid enough, but when in this very chariot Mab gallops through brains, her shell would seem perforce to lose materiality.

We need fear no unfortunate consequence of so working with these tangled elflocks, for they may in fact be ultimately intractable. Their aporias, however, provide a good taste of the volatility of Shakespeare's metaphorical imagination and a good foil of the more ostensibly sedate metaphors, "by the book," of the sonnet comprised in the interchange between Romeo and Juliet in the next scene. I say ostensibly sedate, for many university students come to the play with prepackaged notions of these metaphors—and of hands, lips, and pilgrims as haloed flowers of poesy—and Queen Mab may help students see the strangeness of the famous lines in which hands have lips, and so do lips.

It can also be productive to sound Mercutio's bawdy metaphors, especially with respect to the cultural, critical, and editorial history of the play's presentation of sexuality. Here I often use Mercutio's speeches to Benvolio in 2.1, focusing on lines 23–29 or 33–41. In the first lines, Mercutio claims that he conjures only to raise up Romeo and not to raise a spirit of some strange nature in Rosaline's circle. I elucidate the double entendres in the sexual ("obscene" according to Greenblatt in the Norton edition) wordplay and then lead the class to consider (1) how and why the sexual organs are more insistently metaphorized than anything else in our universes of discourse, with even denials of metaphor—"Sometimes a cigar is just a cigar" or "A rose is a rose is a rose"—proving almost irresistibly genital, and (2) bowdlerization, from early on through Greenblatt's "obscene."

These approaches also work well with Mercutio's following speech: "O Romeo, that she were, O that she were / An open-arse, and thou a popp'rin' pear" (2.1.37–38). If we discuss both speeches, the difference in their kinds of metaphoricalness can come to the fore. If "To raise a spirit" seems comparatively straightforward, Mercutio's optatives take the second figure into the same metametaphoric hinterlands occupied by Juliet's "Take him and cut him out in little stars" (3.2.22), which stands in contradistinction to Romeo's figure of Juliet as the sun. The optative transformations serve in both Mercutio's and Juliet's figures to reify, as it were, the metaphorical process itself.

The notorious "open-arse," furthermore, repays attention as a site of the sexual politics of editing and commentary. If the orthographic and compositorial niceties behind the et cetera–arse alternatives glaze some eyes, few wink when discussion turns to Eric Partridge's reading of open-arse as vagina (101–02) or to the subjects of sodomy and homosexuality as treated in my *Shakespeare's Mercutio* and in Jonathan Goldberg's "Romeo and Juliet's *Open Rs.*"

Another way of treating metaphor in *Romeo and Juliet* could be called intertextual or even, with the aid of electronic databases and searches, hyperintertextual. Electronic databases enable students to make potentially important discoveries about the rich intertextual web in which metaphor may resonate through a particular play or poem, and through earlier and later works, and often through the entire corpus. Under the rubrics of image cluster and iterative imagery, a published intertextual study—for example, Edward Armstrong's *Shakespeare's Imagination*—may be assigned to whet students' appetites. It is advisable to show enthusiasm for the recent increase—of an order of magnitude?—in the quantity of raw factual information now available. From there, classes can proceed to analysis and evaluation, framing answers to questions like, How conscious may these metaphoric resonances have been in Shakespeare's mind? In his companies' and audiences' minds? What effects and significances do the resonances have? What differences might they make? The specter of smug reductionism may raise its sophomoric head here: "So what?" Then I see my task as turning that rhetorical question into a real one.

In the study of Shakespearean metaphor, the resolution may be considerably increased by recourse to Donald Foster's *Shaxicon* (see Foster, "The Webbing of *Romeo and Juliet*"). Foster's database and program make it possible to distinguish layers of revision in multitext and even single-text plays, so that we have within our scholarly grasps a fine-grained tracing of how given metaphors form and change through the Shakespearean decades. Graduate students and advanced undergraduates interested in the evolution of Shakespeare's metaphors may do background readings in the recent "new revisionism," such as John Jones's *Shakespeare at Work,* and all students can thrill to the chase if we merely describe for them the new wealth of information available and the light it sheds on Shakespeare's thought.

Furthermore, with such resources as the electronic OED, the Vassar Electronic Text Archive, and the Chadwick-Healey full-text databases of English poetry, English verse drama, and English prose drama, it is now becoming possible to situate verbal entities of whatever sort in the "shared matrix of influence" linking text to text through early modern English and beyond (Foster 147). Thus, for instance, particular Shakespearean metaphors, from the nonce and idiosyncratic ("well-apparelled April" treading "on the heel / Of limping winter" [1.2.25–26]) to the widely shared (such as that of the person as book [e.g., 1.3.83–90, 3.2.83–84]) may be considered far more systematically and comprehensively than was possible until the very recent past. Students may be encouraged to make what they can and what they dare of similarities and differences between Shakespearean and extra-Shakespearean manifestations of particular metaphors.

Because *Romeo and Juliet* contains no true disguises, no characters assuming false identities—the masks at the Capulet ball merely hiding identity for a moment—nor any twins, students may not immediately appreciate how concerned the play is with the logic of identity and substitution. Once these issues are presented, however, many students will cite Juliet's replacement of Rosaline in Romeo's affection or the Capulets' attempts to replace Romeo with Paris or the questions raised by Juliet's "What's in a name" speech. With some guidance students see that this problematic of identity, foregrounded elsewhere—"still-waking sleep, that is not what it is" (1.1.174), "[t]his is and is not Romeo" (1.1.191), "now art thou what thou art" (2.3.77–78), "I am not I" (3.2.48)—is in fact deeply kin to the problematic of metaphor, in which one thing stands in for another. Such prompting may tempt students to think hard about the mind behind the play's metaphors and to broach such tantalizing questions as that of intentionality. Within the fiction of the play, we have examples of what may be called inadvertent metaphor: Gregory's "Draw thy tool," Sampson's "My naked weapon is out" (1.1.29–30), and Peter's "I saw no man use you at his pleasure; if I had, my weapon should quickly have been out" (2.3.140–41). Such metaphors suggest the possibility—probability, even—that elsewhere in the play, and perhaps less comically, the metaphor function may be occurring, in Armstrong's phrase, "below the level of full consciousness," not only for the speaker but also for the author (55).

For example, when Benvolio gives an account to the Montagues of their son's nocturnal perambulations in the sycamores west of Verona, he specifies the time as "an hour before the worshipped sun / Peered forth the golden window of the east" (1.1.111–12). This picture (not in Brooke) is charged in several respects—by the unnamed trouble in Benvolio's own mind that has driven him into a predawn ramble and by Romeo's unknowing reprise of the image in "what light through yonder window breaks? / It is the east, and Juliet is the sun" (2.1.44–45). Might then the exceptional freighting, or imaginative pressure, of Benvolio's metaphor have caused some part of Shakespeare's mind to respond, if perhaps not yet consciously, to the buried metaphor in Benvolio's "window" (itself metaphorical)? If so, the same buried metaphor may stir in the later literal windows, which contribute to the play's emphasis on the liminal, on thresholds between inside and outdoors, private and public, and night and day. At the same time, may not the buried "wind eye" metaphor resonate in all the play's winds and eyes and, further, ground a certain epiphenomenal hypermetaphor that obtains more or less throughout the play (and elsewhere in Shakespeare's drama, though not in his nondramatic verse), that is, the paradoxical legibility, and hence writtenness, of the airy spoken word?

In teaching *Romeo and Juliet*, it seems appropriate to pay special attention to the protean realm of metaphor. In braving that realm with students, I try to keep us all on the qui vive. In particular I encourage visualization—of the staging of potentially metaphoric (or allegorical or emblematic) action, as when Tybalt thrusts at Mercutio "under your [Romeo's] arm" (3.1.98), and above all of verbal metaphor. Some students (like some scholars) tend to read with minds' eyes closed, but with help students open their eyes and visualize recklessly; they begin to appreciate the strangeness and the beauty of Shakespeare. In *Romeo and Juliet*, Shakespeare, like Romeo, leaves behind the formulaic and accesses reservoirs of force that drive him (rather like Benvolio before dawn) into terra incognita. In teaching metaphor in the play, I have found it productive (and it seems only just) to open myself to the play's spirit of post-formulaic adventure.

NOTE

[1] Citations to *Romeo and Juliet* in this essay are from *The Norton Shakespeare* unless otherwise noted.

Teaching the Books of the Play

Jill L. Levenson

> *Enter Iuliet.*
> *Iul:* Gallop apace you fierie footed steedes
> To *Phoebus* mansion, such a Waggoner
> As *Phaeton*, would quickly bring you thether,
> And send in cloudie night immediately.
> *Enter Nurse wringing her hands, with the ladder*
> *of cordes in her lap.*

In the first quarto of *Romeo and Juliet* (Q1), published in 1597, the opening of act 3, scene 2, takes the unfamiliar form printed above. In the second quarto (Q2), published in 1599, the familiar version contains thirty-five lines of text and a simpler stage direction: *"Enter Nurse with cords."* Modern editions of *Romeo and Juliet* reproduce the longer speech (a variation on the epithalamium), which elaborates the ironies and classical allusions of the Q1 lines. At the same time, they tweak the text with refinements from other quartos. The shorter stage direction often expands with additions from its Q1 equivalent: *"Enter* NURSE, *with cords, wringing her hands"* (Arden Shakespeare, 2nd ser.); *"Enter* NURSE, *with [the ladder of] cords [in her lap]"* (New Cambridge Shakespeare); *"Enter* NURSE, *[wringing her hands,] with the ladder of cords in her lap"* (Norton Shakespeare).

The skepticism that characterizes late-twentieth-century literary theory has influenced bibliographic method and raised doubts about such editorial conflation. Since the late 1970s it has led in particular to a reexamination of Shakespeare's multiple-text plays, a group of eighteen ranging from *Titus Andronicus* to *Othello*. At first scholars concentrated on the two substantive texts of *King Lear*. Now facsimile and modern editions of Q1 and Folio 1 (F1) *King Lear* are available (Warren; Halio) as is a volume with reprints of Q1, Q2, and F1 *Hamlet* (Bertram and Kliman); modern editions of original texts of *Romeo and Juliet* (Oxford Shakespeare) and *Hamlet* (Arden Shakespeare, 3rd ser.) are either in print or under way; and other resources—such as Michael Allen and Kenneth Muir's *Shakespeare's Plays in Quarto*, Charlton Hinman's *The First Folio of Shakespeare*, the Malone Society Reprints, and Michael Best's *The Internet Shakespeare Editions*—offer access to the earliest texts. As a result, instructors and students have the means to become informed critics of the editions they use and the scholarship they read. They can analyze the first printed versions of Shakespeare's plays, compare them with modern renderings, or probe them for information about Elizabethan drama and theater.

In effect, the end of the twentieth century gave new life to Shakespeare studies. Instructors can take advantage of the newest bibliography—its findings and its attitude—to engage their students in a wide variety of projects that will make any play seem immediate: the original texts hold clues to subjects as diverse as early modern printing and early modern theatrical performance; their derivatives reveal the aesthetic, political, and even economic preoccupations of later cultures. Investigation of these subjects revitalizes a sense of the play texts as part of a multivalent and dynamic process. It also demands careful research and logical thinking.

As one of Shakespeare's multiple-text plays, *Romeo and Juliet* provides an excellent site for this kind of project. It originates in two substantive texts (Q1 and Q2) and seven seventeenth-century editions. It has been edited or adapted many times since the Restoration and has enjoyed a remarkable career on the stage since its initial performances at the end of the sixteenth century. The earliest texts allow us a glimpse of the play's course from Elizabethan beginnings to postmodern reconstructions. To make the most of that valuable if restricted view, an instructor needs to prepare in two ways: establishing what is known about the original printed scripts and giving students access to the books and their historical contexts through challenging assignments.

The first task should probably take place in two stages: research into facts about the physical books and a survey of theory about manuscript copy and connections between the earliest quartos. Whereas the research is straightforward if technical, the theoretical survey may be fraught with confusion. This essay offers direction through both stages, considerably more through the latter. As context, it is helpful to know that initially there were five quartos and a folio version of *Romeo and Juliet*. Q1 and Q2, the substantive texts, had variant title pages and different printers: Q1, "*AN EXCELLENT* conceited Tragedie *OF* Romeo and Iuliet" (1597), was produced by John Danter and Edward Allde; Q2, "THE MOST EX-cellent and lamentable Tragedie, of Romeo and Iuliet" (1599), by Thomas Creede for Cuthbert Burby. A third quarto (Q3), dated 1609, reprints Q2; a fourth, dated 1622 by George Walton Williams, reprints Q3 with occasional consultation of Q1; the Folio reproduces an annotated copy of Q3 (Reid); and a fifth quarto, dated 1647, reprints the fourth.

A substantial body of bibliographic scholarship describes the appearance of key books in this sequence—lines of text per page, typeface, ornaments—and re-creates their presswork. For a guide to seminal research until 1984, instructors can turn to the list accompanying John Jowett's introduction to *Romeo and Juliet* in *William Shakespeare: A Textual Companion* (Wells and Taylor 290). Since 1989 W. Craig Ferguson, Chiaki Hanabusa, and Jowett have each published articles on the printing of Q1. For purposes of teaching, the first two quartos are the most important books; significantly, bibliographic study shows nothing particularly unusual or different about their physical properties. But they differ from each other in content: Q1 is about one-fifth shorter than Q2, and many linguistic and theatrical details vary between the two quartos. In short, there are two extant versions of *Romeo and Juliet* that represent the Elizabethan play, two witnesses to distinct phases of its career in the late sixteenth century.

Critics since Pope, focusing attention on textual differences, have attempted to identify the phases and evaluate the quartos. Bearing the imprints of these critics, *Romeo and Juliet* has actively registered changing editorial styles and bibliographic theories, from eighteenth-century eclecticism to contemporary revisionism. Throughout the twentieth century, editors and textual critics have proposed a number of theories—Paul Werstine calls them "narratives"—to explain relations among the texts ("Narratives," "Touring"). But for most of this period, the play has been under the influence of the New Bibliography, which has set the agenda of textual studies for *Romeo and Juliet* and other multiple-text plays.

The New Bibliographers, emphasizing the material book rather than its literary content, intended to analyze textual transmission by technical means such as typography and other features of book production. Nevertheless, subjectivity has colored their impressions of the *Romeo and Juliet* and other quartos. They have often expressed disappointment with the short quarto, ostensibly because it falls below what they regard as accepted standards of literary value, but more likely because it obscures manuscript copy and traces of Shakespeare's work to a greater extent than Q2 does (Walton 16–17). Rationalizing their disappointment, they have raised questions about both the quarto's authenticity and its presswork. Alfred W. Pollard, who first categorized Shakespeare's quartos as "good" and "bad," identified Q1 as bad for two reasons: it had no entry in the Stationers' Register, and it disagreed with the Folio (65, 69). Yet not being entered in the Register says nothing about copyright or the way Danter acquired this version of *Romeo and Juliet,* and disagreement with the Folio does not automatically signal an inferior play.

The New Bibliography has taken little notice of such qualifications. By the 1980s conjectures about the two substantive versions of *Romeo and Juliet* formed a received narrative about the play's textual history, a theory that appears again and again in editions and textual studies. The theory began to take shape in the mid–twentieth century, when Harry R. Hoppe determined the fate of the 1597 quarto with the title of his monograph, *The Bad Quarto of* Romeo and Juliet: *A Bibliographical and Textual Study.* He argued that Q1 printed a manuscript reconstructed from the memories of two actors. During the 1940s and 1950s, W. W. Greg had endorsed the legitimacy of the 1599 quarto, giving his distinguished imprimatur to a view first advanced in 1879. He claimed that most of the second quarto derived from Shakespeare's holograph; only one reprinted passage and occasional bits depended on the first quarto (*Editorial Problem* 61–62; *Shakespeare First Folio* 229–31). Once the substantive texts had been characterized as bad and good, scholars who followed Hoppe and Greg concentrated on figuring out the relation of the quartos to each other and their common original. Jowett's Lachmann-like genealogy in *Shakespeare: A Textual Companion* (Wells and Taylor 288) illustrates the trend in scholarship.

As a logical argument the received narrative itself raises questions for lack of evidence. Evidence consists of three disparate facts: the dates on the title pages indicate that Q2 was printed after Q1; the two texts differ in length and expression; and one long segment as well as a number of short passages are virtually identical in the two quartos. Moreover the data, meager as they are, generate complex problems and lead to an impasse. For instance, correspondences between the two texts reveal that Q1 served as copy for Q2 at least once, for a passage of more than eighty lines (see Williams's edition 105); Q2 follows this passage in wording, capitals, punctuation, spelling, and typography, in particular the odd use of italics for the speeches of the Nurse. It appears that Q2 printers may have consulted Q1 elsewhere besides: for example, 2.1.13, 2.4.101–03, and 3.5.27–31 (see Gibbons's edition 21–23). As a result, bibliographers agree, in an uncommon consensus with serious implications, that the first quarto influenced the second to an extent that cannot be measured with accuracy.

Another critical unknown obstructs the New Bibliographers' argument: the variety of nonauthorial interventions possible in early play manuscripts. To borrow J. Dover Wilson's terms, plays are "standing copy" or "continuous copy" that undergoes change in the theater (qtd. in Grazia 79–80). As Wilson and others enumerate, many persons could have "rehandled" (80) the manuscript of a Shakespearean play, from Shakespeare and his fellow actors to adapters, revisers, bookkeepers, and censors to compositors and proofreaders. How can anyone trace a play's line of descent without precise facts about the construction of the manuscript copy for each printed version?

Parts of the received narrative raise other questions. Perhaps the most debatable argues memorial reconstruction of the first quarto, a theory of transmission that originated with Tycho Mommsen in the *Athenaeum* in 1857. Since Hoppe's application it has gained wide acceptance, and recent scholarship endorses it (see, e.g., Irace). Briefly, the theory holds that an actor or actors, probably disaffected, reproduced the play from memory either for production (possibly by Pembroke's company or on provincial tour) or for publication as Q1. The original was a form of *Romeo and Juliet* represented by Q2; the actor(s) would have remembered this original from taking part in performance or reading the script. Memory may have faltered, a lapse explaining the shortness of the Q1 text. In some versions of the theory, doubtful motives, ascribed to Danter and the reporter(s), contribute to assessment of the quarto as bad.

The case for memorial reconstruction as a means of transmitting play texts has been challenged on several grounds since the 1970s and repeatedly in the 1990s. Uncertainty persists about both external and internal evidence, especially that connected with theatrical performance, with the publication of dramatic quartos, and with the textual criteria for identifying plays re-created from memory. First, no contemporary data survive to verify that any actor(s) ever reconstructed a play from memory, and it seems unlikely that reporters would have forgotten their own lines and cues (Halio, "Handy-Dandy" 123–28). Second, none confirm that a manuscript was ever taken from Shakespeare's company without permission; furthermore, it seems unlikely that actor(s), stationer, and printer would have risked so much for the small profits yielded by a playbook (Blayney). Third, many of the textual features used to identify memorial reconstructions—from various forms of repetition to descriptive stage directions and vestigial characters—prove ambiguous under examination (Maguire, pt. 2).

Among challengers of the received narrative, some argue from two minority positions that raise their own questions. Pope introduced the idea that Shakespeare revised and enlarged early versions of the plays, a theory prevalent during the nineteenth century and supported by a small but growing number of scholars since the 1980s (Hoppe 58–64; Irace 95–114). According to this theory, Q1 served as a first draft for Q2. By contrast, a few scholars have argued lately that Q1 is a deliberate abridgment of Q2, made by a redactor or by Shakespeare himself from a holograph basically the same as the copy for Q2 (see, e.g., Farley-Hills; Halio, "Handy-Dandy"). They emphasize the efficiency of the cuts, which reduce poetry and rhetoric but accelerate the action: abbreviation results in a quickly paced, popular version of the play for performance on a provincial tour or in London. Whatever course revision may have taken, in view of these theories the first quarto acquires legitimacy. Both minority rationales accept as intentional most of the differences between the first quarto and the second—hundreds of variations that make the extant texts seem like two forms of the same play.

Critics unconvinced by Pope's idea argue against it from the majority position. Sometimes they use textual criteria for uncovering memorial reconstruction to show that Shakespeare could not have composed such a text (see, e.g., Irace). The editors of the Oxford Shakespeare find untenable the methodology of recent scholarship that has elaborated on Pope (Wells and Taylor 27). However, none of these objections sabotages the theory that ascribes textual alterations to the author or a redactor, because all of them rest on hypotheses or taste. With slight adjustment of perspective, some permit both quartos to represent the same original manuscript. The question that does remain is whether a playwright or redactor would have made more than fifteen hundred changes —cuts or additions and other modifications—some quite minor and not all obvious improvements. Without firm or external evidence, that question can have no definitive answer.

In view of all these questions and contingencies, what can we conclude about the manuscripts behind the quartos and the relation between the printed books? Q2 offers some hints about its origins: evidence of revision, first and second thoughts preserved in the printed book, has convinced most scholars that Q2 text independent of Q1 derives ultimately from Shakespeare's own manuscript, possibly transcribed. Scattered throughout Q2 are well-known duplications that occur between and within speeches; they appear at the end of 2.2 and the beginning of 2.3, where Romeo and Friar Lawrence greet the dawn in very similar four-line passages; they mark Romeo's complaint in Friar Lawrence's cell (3.3.29–51) and Romeo's farewell to Juliet in the tomb (5.3.90–120). (See Pearlman for additional evidence of revision.) By comparison, Q1 is not forthcoming beyond its physical properties. It may look like playhouse copy, but if we abandon accepted theories about the origins and features of quartos labeled bad—encouraged by critics like Janette Dillon and Werstine ("Narratives," "Touring")—we have no grounds for associating these books with the stage. Lack of firm evidence baffles attempts to identify copy for Q1 or to make a connection between the substantive texts.

During the early 1980s, in reviews of the Arden *Romeo and Juliet*, second series, some revisionists began to inspect the textual evidence and the received narrative. At the end of an essay that signified a turning point, Randall McLeod (writing as Random Cloud) proposed a new formulation: the two substantive quartos witness the multiplicity of what Shakespeare wrote; the playwright may have created *Romeo and Juliet* over time and through different phases, "perhaps in several different manuscripts, each perhaps with its own characteristic aesthetic, offering together several finalities" (429). By 1988 Jonathan Goldberg extended his own review into a full-length paper that argued for a related kind of multiplicity: "Q2 is a different version—or, rather, different versions—of the play. It is a selection from or an anthology of a number of productions of *Romeo and Juliet,* one of which was close to the performance represented by Q1 [. . .]" ("'What?'" 186).

Of course these two hypotheses are as impossible to prove as those that support the narrative of good and bad quartos, but linguistic evidence (see Foster) and data about Elizabethan theater practice make them seem more persuasive. Of greater consequence, the arguments behind these revisionist speculations— raising questions and expressing doubts—release the quartos from limiting categories. They allow the early texts of *Romeo and Juliet* to be viewed as important records of a tragedy that underwent many changes when first written and performed, beginning a process still vital after four centuries.

From this new perspective, differences among the early texts of *Romeo and Juliet* look like signs of the collaborative efforts we now identify as theater. They interest students, making the play accessible as a work in progress rather than a finished work of art. Obviously all plays change in the theater, influenced by the responses of actors and audiences to the texts, but since the Restoration, staging has become more or less set for a series of performances. Like other dramatic works of its era, *Romeo and Juliet* may have changed more radically in its earliest productions than it would in later runs. It probably appeared in both long and short versions (Foster); it certainly left performance decisions for each revival to the acting company. Introducing students to the original texts encourages them to see that even the most famous Elizabethan plays were created not as enduring monuments but as dynamic events.

Unquestionably, students' introduction to the texts should be appropriate to their level of acquaintance with *Romeo and Juliet* in particular and with early modern drama in general; imaginative instructors will be able to devise a range of preliminary activities. The rest of this essay outlines a number of increasingly complex assignments that may serve as models. The unusual angle of these assignments may cause some unease among students. To reduce the discomfort and eliminate other obstacles, I make the original texts readily available in more than one sense. I place Michael Allen and Kenneth Muir's edition of Shakespeare's quartos and Charlton Hinman's edition of the Folio on reserve in the library. At the same time students can be directed to Michael Best's Web site (*Internet Shakespeare Editions*). When explaining an assignment, the instructor has the opportunity to contextualize the earliest versions of *Romeo and Juliet* by locating them in the history of the book or the history of the theater or the history of late-sixteenth-century England.

The simplest introduction might ask for a comparison of corresponding passages, twenty to twenty-five lines or so in length, between the first two quarto texts. In my undergraduate Shakespeare class, a second-year course, each student prepares a tutorial presentation during the spring term. For twenty minutes (plus a five-minute question period) the student holds forth in front of a small group from the class, explicating a short passage from one of the tragedies we read and teaching the other students the lines. The explication includes analysis of components from staging to prosody and always contains a comparison of the original texts. With *Romeo and Juliet,* if the lines are virtually the same there may be more than one explanation: they come from part of the play where Q1 served as copy for Q2, or they represent a passage that appears to have undergone little revision. Some differences can be striking and provocative. For instance, where the quartos are unequal in length, Q1 speeches may seem more abrupt than their Q2 equivalents. Good examples of this difference are the speech that opens this essay; the rest of act 3, scene 2; and act 4, scene 3, when Juliet prepares to drink Friar Lawrence's "distilling liquor." Moreover, portions of the play appear to have been completely rewritten: the wedding scene in act 2, scene 6, is one, and Mercutio's death speeches in act 3, scene 1, another. In addition, passages with duplications or other signs of revision, like Mercutio's Queen Mab speech in act 1, scene 4, make effective points of departure for broader considerations of differences between the earlier versions.

Such considerations can take the form of dialogue supervised in the classroom or essay topics pursued elsewhere. For an advanced examination of the original texts, students might interpret the effects of the differences on key features of drama such as character or motif. They can do this kind of assignment without adopting a theoretical position on the relation of the first two quartos: the object is to recognize the singularity of each script and its impact on elements of *Romeo and Juliet* that may seem familiar to the point of cliché. If students trace either protagonist through a few critical scenes or (a more ambitious project) through the tragedy as a whole, they will almost inevitably receive distinct impressions from the earliest quartos. By virtue of its length Q1 contains less verse, the carefully regulated medium that conveys psychological states in Q2. Consequently, the characters reveal less of themselves and speak in voices less individualized from the other voices in Verona. There are subtler, more local modulations as well. At the end of act 1, scene 3, Q2 has a brief exchange among a Servingman, Juliet's mother, and the Nurse: he urges them to make haste to Capulet's party, his urging perhaps an indication that Juliet hangs back for a moment (Urkowitz, "I Am" 91–92). In Q1 the women do not speak during this transition and the hint of gesture disappears. At the end of act 1, scene 1, Q2 gives a more complex portrayal of Romeo than Q1 does, specifically in his relationships with both Benvolio and Rosaline: Q1 concludes with line 216, "That when she dies with beautie dies her store"; Q2 elaborates with seven additional speeches in which the cousins spar verbally over the unattainable lady and the repercussions of unrequited love.

Of course, it is possible to trace secondary characters as well: Mercutio, the Nurse, Friar Lawrence, Capulet, or Capulet's wife. But characterization provides only one fruitful topic for comparison. Another line of inquiry might follow a central motif like violence (the modern theme conceivably more piquant than love), fate, or the conjunction of these motifs. In some ways these topics can be more abstract, and perhaps more demanding, than characterization: differences between the quartos and their effects may seem less obvious. For example, violence features as a commanding motif in both texts because it is intrinsic to the plot, which is identical in the two quartos: twelve incidents in the same order. The protocols of fighting inform this narrative, not only facilitating its mechanics but also adding political implications. In both quartos there are three dangerous confrontations: one in the third act, derived from Shakespeare's source(s), and two others in the first and fifth acts, invented by Shakespeare. Weapons and fighting occur in both the action and the dialogue, which they furnish with content as well as metaphors. Comparing the motif of violence in the early texts may uncover different shades of meaning rather than different meanings.

For such a project students might isolate relatively short passages, considering details of staging and speech. The opening stage directions, after the prologue, make a good starting point: "*Enter 2. Seruing-men of the* Capolets" (Q1) versus "*Enter* Sampson *and* Gregorie, *with Swords and Bucklers, of the house of* Capulet" (Q2). In Q2 the weapons signify not only social rank but also a form of recreational fighting (Edelman 34–35). Later, as the brawl gets under way, Q1 has a three-line stage direction that disposes characters on the stage; Q2 spreads several stage directions through more than two dozen additional lines of dialogue that enhance the symmetry of the entrances and make specific reference to dueling practices. Similarly, Benvolio's eight-line recapitulation in Q2 gives a circumstantial account of the duel the audience has witnessed between Benvolio and Tybalt. What is the effect of the additional information about fencing decorum and style on our impression of events? How does the quality of violence differ in the quartos? Variations in dialogue and staging are not as pronounced in the duel scenes of acts 3 and 5, but they give comparable inflections to the violence in those episodes: Q1 places less emphasis on the procedures and ethics of fighting than Q2 does.

Stage directions, printed as discrete signals or incorporated in dialogue, furnish valuable clues not only to different effects produced by early texts but also to important aspects of the play's original performances. If students compare these data in the first two quartos of *Romeo and Juliet,* they will discover many correspondences. As scripts both are flexible, characteristic of Shakespeare's practice and typical of Elizabethan play texts. On the one hand, they make demands that the theater had resources to fill; on the other, they themselves are tractable. In many ways they allow for interpretation and variables, particularly in their directions to actors. They have a wide range of requirements, some slightly more unusual than others. As Andrew Gurr has emphasized, both quartos made heavy demands on contemporary theatrical venues, especially for the closing scenes: they required means to represent bed, balcony, and tomb ("Date"). They also call for a variety of modest but emblematic handheld properties and distinctive but uncomplicated items among the stock of Elizabethan costumes. Like many other contemporary playbooks, both quartos left the specifics of deploying supernumeraries and other minor parts to the acting company. The same adaptability is evident in their directions to performers. Although each quarto has a distinct style of address, both permitted the actors to exercise their skills in the representation of characters and events. In both early quartos the dialogue contains many cues.

Nevertheless, Q1 adds stage directions to the dialogue at more than twenty points. A dozen times or so it supplements what the characters say and in the process makes timing more precise. At a climactic moment in act 3, scene 1, it describes Mercutio's deathblow several lines before Mercutio does: *"Tibalt under Romeos arme thrusts Mercutio, in and flyes"* (F1^v). Later it tells Romeo when to rise from the floor in act 3, scene 3 (G1^r), when to descend in act 3, scene 5 (G3^v), and when to open the tomb and fight with Paris in act 5, scene 3 (K1^r, K1^v); it tells Juliet when to kneel in act 3, scene 5 (H1^r) and in act 4, scene 2 (H4^r).

While the first quarto makes cues prominent, however, it still leaves a great deal to the actors' judgment. This openness distinguishes the Q1 stage directions, which elaborate dialogue rather than repeating it. Often reprinted by editors, many of these stage directions have become well-known. They add detail to moments that are vaguer in Q2. In the Q1 version of act 1, scene 5, for example, Romeo's party make their farewells to Capulet with a particular signal: *"They whisper in his eare"* (C4^r). Mercutio gives a fillip of impudence to his exchange with the Nurse in act 2, scene 4: *"He walkes by them, and sings"* (E2^v). When Romeo threatens suicide in act 3, scene 3, it is specifically the Nurse who intervenes: *"He offers to stab himselfe, and Nurse snatches the dagger away"* (G1^v). As all these illustrations show, stage directions in the first quarto are more descriptive than those in the second, but they are hardly more prescriptive. In J. L. Styan's assessment, the instructions are rich and precise in both texts but never indispensable except for entrances and exits (*Stagecraft* 198, 53). John Russell Brown is probably right to conclude that nothing subtle or elaborate in the actors' business, movements, gestures, pauses, or inflections could have been fixed (*Free* 52).

Staging offers an approach to early texts that is adaptable to the students' level: the more of the first two quartos students analyze, the more extensive and complex the results. It also combines with other strategies that demonstrate how physical books contain volatile texts. In Bibliography I, an introductory course for graduate students at the University of Toronto, I assign an exercise that I originally created for a workshop at a meeting of the Shakespeare Association of America. The students produce a modern edition of *Romeo and Juliet* 1.2.26–33, a short passage with more than one crux. For the assignment they receive photocopies of the lines in Q1, Q2, and F1; Clifford Leech's essay "On Editing One's First Play"; John Jowett's commentary in *Shakespeare: A Textual Companion* (Wells and Taylor 288–90); and a lecture about editing that attempts to place all this material in context. Students decide which text to modernize (that is, they determine their "copy text" or "control text"), provide it with a collation and gloss, and compare their results with the passage in one edition of Shakespeare published before 1850 and one modern scholarly edition. In the Renaissance section of Bibliography II, a course for PhD candidates, my students have edited a twenty- to twenty-five-line passage of their own choice, writing a textual introduction for it.

Finally, graduate students doing either exercise need to decide which words and punctuation they will print on the page to represent specific lines of *Romeo and Juliet*; the process allows them to feel the weight of editorial responsibility. There is nothing like this type of assignment to make them focus on the material and elusive qualities of early modern books, in particular the indeterminacies. By attempting to establish a text, students experience its instability and the disorientation of getting their bearings in what Leah S. Marcus has described as "a 'field' of force" (51). Their observations should leave them in a healthy state of doubt.

DRAMATIC TECHNIQUE AND PERFORMANCE ART

Provoking Thought: Teaching *Romeo and Juliet* through Dramatic Technique

James Hirsh

Shakespeare's plays invite or challenge playgoers to exercise their imaginative powers, and in teaching a play I attempt (however feebly) to imitate this process by encouraging students to exercise their imaginations. By imagination I do not mean idle speculation; I mean putting two and two together and drawing inferences from specific implications of specific dramatic elements. I direct students' attention to particular elements or combinations of elements and then ask students to make appropriate inferences. By progressing in small steps, students can, with my help, construct fairly complex chains of inferences that lead to sophisticated conclusions.

One major difficulty in teaching *Romeo and Juliet* is that most students have a vivid preconception about the play. Long before they have ever experienced the play itself, they gain the impression from countless references in popular culture that the play is a sappy love story. This preconception is so strong that it is likely to survive students' reading of the play itself because students tend to ignore those features of the play that undermine the preconception. But the impression created by popular culture is wrong and can interfere with a student's ability to respond imaginatively to the play. The play is indeed a love story, but not a sappy one, and it is more than a love story. It counteracts both cynicism and sentimentality. *Romeo and Juliet* is actually underrated as a work of dramatic art. Instead of being a disadvantage, the popular misperception of the play can be turned to advantage by a teacher. Class sessions on the play can themselves be dramatic, involving conflict (between the simplistic conception of the play promoted by popular culture and the complexity of the play itself) as well as suspense (about whether the teacher will enable students genuinely to overcome the popular misconception). The procedure I follow in class is to engage students in the careful consideration of evidence of the complex and subtle dramatic technique of the play.

One example of Shakespeare's subtlety involves his dramatic use of rhyme. I ask students to comment on Romeo's speech in the ball scene, beginning "O, she doth teach the torches to burn bright! / It seems she hangs upon the cheek of night" (1.5.44–45). Students quickly notice that Romeo's first expression of love for Juliet takes the form of a series of rhymed couplets. How sweet! But the sweetness of the passage is complicated by its dramatic context, for this speech inadvertently alerts Tybalt to the presence of a member of the enemy family and arouses his hatred and lust for violence: "This, by his voice, should be a Montague. / Fetch me my rapier, boy" (54–55). Also disturbing is the fact that Tybalt eventually adopts rhymed couplets to express his hostility: "Now, by the stock and honor of my kin, / To strike him dead I hold it not a sin" (58–59). Rhyme is not so sweet now as it was before. Shakespeare has desentimentalized the poetic device. That Romeo's love and Tybalt's hate are both expressed in rhymed couplets amounts to a metaphoric rhyme. Just as rhyming words may have opposite denotations (bright, night), Romeo and Tybalt use rhyme to convey opposite emotions. This similarity seems designed to encourage playgoers to recognize a deeper and more disturbing similarity—both young men are overwhelmed by emotion and inclined to impetuous action. And this is only the beginning of Shakespeare's dramatic use of poetic devices in the episode.

As many commentators have pointed out, the first fourteen lines spoken by Romeo and Juliet to each other form a sonnet (1.5.93–106). After rhymed couplets become tainted by being used to express hatred earlier in the scene, Shakespeare provides the lovers with a more complex poetic pattern. How sweet! This may seem to confirm the notion that the play is a sentimental love story; real lovers do not spontaneously collaborate on sonnets in the course of a conversation. But initial exchanges between real people who are attracted to each other at a party often do involve artifice. Some real people even practice pickup lines in advance. Earlier in the play Romeo adopted the contrived pose of the unrequited lover. His first exchange with Juliet dramatizes the fact that Romeo has not completely transcended artificiality even after he transfers his ardor from Rosaline to Juliet. Juliet's responses also have a conventional element—she adopts the pose of the coy mistress, overtly discouraging Romeo's advances but encouraging him by holding up her end of the metaphorical dialogue. The passage is lovely despite its artifice (it is helpful to have Shakespeare around to compose one's pickup lines), but its very artificiality dramatizes the unsentimental and perhaps disturbing fact that artifice cannot be entirely transcended in even the most genuine expression of emotion.

The passage becomes even more dramatic and complex in its context. Immediately following the sonnet are these lines:

ROMEO.	Thus from my lips, by thine, my sin is purg'd.
JULIET.	Then have my lips the sin that they have took.
ROMEO.	Sin from my lips? O trespass sweetly urg'd!
	Give me my sin again.
JULIET.	You kiss by th' book.
NURSE.	Madam, your mother craves a word with you.
ROMEO.	What is her mother?
NURSE.	Marry, bachelor,
	Her mother is the lady of the house. (1.5.107–13)

Describing the poetic form of this passage as simply four lines of alternating rhyme and three lines of blank verse ignores the temporal and dramatic features of the lines. A more accurate description would be that Romeo and Juliet begin a second sonnet that is interrupted by a message from Juliet's mother, the matriarch of the family that is feuding with Romeo's family. Romeo and Juliet get to complete only one sonnet before the forces that threaten their love intervene. In a subtly analogous plot development, Romeo and Juliet get to consummate their marriage in only one night of lovemaking before the forces that threaten their love again intervene. Like simple rhymes, sonnet form can be used as part of a complex pattern in which sweetness is dramatically blended with sourness.

This analysis of poetic forms demonstrates to students at least two other general principles. First, elements that are usually regarded as purely formal or ornamental can become specifically dramatic devices if they conflict with one another and thus reflect dramatic conflicts between characters. Rhyme patterns are intrinsically poetic devices, but in *Romeo and Juliet* 1.5 Tybalt usurps couplets to express hatred, and the Nurse interrupts the sonneteering of the young lovers. Second, the particular functions of a dramatic device are not preset but rather are determined by context. Any device can, for example, be used ironically and therefore can have opposite effects in different contexts. Thus Tybalt's rhyming reverses the polarity of Romeo's.

If I am lucky, some student will protest, "How could a playgoer recognize poetic forms and make all these inferences during a theatrical performance?" This legitimate and thoughtful question allows me to discuss some other features of the play, to introduce some elements of cultural context, and to raise some further theoretical issues. I point out that it is unlikely that a sonnet would show up accidentally in a piece of writing. Shakespeare wrote over 150 sonnets, and he would know when he was writing one. This suggests that Shakespeare deliberately wrote the first exchange between Romeo and Juliet as a sonnet and that he intended it to have some effect. He reasonably could have expected at least some playgoers to recognize a sonnet. At the time *Romeo and Juliet* was written, the sound of sonnets was as much in the air as the sound of disco was in the 1970s and the sound of rap was in the 1990s. Even without a current craze, people are capable of recognizing poetic form. At this point I recite a limerick and ask if anyone can identify the form—and many students can. Furthermore, because Shakespeare uses the sonnet form for the opening choral speech of *Romeo and Juliet,* playgoers would have the form freshly in their minds. As a retroactive reminder, Shakespeare includes another choral speech in the form of a sonnet immediately after the scene in which Romeo and Juliet share their sonnet. These choral sonnets desentimentalize the form by extending its use beyond the expression of love (as do some of the sonnets in Shakespeare's collection). The choral sonnets' intimations of doom play off against the sonnet on which the lovers collaborate. The lovers' sonnet is also dramatic because Juliet participates in its creation. In most sonnets written in the period, a male speaker pleads with or complains about a woman, but here the sonnet is jointly constructed.

Despite the currency of the sonnet form and despite the reminders of the form elsewhere in the play, many playgoers of Shakespeare's time would probably still not have recognized a sonnet in the midst of dialogue. This fact illustrates another important principle of Shakespearean drama. Shakespeare included numerous and subtle complications in his plays even though he realized that many in the audience would not notice them and that no one would respond to them all. Different playgoers notice different complications, and so every playgoer's experience is unique. Instead of trying to enforce a single experience on all playgoers, Shakespeare went out of his way to create a diversity of responses.

Another principle is suggested by the occurrence of a choral sonnet *after* the one shared by Romeo and Juliet. If at least one function of that choral sonnet is to help playgoers become aware that they have just heard a sonnet in the midst of dialogue, this suggests that Shakespeare wanted playgoers *retroactively* to reconsider what they have witnessed at an earlier moment of the play. A great deal of evidence suggests that Shakespeare intended his plays to be thought-provoking, to be incitements to consideration and reconsideration and not merely moment-by-moment disposable experiences to be quickly forgotten. No playgoer could immediately pursue all lines of thought opened up by an episode. Shakespeare seems to have hoped that a playgoer's response to a scene would be revived and reconsidered during later scenes and would continue to develop even after the performance was over. Thus a playgoer might attend more than one performance of a play, not to repeat the initial experience, but to experience the play in the light of the thoughts provoked by the first experience and to be provoked into further thoughts by elements unnoticed at the first performance.

Examination of other dramatic techniques can make class sessions themselves dramatic by exposing the conflict between the sentimental view of the play and the play itself. A thoughtful examination of Shakespeare's methods of characterization reveals that Juliet is not a sappy love-story heroine. Students first encounter Juliet in 1.3. Because they are prepared to see Juliet as merely a

sweet young thing and because she speaks only 7 of the 105 lines in this confrontation with two mother figures, Lady Capulet and the Nurse, they are apt to
perceive Juliet as meekly obedient. But the Juliet portrayed in this episode is
engagingly tart and shrewd. In response to the long and embarrassing anecdote
in which the Nurse comically repeats that the young Juliet "stinted and said,
'Ay' " (48, 57), Juliet wittily turns the Nurse's words back on her by saying, "And
stint thou too, I pray thee, nurse, say I" (58). If Shakespeare wished our first impression of Juliet to be one of mere sweetness, he bungled the job. Later in the
episode, when Lady Capulet attempts to wheedle a commitment from Juliet
that she will agree to marry Paris, Juliet shows herself to be an adept politician.
She adroitly evades making any advance commitment about marriage in general:
"It is an [honor] that I dream not of" (66). When Lady Capulet argues at length
in favor of the match with Paris, Juliet responds in the language of obedience:

> I'll look to like, if looking liking move;
> But no more deep will I endart mine eye
> Than your consent gives strength to make [it] fly. (97–99)

Even though Lady Capulet has urged her to like Paris, Juliet says that she will
not like Paris more than her mother wishes and will only like him if she is
moved to do so by her own inclination. Many politicians would envy Juliet's
ability to temporize. Shakespeare's clever Juliet is much more interesting and
attractive than the insipid Juliet fabricated by post-Renaissance popular culture. And Shakespeare manages to construct this more complex character in
only seven lines.

A dramatist whose main goal was to romanticize the lovers would have made
the suitor promoted by Juliet's parents a foolish or vile character. But
Shakespeare's Paris is an appealing figure, if a bit conventional. He has at least
as much going for him as Lysander, Demetrius, Bassanio, and other successful
suitors in Shakespeare's plays. When he dies ironically believing he is defending
Juliet's tomb from desecration by a member of the family feuding with hers, the
play becomes for a brief moment "The Tragedy of Paris." A less daring dramatist would not have risked diverting and diluting playgoers' sympathies in this
fashion.

Similarly, a dramatist whose goal was to glamorize Romeo and Juliet would
have made Capulet a simple domestic tyrant. But Shakespeare's Capulet is a
complex figure. In his early meeting with Paris, his apparently sincere insistence that Paris obtain Juliet's consent to marry seems enlightened for an age in
which well-to-do parents commonly arranged marriages for their children. At
the ball, Capulet prevents Tybalt from attacking or showing discourtesy to
Romeo even though the son of Montague has invaded his very home.
Chastened by the Prince's warning in 1.1., Capulet seems genuinely ready to
end the feud. He actually praises Romeo:

> Content thee, gentle coz, let him alone,
> 'A bears him like a portly [dignified] gentleman;
> And to say truth, Verona brags of him
> To be a virtuous and well-govern'd youth.   (1.5.65–68)

Capulet's actions and words in this scene raise the possibility that, if Juliet had only trusted her father with the news that she was in love with Romeo, Capulet might have agreed to their marriage. In addition to pleasing his daughter, the match would formally end the feud in a manner that would save face and would please the Prince. Shakespeare's characterization of Capulet in 1.2 and 1.5 encourages playgoers to imagine this lost opportunity to avert the tragedy, one of countless such opportunities that occur in the play.

At this point I invite students to consider the question, if Capulet is such a decent fellow, why in 3.4 does he violently demand that Juliet marry Paris against her wishes? The lazy answer is that this scene is necessary for the plot and that Shakespeare either did not notice this inconsistency in characterization or hoped that playgoers would not notice. A more likely possibility is raised by the further question, does anything happen between 1.5 and 3.4 that makes Capulet's transformation psychologically credible? When this question is put to students, they realize that in 3.4 Capulet is in a panic. The feud has flared up again, and this time Mercutio, a kinsman of the Prince, has been killed by Tybalt, a member of the Capulet faction. In 1.1 the Prince told the patriarchs of the feuding families, "If ever you disturb our streets again / Your lives shall pay the forfeit of the peace" (96–97). The Prince did not seem to be kidding around. In 3.4 Capulet has reason to believe his life is in danger. But it is possible the Prince will be placated if Capulet's daughter is quickly wed to Paris, another kinsman of the Prince. Capulet's rough treatment of Juliet may be the result of his shame at having to save his own life at the expense of his daughter's freedom of choice. His desperation to bring about this match as soon as possible does not entirely excuse his treatment of Juliet, but it does explain how the Capulet of 1.2 and 1.5 could act as he does in 3.4. Shakespeare did not have Capulet explain all this in a soliloquy because he wanted playgoers to put two and two together on their own. No playgoer rises to every occasion, but Shakespeare includes so many intriguing complications in each of his plays that few playgoers fail entirely to be provoked into thought. Once students get the hang of it, they themselves locate other complications that individualize even most minor characters.

In teaching *Romeo and Juliet* through dramatic technique, I remind students of certain Renaissance stage conditions. One such condition was the absence of elaborate fixed sets. It would be misleading to say that Renaissance playgoers formed mental images of missing physical settings. Shakespeare did encourage and challenge playgoers to use their imaginations, but what he expected them to imagine were mainly the personalities, motives, and interrelationships of the characters; the imagery and figurative language used by the characters; and the thematic implications of the plot. As already indicated, in 1.3 playgoers are invited to imagine Juliet's complex character on the basis of only seven lines. Shakespeare did not encourage playgoers to waste their efforts picturing irrelevant details of the decor of the Capulet household.

There were, however, some moments in which the physical features of Shakespeare's theater were dramatically important. The balcony area in the rear wall of the stage was put to memorable use in several plays. Because playgoers would not have been able to see far into this area, it was almost never used as the exclusive focus of stage action; it was almost always used in conjunction with the main stage. Its most common use was in dramatizing a siege. A few actors at the front of the balcony portrayed the defenders of a castle or walled city who parleyed with leaders of a besieging army on the main stage. Although the most famous balcony scene in world drama involves Romeo and Juliet, in the original performance of the play the use of the balcony for a love scene would have been unconventional. Experienced playgoers of the time would have been reminded of the more common use of the balcony and hence in the midst of the eloquent love scene would have recalled violence and aggression, forces that threaten the lovers.

Another feature of the balcony scene as Shakespeare constructed it undermines sentimentality: the balcony "scene" is not a scene but part of a continuous dramatic sequence that begins with the entrance of Romeo alone after the exit of the Chorus. Romeo speaks two lines that indicate how deeply he is in love with Juliet, and then Benvolio and Mercutio enter. Instead of joining his friends, Romeo hides, dramatizing a serious and unsentimental consequence of intense romantic love: such love can isolate one even from one's closest friends. Romeo's separation from his friends continues for the rest of the play. Romeo never tells them about the most important event of his life, his love for Juliet, and Mercutio dies still believing that Romeo is smitten with Rosaline. As Romeo hides, he eavesdrops on his friends, and what he hears is cynical mockery of love and a series of sexual innuendoes. A mere five lines before leaving, Mercutio refers to Rosaline as an "open-arse" (a term so vulgar that it was printed as "open Et caetera" in the first quarto of the play) and to Romeo as a phallic "pop'rin pear" (2.1.38). After Benvolio and Mercutio exit, Romeo remains onstage and soliloquizes about Juliet, who then appears on the balcony. There is no cleared stage, no break in dramatic continuity, between the exit of Romeo's friends and the misnamed balcony "scene." Shakespeare undermined a simplistic, sentimental response to Romeo and Juliet's encounter by constructing a single, continuous sequence in which are voiced sharply conflicting attitudes about love and in which the effect of Romeo's love for Juliet on his other relationships is vividly dramatized. Unfortunately, editors have been sentimentalists. Thomas Hanmer, in his 1743–44 "Carefully Revised and Corrected" edition of Shakespeare's works, inserted a scene division at the moment when Benvolio and Mercutio leave, even though Romeo remains on stage and the first line Romeo speaks after the others depart rhymes with Benvolio's exit line. Subsequent editors have retained Hanmer's interpolated division, which insulates for readers the lovely balcony "scene" from the cynicism of Romeo's friends, an insulation that Shakespeare sought to avoid by making the two episodes parts of one continuous scene.

In the open-air, arena theaters of Shakespeare's day, two large pillars held up a roof that covered part of the stage. An unimaginative dramatist would be inclined to regard these pillars merely as inconvenient obstructions to playgoers' views. But Shakespeare used the pillars to provide built-in hiding places, a strategy that partly explains the extraordinary number of eavesdropping episodes in Shakespeare's plays. *Romeo and Juliet* contains several such episodes, which are interesting both individually and in comparison with one another. The most famous example is the balcony episode, for part of which Romeo eavesdrops not only on Juliet but also on his friends a moment earlier, and, as already noted, Shakespeare encouraged playgoers to connect and compare these episodes. Late in the play, Paris eavesdrops on Romeo and Balthasar. This episode ironically recalls the earlier one in which Romeo eavesdropped on two men from whom he had become isolated because of his love for Juliet; here Paris eavesdrops on two men for whom he feels enmity because of his own love for Juliet. Shakespeare encourages playgoers to recognize an ironic parallel between Paris and Romeo that dramatizes the disturbing and unsentimental fact that love can be the cause of aggression.

At any one time, Shakespeare's acting company, the Lord Chamberlain's Men, which later became the King's Men, had about ten members, and a few additional actors were hired for each play. Because most of Shakespeare's plays have many more characters than the total number of actors, some actors played more than one part. This stage condition might have been regarded as a disadvantage because it reminded playgoers that they were seeing a play. Except perhaps for young children, however, playgoers never forgot that characters were played by actors. In an age in which doubling was common, experienced playgoers probably took pleasure in discerning which parts were played by the same actor. A good actor would be inspired rather than discouraged by this condition. If the two characters he portrayed were radically different, he could show off his range as an actor; if the two characters were similar, it would give him an opportunity to show off his ability to make subtle differentiations between characters. Shakespeare, too, evidently regarded doubling as an opportunity. I ask students what possible dramatic function might be served by doubling. Students realize that a good dramatist could use doubling to encourage playgoers to compare two characters portrayed by the same actor. Surviving evidence of specific examples of doubling is scant, but I invite students to consider which parts could have been doubled in *Romeo and Juliet* and what would have been the implications of each pairing. Donald Foster has speculated that Shakespeare himself doubled as the Chorus and Friar Laurence, a suggestive possibility especially since the Friar's first appearance in the play occurs after the last appearance of the Chorus. This pairing has interesting and unsentimental implications. At first, it suggests a similarity between the characters. The Chorus is a dignified figure who observes the characters and their actions from the outside. The Friar is also a dignified figure at first. Exempt from the turmoil of love, he provides Romeo with seemingly wise and objective advice. But as the play progresses, the Friar becomes less detached and more involved in the action, and the wisdom of his behavior becomes more and more questionable. In the final scene he abandons Juliet in the tomb because he does not wish to be found and have his ill-fated machinations exposed. This momentary act of cowardice does not turn him into a villain, but it ironically distances him from the aloof Chorus and dramatizes the unsentimental fact that one cannot become actively involved in the affairs of the world without encountering the contingencies, risks, and tests of character that such involvement entails. The comparison between these two possibly doubled characters turns into an unsentimental and disturbing contrast.

Students and I explore other features of dramatic technique that cannot be described in detail here. For example, most students are surprised to learn that, since women's parts were played by boy actors, the first Juliet was played by a guy. I summarize some of the main features of current scholarly debate about cross-gender casting and invite students to enter into the debate. We also discuss the implications of the curious elements of comic structure in *Romeo and Juliet* pointed out by Susan Snyder and others (see *Comic Matrix*). After I explain the complex conventions governing soliloquies and asides in Shakespeare's plays, we discuss Shakespeare's subtle use of these devices in *Romeo and Juliet*.

My main purpose as a teacher is to enhance each student's imaginative skills, the most important of which is the skill to comprehend complexity. Simplifying a play by Shakespeare in an effort to make it "available" to students is self-defeating. Shakespeare's plays are almost uniquely valuable precisely because, better than most other literary or theatrical works, they capture the genuine complexity of human psychology and social interaction. To eliminate that complexity would be to de-Shakespearize Shakespeare. Fortunately, Shakespeare makes complexity intriguing. Even playgoers who seek pure entertainment are apt to find themselves actively considering the complexities of the characters and their situations. In spite of themselves, such playgoers are enticed or provoked into complex thought. Engaging in complex thought may be arduous, but it is also invigorating. Although much popular culture of our age is simple-minded or mindless, this is not a necessary feature of popular culture. I remind students that Shakespeare's plays were popular at the time they were first performed. *Romeo and Juliet* provides vivid evidence that a work can both demand complex thought and appeal to a wide audience. One way of helping students understand how these seemingly contradictory effects can coexist is by examining the play's dramatic technique.

Textual License and Restraint: (Re)Enacting Stage History

Stephen M. Buhler

The teaching of *Romeo and Juliet* can, at times, profitably build on received cultural associations surrounding the play text. Thanks to countless hackneyed reconfigurations of the balcony scene and to more startling revivals, such as the one offered in Baz Luhrmann's recent film, instructors can anticipate that students enjoy some familiarity with the story—or, at least, with the characters. That familiarity, though, can interfere with students' engagement with the play text: many students decide, on the basis of past experience (however tangential), that they already know the play and need not examine it closely. One way for instructors to break through received notions about the play is to have students reenact less familiar and strongly divergent stage interpretations of selected scenes. By following the implicit or explicit stage directions found in early printed versions of the play and in later acting editions, students can discover what kinds of challenges the play has historically presented to the expectations of performers and audiences, of editors and readers.

As Jill Levenson has noted, Romeo and Juliet are anything but stock characters, and their story, in Shakespeare's version, breaks the bounds of the generic conventions the playwright found in his sources (*Shakespeare* 2–9). The play often resists the theatrical conventions not only of Shakespeare's time but of later times as well. Exploring the dynamics of past stagings allows students to see just how recalcitrant the play can be, despite its enduring popularity, to giving audiences what they want. Students quickly learn as well that the play text itself is far more fluid and far more actively constructed than they initially believe.

In this essay, I focus on classroom exercises involving five versions of one pivotal scene in *Romeo and Juliet*: Romeo's abortive suicide attempt after learning of Juliet's anguished response to his slaying of Tybalt. In groups of three, students enact a portion of the scene as it appears in the First Folio; in the first quarto (Q1); and in acting editions based on stage adaptations prepared by Theophilus Cibber, John Philip Kemble, and Maude Adams. As I present each version here, I discuss the reasons for selecting it, provide some background about the differences among versions and the significance of these differences, and give an account of the decisions and discoveries students have made in rehearsing and performing the restagings. With Steven Urkowitz, my students and I "have found that the substantially variant versions of Shakespeare's plays, laid side by side, disclose theatrically interesting patterns not readily discernable when only a single text is examined" ("Two Versions" 222–23). Slightly variant versions, too, can be instructive about the play and about responses to it.

Despite having iconic status as a symbol of Shakespeare's theatrical oeuvre and being utterly indispensable as a source for other plays, the First Folio rarely serves as the basis for standard or teaching editions of *Romeo and Juliet*.

Most editions are based on the 1599 second quarto (Q2), which was re-printed in 1609 (the third quarto); the folio version merely adds stage direc-tions to the 1609 edition. The folio's iconic status, though, makes the folio a useful version for helping students begin to appreciate the range of textual dif-ferences and begin to understand the long-established desire to control these differences. In the folio (and almost identically in Q2) Romeo's attempt to kill himself appears as:

> *Rom.* Oh tell me Frier, tell me,
> In what vile part of this Anatomie
> Doth my name lodge? Tell me, that I may sacke
> The hateful Mansion.
>   *Fri.*   Hold thy desperate hand:
> Art thou a man? Thy forme cries out thou art:
> Thy teares are womanish, thy wild acts denote
> The unreasonable Furie of a beast.
> Unseemely woman, in a seeming man,
> And ill beseeming beast in seeming both,
> Thou hast amaz'd me.   (Hinman, *First Folio* 67, lines 1921–31; cf.
>   3.3.104–13 in *Norton Shakespeare*)[1]

Your own experience in reading and teaching the play may have already alerted you to a glaring absence in the passage: there is no stage direction following Romeo's "The hateful Mansion." G. B. Harrison's long-enduring edition of *Shakespeare: The Complete Works*, first published in 1948 and based on the Globe edition of 1864, adds "[*Drawing his dagger.*]." Harrison does not indi-cate whether this direction derives from any textual authority (all other stage di-rections in his edition are also in brackets and italics) or whether past or present editorial practice is responsible for the inclusion.

Most students, though, are content to accept the folio's authority and are happy with its lack of specific direction. Along with the open silences involving characters' speech, ably studied by Philip McGuire (*Speechless Dialect* xix–xxiii, 132–42), most Shakespearean play texts also offer open silences involving char-acters' actions. The language may prompt some kind of stage business—as ac-tors seek actions to suit the words—but the nature of that business is, for the most part, left undefined. One group of students used consistent cross-gender casting in this scene, which they started at the Friar's expostulation, "Let me dispute with thee of thy estate" (3.3.63), and continued to the Nurse's exit: Romeo and the Friar were played by women and the Nurse by a man. It is often useful to assign students to groups that don't match the scene's apparent gender requirements and let them sort out the casting. They confront some of the issues raised by Elizabethan stage practice and consider its thematic reson-ances in the plays. (In this case, the woman playing Romeo went on to research later examples of cross-gender casting, writing a paper on Charlotte Cushman's celebrated appearances in the same role.) Following what they considered straightforward prompts in Romeo's and the Friar's lines, students presented a staging in which Romeo physically confronted his "ghostly father" and drew a dagger in defiance of the Friar's attempts at consolation (2.1.233). Friar Laurence, in turn, quickly restrained and disarmed the distraught lover, who collapsed in tears before him. The woman playing the Friar went so far as to retrieve the dagger she had tossed aside and present it to Romeo at the line "Wilt thou slay thyself" (115). Through all this, the Nurse remained merely a spectator, effectively cut off from the action as much by the other actors' physical proximity as by the lack of obvious cues.

Another group worked with the version of events (and language) appearing in the first quarto. Most editions, including the Globe and its successors, rely on the second quarto as the most authoritative (even as they discreetly add some kind of stage direction in this scene), but from the late 1960s on, many editions started to draw from Q1 to provide more extensive business. Both John E. Hankins, in the Pelican edition of *Romeo and Juliet,* and G. Blakemore Evans, in the *Riverside Shakespeare,* interpolate the following direction: "[*He offers to stab himself, and Nurse snatches the dagger away.*]." Although the direction appears in brackets and italics, the textual notes indicate that its inclusion is founded on more than editorial extrapolation—or stage practice. In this instance, among others, the first quarto is accepted as quasi-authoritative. Because of its controversial place among the so-called bad quartos, however, Q1 has not been universally accepted, especially on this point. Brian Gibbons, the Arden second series editor, dismisses the stage direction as not "necessary or defensible," deeming it likely the record of "a gratuitous and distracting bid on the part of the actor in the unauthorized version [of the play] to claim extra attention to himself when the audience should be concentrating on Romeo and the Friar" (180). Most of Gibbons's objections stem from his sense that the first quarto was based not only on an unauthorized text but also on unauthorized (and, it seems, undisciplined) performances of that suspect text. Even though the title page of Q1 bears the name of Lord Hunsdon, then patron of Shakespeare's company, many critics have effectively distanced Shakespeare from this publication. It may also be, though, that Gibbons objects to this version's insistence on reminding the audience of a potentially unsettling presence: the male actor portraying the Nurse. The Friar's subsequent lines are most directly aimed at Romeo, but auditors and spectators could apply them as well to the Nurse—the other "ill-beseeming beast in seeming both" woman and man —especially having just seen the actor intervene in a forceful, masculine manner despite his feminine role.

Alan Dessen argues against Gibbons's decision to leave the Nurse out of the scene as much as possible but concedes that she interrupts "surprisingly." He nevertheless insists that the Nurse's surprising behavior is "imagistically or symbolically consistent or meaningful" ("Q1" 109–10). I am not sure that the experience of consistency ever registers as surprise. What makes the action meaningful is the inconsistency between action and expectation at work in more than just our hero's unheroic behavior. An audience's sense of inconsistency would only be intensified by the realization that a man enacts the character responsible for the unseemly spectacle of a woman disarming a man. The debate over Q1's authoritative status, then, involves several issues related to performance. What authority does an actor's possibly improvised—but then retained—stage business have in relation to the playwright's text? What business do men and women have acting like each other? What impact do Elizabethan stage practices have on our understanding of a play text that has proved itself adaptable to drastically different modes of staging and dramatic interpretation?

This debate and its corollaries impinge on recent attempts at standard editions of the plays. While *The Norton Shakespeare,* based on the Oxford edition of Stanley Wells and Gary Taylor, prints the stage direction about the Nurse without either brackets or comment, David Bevington's 1997 *Complete Works* offers instead a less specific action: "[*He draws a weapon, but is restrained.*]." Bevington's stage direction exercises its own kind of restraint in toning down the surprise that may still attach to the Nurse's intervention. As a result, it leads to a less surprisingly womanish hero: Romeo is most likely prevented from inflicting self-violence by the Friar, who completes the blank verse line initiated by Romeo. This version of the play also reflects the impact of stage history, an accumulation of practices that for the most part have resisted the promptings of the undeniably theatrical first quarto. Jay Halio has proposed that Q1 of *Romeo and Juliet,* unlike early texts of other plays, be seen as "a version of Shakespeare's original script shortened and otherwise adapted for performance" ("Handy-Dandy" 144). Although he acknowledges the collaborative nature of stage adaptation, Halio still wonders if Shakespeare himself was the "reviser-adapter" (137) of Q1, which reads:

> *Rom*: Ah tell me holy Fryer
> In what vile part of this Anatomy
> Doth my name lye? Tell me that I may sacke
> The hatefull mansion?
> > *He offers to stab himselfe, and Nurse snatches*
> > *the dagger away.*
> *Nur*: Ah?
> *Fr*: Hold, stay thy hand: art thou a man? thy forme
> Cryes out thou art, but thy wilde actes denote
> The unresonable furyes of a beast.
> Unseemely woman in a seeming man,
> Or ill beseeming beast in seeming both.
> Thou hast amaz'd me. (Allen and Muir 141, G1v)

Halio calls attention to the stage direction (143) but not to the Nurse's cry or to the regularity of the meter in the Friar's next line. An examination of the meter supports Halio's larger claims that Q1 is, in effect, a performance edition and works against Urkowitz's suggestion that Q2 is a revision of Q1 ("Two Versions" 225–30). The word "desperate" and the clause "Thy teares are womanish," which appear in Q2, do not appear as part of the Friar's fulminations in Q1. The spectacle of Romeo's attempt and the Nurse's interruption may well have made it unnecessary to retain these words, and new words to preserve the meter were not added after these deletions.

Student actors have developed strikingly different stagings of the Q1 scene. One group did cross-gender casting for the Friar and the Nurse; the result retained conventional gender roles for the actors if not for the characters. This Nurse instinctively lunged at Romeo, nearly pinning the actor's arm behind his back and forcing him to drop the dagger. (In rehearsal, the Nurse's "Ah?" became a martial-arts cry.) The Friar remained aloof, and the woman portraying him explained that she took her cue from the character's disdain for "The unresonable furyes of a beast." Another group, though, with the same cross-gender casting had the Friar join in the struggle. Again, the language served as the rationale: for this woman, the Friar could not call out "Hold, stay thy hand" without taking some action as well. The man playing the Nurse drew out the "Ah?" as aural background to the first part of the Friar's line. The Nurse then fell silent as he wrested the dagger away, while the Friar didn't miss an iambic beat. Especially in contrast with the folio version, Q1 has inspired not only lively scenes but also lively discussions about the interplay between gender and genre conventions.

Despite the authority that Halio's theory confers on the early published text, the fact remains that, even if Q1 reflects Shakespearean ideas about performance, stage practice deviated from this version rather soon. The First Folio, following Q2, specifies no stage business—the folio's language makes seamless the exchange between Romeo and the Friar. Later revivals of the play often present a restrained Romeo indeed. Theophilus Cibber's adaptation, presented in 1744 and published four years later, leaves Romeo only contemplating suicide before that option loses the name of action: the stage direction before the Friar's rebuke reads only "[*Laying his Hand on his Sword*" (39). The property has changed, following custom, from a dagger to a sword, and the gesture has changed as well, from one of passionate impulse to one of desperate indecision. Students involved in stagings of this version feel at a decided disadvantage after seeing the physicality felt to be implicit in the Shakespearean play texts. *Romeo and Juliet,* in its variants, provides vivid reminders that the Restoration and Augustan stages, far more than the Elizabethan or Jacobean, were declamatory rather than active. One student discussant made reference to the "Sense and Senility" episode of the English television program *Black Adder III,* an episode that uproariously revisits acting styles (and theatrical superstitions about the Scottish Play). Students have also noticed a practical concern: it is far easier for Romeo to produce a dagger that someone "snatches" away than it is for him to draw a full-length sword, which then becomes the object of a struggle.

This fact becomes even clearer in John Philip Kemble's 1811 acting edition, which is based largely on David Garrick's 1750 adaptation. Garrick does not specify any stage business at this point in the scene; Kemble, in contrast, has Romeo "*Drawing his sword*" (46). This staging still relies on the Friar's verbal rebuke, rather than on more physical restraints, to check the vehemence of Romeo's despair. Thus the awkwardness invited by the change in prop is largely, though not completely, avoided, as it is in Cibber's version. The awkwardness of the sword, however, could conceivably produce an analogue to the unseemliness generated in earlier versions and made explicit in the Friar's words. In-class experiments with staged fights over the weapon generally lead to laughter —especially when a wrapping-paper tube serves as an inexpensive and safe alternative to a sword. Such laughter has led to a consideration of decorum. Several students have suggested that they understand eighteenth-century tastes in this regard: Cibber's and Kemble's Romeos may be comparatively dull, but they are also, in one student's phrase, "less unstable" and therefore more conventional and more easily recognizable as heroes. The same student went on to argue that an "acceptable" hero could make the audience feel more strongly about him and his fate. Other students countered with their response to the death of Leonardo DiCaprio's Romeo (which prompted a review of other stage traditions involving the timing of the character's death), but the point about audience expectation and response was made all the more strongly in the ensuing discussion.

Nineteenth-century attempts to recover more of the Shakespearean play text from the inroads of Cibber (Colley as well as Theophilus) and Garrick also responded to changing expectations and responses: the growing authority accorded Shakespeare led audiences to demand more authentic productions. In this scene, the weapon once again becomes a dagger and action is restored, but the action is regularly assigned to the Friar, not the Nurse. Maude Adams's acting edition, based on New York performances in 1899, shows an almost prostrate Romeo and a determined Friar. Romeo is presented "[*Drawing his dagger, on knees, R.C.* (i.e., right center)" and Friar Laurence delivers his line "Hold thy desperate hand!" while, we are told, "[*Seizing his hand.*]" (76). Student realizations of this version often play on the conventions of melodrama, including gender expectations: the Nurse almost always remains a distant but aghast spectator, approaching the other characters only after the Friar has reestablished conventional roles. By the end of the performances (which can fill two class meetings if all five versions are included), students often find that the Elizabethan approach to stagecraft seems, to them, more easily adaptable to present-day notions of realism than do subsequent approaches.

The foregrounding of variant texts and acting editions can help students investigate more thoroughly the play's explorations of heroism; of manhood and womanhood; and of the interrelations among language, action, and expression. Bringing these materials into active play in the classroom also helps students negotiate the history of changing artistic and social expectations and recognize their own expectations in relation to that history.

NOTE

[1] Citations to *Romeo and Juliet* in this essay are from *The Norton Shakespeare* unless otherwise indicated.

Star-Crossed Generations:
Three Film Versions of *Romeo and Juliet*

Robert F. Willson, Jr.

In an essay defining the term *culture* and its use in literary study, Stephen Greenblatt states that "a full cultural analysis will need to push beyond the boundaries of the text, to establish links between the text and values, institutions, and practices elsewhere in the culture" (226). This approach is particularly attractive when studying and teaching films of a Shakespearean play like *Romeo and Juliet*. Films of the tragedy naturally "push beyond the boundaries of the text" to reveal values and practices of the culture, particularly the popular culture, in which they are produced. Like stage productions, films are of course interpretations that reflect the director's readings of the text; unlike theatrical renderings, they allow us to recover fully the performance and to view and study it repeatedly. While it may be misleading to claim that a present-day audience can fully experience a 1936 film of *Romeo and Juliet*, so removed are we from the earlier audience's zeitgeist, we are enabled by our sophisticated understanding of the medium and its message to recover a good deal. By encountering the cultural values films reflect and create, we are guided more readily to their sites of production. It is particularly important to recognize the power of films, given their large and varied audiences, to influence values.

The approach recommended by Greenblatt also invites teachers and students to reexamine the claim of transcendence that has so often been asserted for the story of star-crossed love told in *Romeo and Juliet*. Shakespearean universality, a condition championed by humanist defenders of the author, has been closely questioned by poststructural critics. The position of new-historicist scholars like Greenblatt, Catherine Belsey, Louis Montrose, and others is that any work must be read and studied with particular attention to the conditions—historical, social, political, and material—of its production. The study of films can help discover these conditions and illuminate how embedded in popular culture Shakespearean themes and characters are.

By placing three films of *Romeo and Juliet* in their cultural settings, reconstructing not only the social worlds the films reflect but also the conventions of performance—elements of the theatrical or filmic culture—the films employ, we can more readily historicize the phenomenon of young lovers victimized by fate. No other Shakespearean play, with the possible exception of *Hamlet,* has had such an immediate impact on youthful members of modern audiences. Indeed, the startling increase in teen suicide, especially in 1970s America, seemed traceable to the popularity of Franco Zeffirelli's 1968 film. Apparently the film, with its young, unknown actors playing hero and heroine and its theme of liberation, gave impetus to the youth movement of the 1960s and at the same time inspired teen lovers to expire in each other's arms. By examining phenomena of this kind, students of Shakespeare can better understand both how film versions are linked to their time and how they influence cinematic treatments and cultural practices.

The 1936 MGM production of *Romeo and Juliet* reflected and influenced a traumatic period in American history. The Great Depression had a devastating impact on the United States' economy and society. Following the stock market crash in 1929, many prominent citizens lost fortunes and committed suicide. Many Americans lost their jobs, were unable to find others, and survived as best they could by, for instance, selling apples on street corners. The lavish movies produced by Hollywood's Dream Factory were almost the only source of escape from these bitter conditions. Among the most elaborate and expensive productions were those of the Metro-Goldwyn-Mayer Studios, where wunderkind Irving Thalberg had established a reputation for turning out epic movies, many of which—like *Little Women* (1933) and *David Copperfield* (1935)—were based on literary classics (Higham 201).

The 1936 *Romeo and Juliet* is just such a spectacle, and Thalberg was inspired to make it because he believed his beautiful wife, Norma Shearer, would prove an unforgettable Juliet. Shakespeare's tragedy would be the producer's vehicle for showing the world that his bride could both break hearts and act. But Shearer was thirty-six years old at the time; her costar, the slight, sensitive British actor Leslie Howard, was forty-three. The tradition of using aged stars to play the young hero and heroine was of course firmly rooted in the theater. It was therefore not unusual to find actors like Howard and Shearer in such parts on stage. Indeed, this fact reveals just how stage centered many Hollywood films of the 1920s and 1930s were. The choice of such mature actors as John Barrymore to play Mercutio and Basil Rathbone to play Tybalt provides further proof that Thalberg envisioned a "screenplay" when he set out to film Shakespeare's classic.

This reverence for Shakespeare as a theatrical icon can also be discovered in

Thalberg's choice of George Cukor as director and Talbot Jennings as screen-writer. Cukor was noted for working with actors as if they were stage perform-ers, and Jennings, who had collaborated with Thalberg on other films, was renowned for his care in retaining the style of literary classics. Some of the raunchiest exchanges between Romeo and Mercutio and between Mercutio and the Nurse were therefore excised from Jennings's script. Jennings also kept most of Shakespeare's poetry and rejected any additional lines of dialogue or playful modernisms. Jennings was aided by the English professor William Strunk, Jr. (later famous for cowriting *The Elements of Style*), whose job it was "to protect Shakespeare from us," in Thalberg's words (Higham xx). Such a re-spectful approach to the text and adherence to traditional stage practices gen-erated a film that has little of the energy or pathos of Shakespeare's tragedy. The approach tends to distance the audience from the characters and freeze the production in time.

Nowhere is this quality more evident than in Cukor's shooting of the balcony scene (2.2). Howard as Romeo approaches the Capulet mansion by a route that takes him first near a reflecting pool, then through a formal garden whose grandeur belies Juliet's warning that "this place is death." The stylized en-counter between the lovers is filmed almost exclusively in close-ups rather than medium shots or two-shots. Cukor employs only a few reaction shots to record the lovers' meeting. Indeed, the camera lingers overlong on Juliet's radiant face, indulging the "male gaze" through which the audience experiences woman as an object rather than a human being (Mulvey 8–9). While a degree of magne-tism can be glimpsed in the actors' relationship, their maturity defeats the mood of the episode, emphasizing the difference between their ages and the youthful passion and anxiety of Shakespeare's lovers. Lines like Romeo's "With love's light wings did I o'erperch these walls" and Juliet's "Thou knowest the mask of night is on my face, / Else would a maiden blush bepaint my cheek" are intended for speakers much younger and more impetuous than these seasoned actors. This discrepancy is enhanced by the medium's inherently naturalistic quality; despite makeup and carefully arranged backlighting, the camera searches out and exposes signs of age in Howard's and Shearer's faces, voices, and gestures. Hollywood's first full-scale treatment of *Romeo and Juliet,* tied to stage conventions and exhibiting reverence for Shakespeare's poetry and repu-tation, reveals the industry's conservative approach to filming literary classics and the period's belief that the playwright is an icon whose work must be pre-served, not reinvented, even when produced for a popular audience.

The director Franco Zeffirelli set out to challenge this theory of filming *Romeo and Juliet* in his 1968 production. His reputation as an auteur and the disappearance of the studio system in Hollywood freed Zeffirelli to attempt a reinvention of the tragedy. In the 1960s, the emergence of a youth movement in America and Europe, the trend toward liberalizing society, and the presence of a strong antiwar sentiment created a culture in which experimentation—with drugs, dress, music, and sex—was encouraged. Zeffirelli's experiment began with the casting of the tragedy's hero and heroine. Leonard Whiting as Romeo and Olivia Hussey as Juliet were relative unknowns, not major stars. More important, they were seventeen and fifteen years old, respectively, close in age to the characters they played. This casting move signaled a radical shift from the stage-centered practice of the Thalberg-Cukor *Romeo and Juliet*. Now audiences could view characters as part of what might be called a naturalized film culture. Whiting and Hussey bring to their parts both innocence and exuberance that make the Capulet ball (1.5) and balcony scenes believable moments of first-love excitement. Even though the action is set in Renaissance Italy and features costumes and locations that recall the period (more realistically than the sound-stage sets of the 1936 film), Whiting and Hussey sport hairstyles that resemble those popular in the 1960s: he wears a modified Beatles cut; she has long, straight hair parted in the middle.

The hairstyles are signs by which Zeffirelli marks his Romeo and Juliet "flower children," a term used in the 1960s to identify pacifist protesters against the Vietnam War. Whiting's Romeo carries a sprig of flowers when he first appears, after the opening street battle between the two families. As he watches the wounded being carried away, he disgustedly declares, "Here's much to do with hate, but more with love," throws down the sprig, and marches off. Zeffirelli takes the line from an earlier speech by Romeo, giving it a consciously chorus-like effect as Romeo speaks it at the close of the scene. Though Shakespeare uses flower imagery to highlight the lovers' beauty, youthfulness, and fragility, here the tragedy's hero appears not only as the victim of the feud but also as a protester against the madness of war. The playwright's localized theme is thus generalized for an audience sensitive to the devastation of a conflict fought not by families but by governments.

Zeffirelli's handling of 3.4, the scene in which Romeo leaves Juliet's bedroom the morning after his banishment, further reveals the liberated nature of the film. We discover the lovers in bed; both are naked and basking in the glow of their wedding-night lovemaking. As Romeo rises and walks to the window to greet the sun, his nakedness is both appealing and innocent, a sign of the free-love spirit of the 1960s. Juliet too is briefly glimpsed in the nude as she moves to try to prevent her husband from leaving. The sequence underscores the truth that these liberated lovers can only briefly escape convention and the gaze of the patriarchal world, a message that was trenchant for a 1960s audience of rebels sensitive to the so-called generation gap.

Zeffirelli's shooting of the balcony scene offers the most compelling evidence of his attempt to reach out to young viewers. Zeffirelli openly breaks with the text and with stage tradition by having Romeo hang from a tree branch, then climb up to the balcony to kiss, embrace, and reluctantly part from his beloved —and quickly repeat that pattern. Romeo's behavior reminds the audience that physical desire—the lovers' "raging hormones"—cannot be controlled. The scene features several reaction shots as well, lending an air of realism to an encounter that had been played as essentially static, with Romeo below and Juliet above. In addition, Zeffirelli's treatment of Juliet's gaze suggests, as Peter Donaldson points out, a balanced representation of desire between the genders (167). Juliet is no longer, as she was in the MGM version, an object of male desire; instead, her anxiety, exuberance, and energy match those qualities in Romeo. Perhaps this method of representation echoed not only the rise of feminism but also the unisex phenomenon in dress and lifestyle that characterized the 1960s.

In evaluating Zeffirelli's version of *Romeo and Juliet,* we must acknowledge the youth culture, antiwar, and gender movements that the film both reflects and influences. No other rendition of the tragedy has proved so popular with young people, in America or around the world. Yet it should be said that Zeffirelli's film has qualities—a memorable musical score and theme; stylish, colorful costumes; historical authenticity—associated with Hollywood extravaganzas of an earlier period. While Zeffirelli can be called independent and his approach experimental, his product has many of the commercial qualities of studio-driven films. The production may allude to the 1960s, but it is certainly not set in that world.

Baz Luhrmann's 1996 reinvention, by contrast, places the story in contemporary society. Luhrmann, an Australian director known for his sleeper hit *Strictly Ballroom* (1993), follows Zeffirelli's lead by casting young actors in the main roles. But these actors were not unknowns. Leonardo DiCaprio had won an Oscar nomination for best supporting actor for his role in *What's Eating Gilbert Grape* (1993), and Claire Danes was a Golden Globe Award winner for her role in the popular TV drama *My So-Called Life.* Their casting reflects a phenomenon of 1990s culture: the emergence of young audiences as a distinct commercial market. The film's early box-office success was based almost exclusively on ticket sales to teenagers (Corrigan 16). In addition, these two actors are strongly identified with generation X; the characters they have played tend to be moody, passively rebellious, alienated, and underachieving outsiders. Unlike Zeffirelli's film, this *Romeo and Juliet* (styled in the title *Romeo + Juliet*) not only appeals to teenagers but also is directed toward them as a discrete market.

Luhrmann recontextualizes the plot and characters in a thoroughly postmodern setting. The location is Verona Beach, an urban scene marked by gang wars and corruption, where crosses both appear on churches and are worn as costume jewelry. A Renaissance Italian town here becomes a decadent, Miami-like metropolis in which gangs in low-riders cruise the streets looking for trouble. Shakespeare's feuding merchant families become corrupt crime families. In this setting Romeo and Juliet qualify more as loners than simply as passion-blinded, parent-controlled innocents. They identify, moreover, with other alienated teenagers who have created and thrive in their own, marginalized world.

In an attempt to find cultural equivalents for Shakespeare's framing style, Luhrmann establishes a mood of tabloid television by opening the film with a TV anchorwoman delivering the prologue. Narrated in this manner, the story of the lovers' tragedy is immediately framed and distanced, emphasizing their roles as victims. This semidocumentary style can likewise be seen in Luhrmann's treatment of the opening battle between the Montagues and Capulets, which is staged as an encounter between rival gangs at a gas station. Rap music and leather gear set the scene for a shoot-out in which the participants use silver-plated pistols with the brand name Sword. We almost believe we're watching a TV news special. The Capulet ball is shot as a costume party at which Lady Capulet (Diane Venora dressed as Cleopatra) cavorts with young studs and snorts cocaine while Mercutio (Harold Perrineau) shows up in drag. These scenes and others move at a rapid pace, which some reviewers of the film describe as similar to that of MTV videos.

Unlike earlier directors, Luhrmann relies on other films and film genres to evoke certain qualities in characters and scenes. He conceived of Capulet (Paul Sorvino, who played a mob boss in *GoodFellas*) as a *Godfather*-like patriarch and of DiCaprio's Romeo as a James Dean rebel. Allusions to Busby Berkley musicals and films from the European expressionist tradition can also be discovered in this version. Such reflexive, self-conscious referencing places Luhrmann's *Romeo and Juliet* squarely in today's film culture, which often seems to treat earlier cinema as a catalog for knowing, campy allusion. The homages also enhance the cultlike status of *Romeo and Juliet* (Eco 446–47).

As might be expected, Luhrmann's handling of the balcony scene is likewise unconventional. Instead of using a balcony, Luhrmann arranges for the lovers to meet and cavort in the Capulets' swimming pool. There, as they try to avoid detection by the family's security system, they exchange lines that are punctuated by frequent dives below the water's surface. Luhrmann establishes a symbolic link between the lovers and water at their first meeting, when they glimpse each other through an aquarium filled with brightly colored tropical fish. The symbolism underscores the truth that Romeo and Juliet are beautiful prisoners trapped in a tank where they can be observed but from which they cannot escape. The setting and characterizations create the impression that the lovers' relationship is tolerated only if it doesn't violate the codes established by their powerful families. In this 1990s reenvisioning, Romeo and Juliet are signs of the victimhood of young people caught in a destructive, materialist world where their tragedy becomes just one more story on the eleven o'clock news (video of their bodies being put into an ambulance accompanies the narrative). Of the three films discussed here, only Luhrmann's projects the vision of a culture that both reveres and despises the media and that has lost the ability to nurture and protect the children who will inherit the culture.

Teaching *Romeo and Juliet* using these film versions of the play allows teachers and students to go beyond conventional discussions of character and theme. Besides making the tragedy more accessible, the films encourage students to rediscover the cultures in which the films were made. In turn, students realize that there is no one *Romeo and Juliet* but rather that there are many; the many versions are, moreover, the means to understand both how the play has been interpreted and how it has influenced cultural practices over time. Above all, study of this kind can foster an appreciation of how extensively the *Romeo and Juliet* phenomenon has infiltrated American popular culture. Shakespeare can therefore be said to speak directly to students through the language of film.

Teaching Musical and Balletic Adaptations of *Romeo and Juliet*; or, Romeo and Juliet, Thou Art Translated!

R. Alan Kimbrough

The growth of interdisciplinary studies at all levels of the curriculum has fostered opportunities for exploring classic literary texts and themes in the light of later permutations. Such exploration is the logical outgrowth of a much more established tradition in literary study: probing earlier and contemporary sources and analogues for useful contexts. Shakespeare's *Romeo and Juliet* is particularly well suited for interdisciplinary analysis. A highly useful introduction to such an approach is the excellent 1990 collection of essays *Teaching Literature and Other Arts,* edited for the MLA by Jean-Pierre Barricelli, Joseph Gibaldi, and Estella Lauter. We stand to learn more about *Romeo and Juliet* by locating what has been added, what has been omitted, and what has been changed as Shakespeare's play is translated into other languages, including the languages of music and dance.

Three such translations of *Romeo and Juliet* are especially accessible, since all three exist in both audio and video formats convenient for classroom or individual use: Leonard Bernstein's *West Side Story,* which translates *Romeo and Juliet* into the language of mid-twentieth-century American musical theater; Charles-François Gounod's *Roméo et Juliette,* which translates *Romeo and Juliet* into the language of nineteenth-century French grand opera; and Sergei Prokofiev's *Romeo i Dzhuletta,* which translates *Romeo and Juliet* into the language of twentieth-century Russian ballet.

Of the three, Bernstein's 1957 musical (especially the Academy Award–winning 1961 film version of it) is, for Americans, both the most familiar and the most accessible—in language, in setting, and in genre. Few readers of the present volume need much help in formulating the questions that prompt useful classroom discussions: What happens when Shakespeare's Verona is translated into New York City? What happens when Shakespeare's socioeconomic context is translated from one of aristocratic privilege to one of working-class and immigrant deprivation? (Is Bernstein seeking to confirm Arthur Miller's insistence that tragedy transcends class?) What happens when Shakespeare's dominating parental figures disappear? What happens when Shakespeare's Friar Lawrence, an emblem of the religious establishment, is replaced with the ineffectual store owner, Doc? What happens when Shakespeare's figure of reason and civil authority, Prince Escalus, is replaced with the hostile Officer Krupke and the largely absent Lieutenant Schrank? What happens when suicide is replaced by homicide? What happens when Maria is allowed to survive at the end? How clearly does the musical distinguish between victims and agents of fate, particularly in the light of what tragedy demands or can accommodate? (For answers to some of these and other questions, see Hapgood, "*West Side Story*"; Miller 220–37).

Beyond conceptions of tragedy and issues of plot, theme, and characterization, *West Side Story* suggests other important questions: In audience demographics (particularly with regard to educational level, cultural assumptions about morality, and ethnicity), how closely does the London citizenry that flocked to Shakespeare's Globe parallel the Broadway or film audiences of the 1950s and 1960s in the United States? How closely does Shakespeare's balance between maintaining artistic integrity and attracting and pleasing ticket-buying audiences parallel Bernstein's balance between commercial appeal and musical sophistication? The sociopolitical agenda of *West Side Story* is relatively easy to identify. Can one find a parallel agenda in *Romeo and Juliet,* given the historical and political realities of late-sixteenth-century England? Finally, what constitutes sentimentality (see, e.g., Richards 241–54), and how vulnerable are Shakespeare and Bernstein to such a charge of artistic compromise?

The remaining two translations are less accessible—because they are examples of the so-called elite genres of opera and ballet, because they are European rather than American, and because they are more remote (in setting and in time of composition) from the experience of American students. Both works thus invite investigation into the demands of these less-familiar art forms.

Roméo et Juliette (1867) is the ninth opera by Gounod (1818–93) and one of several collaborations between Gounod and the librettists Jules Barbiere and Michel Carré, who worked together on several projects, including Gounod's earlier success, *Faust* (1859). One question naturally arises: To what extent might some of the differences between Shakespeare's play and Gounod's opera stem from the differences between the way a comparatively young playwright, early in his career, looks at the young lovers and the way a much older composer, late in his career, looks at them?

Many of the differences between the two works, however, can be traced to important distinctions between the stages for which Shakespeare and Gounod wrote. The bibliography of studies on opera librettos and the processes of adapting literary texts for operatic treatment continues to grow; one important full-length exploration is Gary Schmidgall's *Shakespeare and Opera,* which devotes a chapter, "Wherefore *Romeo*?", to the many operatic versions of the tragedy. Recent study of Gounod has not been nearly so extensive, and the only major work in English remains Steven Huebner's *The Operas of Charles Gounod.* Huebner's opening chapters, tracing Gounod's operatic career, contain much valuable information about the conventions of serious opera in Paris in the mid–nineteenth century; chapter 9 is devoted entirely to *Roméo et Juliette* (155–74).

The key to operatic adaptation of literary texts is, of course, compression. A useful exercise is to line up Gounod's libretto with Shakespeare's text and discover what has been cut: whole scenes, a number of characters (including all the parents except Juliet's father), and massive sections of dialogue. Two complementary results should be readily apparent. First, the opera's focus is almost entirely on the love relationship between the protagonists, allowing for an unusually high proportion of duets in the score. (Rossini observed that Gounod's opera "is a duet in three parts: one *before,* one *during,* and one *after*" [qtd. in Schmidgall 293].) Second, and consequently, two of the most important contrapuntal elements in Shakespeare disappear: the contrasts between the voices of the older generation and those of the younger generation and the contrasts between the ardor of the young lovers and the low comedy, even horse-play, in the lovers' social context. What is perhaps thus all the more remarkable is how many of Shakespeare's memorable speeches (and even how much of his notable imagery) Gounod's librettists retain.

Particular conventions of French opera in Gounod's era may help explain other features in *Roméo et Juliette.* Four conventions stand out: a five-act structure, a prominent role for the famous opera house ballet companies, elaborate mise-en-scène and dramatically theatrical technical effects, and accommodation for two prominent female roles. The last of these accounts for one of Gounod's most obvious additions—the character of Stephano (Romeo's page), a "trousers" role that could be assigned to a *dugazon,* a female performer who could act but whose voice was not well enough developed to handle the vocal pyrotechnics of the other roles. (Cf. the similar role of Siébel in *Faust.*)

An even more particular idiosyncrasy of the opera house for which Gounod wrote *Roméo et Juliette* may well explain another clear difference between Gounod's opera and Shakespeare's play. Gounod's lead soprano at the Théâtre Lyrique in Paris was the wife of the theater's director, that is, someone whose demands for additional arias had to be taken seriously. Gounod dutifully supplied her with the act 1 valse arietta "Je veux vivre" ("I Want to Live"), which effectively establishes Juliette as a very young girl intent on experiencing the joys of youth to their fullest and shifts the principal focus to her all too rapid journey from adolescence to maturity.

In the introduction to *Romeo and Juliet* in *The Riverside Shakespeare,* Frank Kermode emphasizes Shakespeare's ability to transform the highly simplistic moral context of the play's primary source, Arthur Brooke's 1562 narrative poem, into a much richer, more complex, more thoughtful moral vision. Gounod's opera depicts a moral world that embodies additional changes in the way it assesses the young lovers, and it raises additional questions by its frequent use of explicitly religious language and imagery: Roméo and Juliette are married on stage; their dialogue contains repeated prayers for God's blessings; they die anticipating new life together at the gates of heaven; their last words are a prayer for God's forgiveness. The contrasts with Shakespeare present underlying implications of a very different understanding of tragedy.

Finally, Gounod's denouement contrasts with Shakespeare's. In Gounod's opera, Roméo does not murder Paris outside Juliette's tomb. And Gounod lets Juliette revive while Roméo is still alive, so that the two can die together, with an ecstatic duet and a final kiss sealing their love. Shakespeare's reliance on boy actors may partially explain his avoidance of such a physically impassioned ending, but the larger differences between the two endings also suggest different attitudes toward pathos and toward the importance of restoring moral and civil order at the end of the tragedy.

The full-length (fifty-two–scene!) ballet *Romeo i Dzhuletta* (1935), by Prokofiev (1891–1953), offers a third translation of Shakespeare's *Romeo and Juliet,* particularly important because this translation abandons the verbal text altogether and relies entirely on the languages of music and dance. Prokofiev began work on the ballet with a commission from the Kirov Theater in Leningrad and finished the ballet for the Bolshoi in Moscow. The most accessible performance version for study, however, is the famous 1966 film of the Royal Ballet Covent Garden production featuring Margot Fonteyn and Rudolf Nureyev, with choreography by Kenneth MacMillan. (An especially fine recording of the full score is that by Seiji Ozawa and the Boston Symphony Orchestra, issued by Deutsche Grammophon with a lengthy and informative analysis of the score by Rita McAllister.)

Many topics already raised in relation to Gounod's opera are equally important in the study of Prokofiev's ballet. Prokofiev, like Gounod, clearly focuses on his heroine's maturation from spirited young girl to tragic heroine. The ballet score associates a melodic motif with each of the lovers, weaving the motifs together in the pas de deux episodes that trace the development of Romeo and Juliet's relationship and parallel the extended duets of Gounod's opera. And Prokofiev, like Gounod, creates numerous opportunities for great theatrical spectacle, often taking advantage of the full corps de ballet.

Prokofiev, too, struggled with Shakespeare's denouement, initially producing a ballet with a happy ending, reuniting the lovers as Juliet awakes and Romeo arrives at her tomb. The usual explanation for this ending, credited to Prokofiev, reflects the importance of theatrical exigencies in his artistic choices: "living people can dance; dead ones can't" (McAllister). His revised score, however, restores the tragic ending. Having been convinced that the deaths of Romeo and Juliet could be effectively choreographed, Prokofiev follows Shakespeare in having Romeo die before Juliet revives. Her death ends the ballet; Prokofiev, like Gounod, omits all the closing activity in Shakespeare.

But Prokofiev, composing *Romeo i Dzhuletta* on the eve of his permanent return to the Soviet Union, clearly looked at Shakespeare's play through twentieth-century eyes. And his ballet—both its music and its choreography—returns attention to some of the complexities in Shakespeare's text. Two instances are noteworthy. First, the authority of the state, embodied in the figure of the Prince, is inescapably prominent in the ballet, particularly in number 7 ("The Prince's Decree") and number 8 (the "Interlude" signaling the transition from the opening marketplace scene to Juliet's anteroom). That authority, markedly masculine and aggressive, returns in the "Knights' Dance" (no. 13), which interrupts the gaiety of the Capulets' ball and will be echoed later, always as a dire portent. Second, the psychosocial dimensions of male bravado, bonding, feuding, and obligatory revenge in the world that destroys the young lovers get full attention, dominating the opening scene, punctuating the Capulets' ball, and erupting in the marketplace fight of act 2, scene 3, during which both the madcap Mercutio and the satanic Tybalt are killed.

Prokofiev's elaborate and extensive use of musical leitmotifs is worthy of the kind of extended analysis that Wagnerian opera has received. Prokofiev's clarity of melodic line, distinctive use of instrumentation (for instance, Juliet's themes are most often given to a flute), and variety of rhythmic patterns may not be beyond the apprehension of musically untrained listeners. The expansiveness of a full-length score allows Prokofiev to include significant attention to and exploration of characters like the Nurse, Mercutio, and Tybalt, showing Prokofiev's considerable appreciation of Shakespearean characterization and of the larger contextual complexities of Romeo and Juliet's world. Despite the absence of words, Prokofiev's ballet in many ways remains truer to and more illuminating of Shakespeare's tragedy than either Bernstein's musical or Gounod's opera does.

The Shakespeare play most nearly contemporary with *Romeo and Juliet* is *A Midsummer Night's Dream*. The two plays are closely linked: "Pyramus and Thisby," the playlet presented by the rude mechanicals in the last act of *A Midsummer Night's Dream*, reads like a parody of *Romeo and Juliet*. But another possible link lies in the theme of translation, a theme that preoccupies Bottom. His reflections on his experiences lead him only to amazement and confusion: "The eye of man hath not heard, the ear of man hath not seen, man's hand is not able to taste, his tongue to conceive, nor his heart to report, what my dream was" (4.1.209–12). Ultimately, Prokofiev's translation of Shakespeare's text into music and dance can, like Bernstein's musical and Gounod's opera, send thoughtful audiences back to Shakespeare with eyes, ears, and minds more receptive to and appreciative of the nuances of *Romeo and Juliet*.

NOTES ON CONTRIBUTORS

James R. Andreas, Sr., professor of English at Clemson University and director of the Clemson Shakespeare Festival, has been the editor of the *Upstart Crow: A Shakespeare Journal* since 1983. He has published many critical and pedagogical essays on Shakespeare and on Chaucer in journals such as *Chaucer Review* and *Hamlet Studies*. He is currently writing a book on African American appropriations of Shakespeare's plays.

Michael Basile, assistant professor of English at New Jersey City University, recently published an article, "Semiotic Transformability in *All God's Chillun Got Wings*," in the *Eugene O'Neill Review*. He is currently writing about certain formalist aspects of Tom Stoppard's early plays. He was formerly a professional actor and director.

Thomas H. Blackburn, Centennial Professor of English at Swarthmore College, has published numerous articles and reviews in *Milton Studies, Review of English Studies, Studies in Philology, Renaissance Quarterly,* and *Shakespeare in the Classroom.* His current scholarly project is titled "Eve and Narcissus: Through a Glass Darkly in *Paradise Lost.*"

Douglas Bruster, assistant professor of English at the University of Texas, Austin, published *Drama and the Market in the Age of Shakespeare* (1992). He has also written a forthcoming book titled *Quoting Shakespeare: Form and Culture in Early Modern Drama* and has edited the text of a forthcoming Oxford edition of Middleton and Rowley's *The Changeling.* He is currently preparing an edition of Robert Joyner's 1598 book of epigrams, *Itys.*

Stephen M. Buhler, associate professor of English at the University of Nebraska, Lincoln, has published articles in many journals, including *Shakespeare Quarterly, Journal of English and Germanic Philology, Cahiers Elisabéthains,* and *Milton Studies.* At present, he is engaged in two studies, one on the subject of Milton, music, and authority and the other on the topic of interpretive strategies in Shakespeare films.

Sara Munson Deats, Distinguished University Professor and chair of the Department of English at the University of South Florida, published *Sex, Gender, and Desire in the Plays of Christopher Marlowe* and has coedited four books. She has also published over two dozen articles on Shakespeare and Marlowe in books and refereed journals, including *Theatre Journal* and *Literature/Film Quarterly.*

James Hirsh, professor of English at Georgia State University, has published *The Structure of Shakespearean Scenes* (1981) as well as articles in *Modern Language Quarterly, Shakespeare Quarterly, Studies in the Novel, Essays in Theatre* and elsewhere. He also edited the Spring 1993 issue of *Studies in the Literary Imagination.* He is currently working on a book on Shakespeare and the history of soliloquies.

Maurice Hunt, professor of English and head of the English department at Baylor University, has published *Shakespeare's Romance of the Word* (1990) and *Shakespeare's Labored Art* (1992) and edited three books, including *Approaches to Teaching Shakespeare's* The Tempest *and Other Late Romances* (1992). He has also published eighty essays on topics in Shakespeare, Webster, Beaumont and Fletcher, and Spenser.

Ivo Kamps, associate professor of English at the University of Mississippi, is currently coediting for St. Martin's Press a collection of early modern narratives about travel to the East, titled *Travel Knowledge.* He has published *Historiography and Ideology in Stuart Drama* (1996) and coedited *Shakespeare and Gender* (1995).

Dorothea Kehler, professor of English at San Diego State University, has coedited *In Another Country: Feminist Perspectives on Renaissance Drama* (1991) and edited A Midsummer Night's Dream*: Critical Essays* (1998). She has also written some three dozen articles, chapters, and notes, primarily on Shakespeare. At present she is completing a book on widows in Shakespeare's plays.

R. Alan Kimbrough, professor of English and director of the University Honors and Scholars Programs at the University of Dayton, codirected a 1991 NEH Summer Institute in Vienna titled "Mozart and His Operas." His teaching interests include English Renaissance poetry and drama, especially the works of Shakespeare; Milton and the Metaphysical poets; and literature and music, especially opera.

Arthur F. Kinney, Thomas W. Copeland Professor of Literary History and director of the Massachusetts Center for Renaissance Studies at the University of Massachusetts, Amherst, recently published *Renaissance Drama: An Anthology of Plays and Entertainments* (1999) and prepared *The Cambridge Companion to English Literature, 1500–1600* (2000). His current projects include *A Companion to Renaissance Drama,* a book on *Macbeth,* and a collection of essays on *Hamlet.* He is coediting *Tudor England: An Encyclopedia* with David Swaim (2000).

Jill L. Levenson, professor of English at the University of Toronto, has published many articles and essays on early modern and modern drama. She also published *Shakespeare in Performance:* Romeo and Juliet (1987) and edited the new Oxford *Romeo and Juliet* (2000). Her current projects are a book on Shakespeare and modern drama for Oxford University Press and a volume titled *Shakespeare Bibliographies:* Romeo and Juliet *and* Othello.

Jennifer Low, assistant professor of English at Florida Atlantic University, is the author of "Cutting Both Ways: Society and Self-Creation in Margaret Cavendish's *The Claspe*" (*Philological Quarterly*, 1998). She is in the midst of completing a book, provisionally titled *Manhood and the Duel: Constructing Masculinity in Early Modern Drama.*

Cynthia Marshall, professor of English at Rhodes College, is the author of *Last Things and Last Plays: Shakespearean Eschatology* (1991) and has published many articles and essays on Shakespeare, most recently in *Shakespeare Quarterly.* She is currently engaged in a study of the appeal of violence in Renaissance literature and remains interested in the conjunctions between literary theory and Renaissance literature.

Thomas Moisan, professor of English at Saint Louis University, has published approximately twenty articles on Shakespeare's plays and Robert Herrick's poetry in journals such as *Shakespeare Quarterly, Shakespeare Studies,* and *Renaissance Drama.* He is coediting a Festschrift in honor of G. Blakemore Evans and preparing a book-length study titled *Herrick in Pieces: The Miscellaneous Fabric of Robert Herrick's Poetry.*

Joseph A. Porter, professor of English at Duke University, has written *The Drama of Speech Acts: Shakespeare's Lancastrian Tetralogy* (1979) and *Shakespeare's Mercutio: His History and Drama* (1989) and edited *Critical Essays on Shakespeare's* Romeo and

Juliet (1997). He is the editor of the MLA *New Variorum* Othello. His interests include characterology and pragmatics in drama.

Nicholas F. Radel, professor of English at Furman University, is interested in seventeenth-century tragicomedy, gay and lesbian studies, queer theory, and modern drama as well as the relations among these topics. Articles based on these interests appear in *Shakespeare Quarterly, Renaissance Drama,* and *Medieval and Renaissance Drama in England* and in an edited volume titled *Theory in Practice:* Measure for Measure.

Paul J. Voss, assistant professor of English at Georgia State University, has published essays in *Sixteenth Century Journal, Journal of English and Germanic Philology, Ben Jonson Journal, Cithara, Literature and Theology,* and *English Language Notes.* He recently completed a manuscript on Elizabethan news quartos (forthcoming from Duquesne UP) and coedited a special issue of *Studies in the Literary Imagination* (Spring 1999) titled *The Poetics of the Archive.*

Robert F. Willson, Jr., professor of English at the University of Missouri, Kansas City, has published a multitude of essays on topics mostly Shakespearean, especially those involving film. His recent books include *Shakespeare's Reflexive Endings* (1990) and *Entering the Maze: Shakespeare's Art of Beginning* (1995). His *Shakespeare in Hollywood, 1929–1956* appeared in 1999.

Karl F. Zender, professor of English at the University of California, Davis, served as chair of the English department from 1993 to 1998. His book *The Crossing of the Ways: William Faulkner, the South, and the Modern World* appeared in 1989. He has published articles on Faulkner, Shakespeare, and other writers in journals such as *PMLA, SEL, Philological Quarterly,* and *American Literature.* His current project is a book entitled "Faulkner and the Politics of Reading."

SURVEY PARTICIPANTS

The editor thanks the following scholars and teachers of Shakespeare, whose generous help and support made this volume possible.

James R. Andreas, Sr., *Clemson University*
Frances Barasch, *Baruch College, City University of New York*
Michael Basile, *Seton Hall University*
Laura R. Bates, *Indiana State University*
Thomas H. Blackburn, *Swarthmore College*
Mary Bly, *Washington University*
Douglas Bruster, *University of Texas, Austin*
Stephen M. Buhler, *University of Nebraska, Lincoln*
Kathleen Campbell, *Austin College*
Michael Collins, *Georgetown University*
Herbert Coursen, *University of Maine, Augusta*
Renée R. Curry, *California State University, San Marcos*
Sara Munson Deats, *University of South Florida*
Matthew DeCoursey, *Catholic University of America*
Christy Desmet, *University of Georgia*
Robert F. Fleissner, *Central State University*
Charles R. Forker, *Indiana University, Bloomington*
Michael D. Friedman, *University of Scranton*
Arthur Graham, *University of Kentucky*
Douglas Green, *Augsburg College*
Jay Halio, *University of Delaware, Newark*
R. Chris Hassel, Jr., *Vanderbilt University*
James Hirsh, *Georgia State University*
Delmar C. Homan, *Bethany College, KS*
Lisa Hopkins, *Sheffield Hallam University*
Ivo Kamps, *University of Mississippi*
Dorothea Kehler, *San Diego State University*
R. Alan Kimbrough, *University of Dayton*
Arthur F. Kinney, *University of Massachusetts, Amherst*
Douglas Lanier, *University of New Hampshire, Durham*
Jill L. Levenson, *University of Toronto*
Naomi C. Liebler, *Montclair State University*
William T. Liston, *Ball State University*
Jennifer Low, *Florida Atlantic University*
James P. Lusardi, *Lafayette College*
Leah S. Marcus, *Vanderbilt University*
Cynthia Marshall, *Rhodes College*
William D. McGlone, *Iona College*
Sheree L. Meyer, *California State University, Sacramento*
Thomas Moisan, *Saint Louis University*

Michael Mooney, *University of New Orleans*
Georgeann Murphy, *University of New Hampshire, Durham*
Wayne Narey, *Arkansas State University*
Lori H. Newcomb, *University of Illinois, Urbana*
Elizabeth Oakes, *Western Kentucky University*
Joseph A. Porter, *Duke University*
Nicholas F. Radel, *Furman University*
William R. Rampone, Jr., *Quinsigamond Community College, MA*
Hugh M. Richmond, *University of California, Berkeley*
Jeanne A. Roberts, *American University*
Edward L. Rocklin, *California State Polytechnic University, Pomona*
Karen Saupe, *Calvin College*
George Slover, *University of Massachusetts, Harbor Campus*
M. Dorothy Smith, *Nazareth College, MI*
Mark Stavig, *Colorado College*
Frances Teague, *University of Georgia*
Grace Tiffany, *Western Michigan University*
Paul J. Voss, *Georgia State University*
Paul Whitfield White, *Purdue University, West Lafayette*
George Walton Williams, *Duke University*
Robert F. Willson, Jr., *University of Missouri, Kansas City*
Nancy G. Wright, *Austin Peay State University*
Karl F. Zender, *University of California, Davis*

WORKS CITED

Books and Articles

Adams, Maude. *Acting Edition of* Romeo and Juliet. New York: Russell, 1899.

Adelman, Janet. *Suffocating Mothers: Fantasies of Maternal Origin in Shakespeare's Plays,* Hamlet *to* The Tempest. New York: Routledge, 1992.

Allen, Michael J. B., and Kenneth Muir, eds. *Shakespeare's Plays in Quarto: A Facsimile Edition of Copies Primarily from the Henry E. Huntington Library.* Berkeley: U of California P, 1981.

Alter, Robert. *The Pleasures of Reading in an Ideological Age.* New York: Norton, 1996.

Amussen, Susan Dwyer. *An Ordered Society: Gender and Class in Early Modern England.* Oxford: Blackwell, 1988.

Andreas, James R. "The Neutering of *Romeo and Juliet.*" *Ideological Approaches to Shakespeare: The Practice of Theory.* Ed. Robert Merrix and Nicholas Ranson. Lewiston: Mellen, 1992. 229–42.

———. "Silencing the Vulgar and Voicing the Other Shakespeare." *Nebraska English Journal* 35.3–4 (1990): 74–88.

———. "Wordplay and Swordplay: The Verbal and the Violent in *Romeo and Juliet.*" *Arkansas Quarterly: A Journal of Criticism* 2.2 (1993): 88–108.

Andrews, John F. "Falling in Love: The Tragedy of *Romeo and Juliet.*" Andrews, Romeo and Juliet: *Critical Essays* 403–22. Rpt. in *Classical, Renaissance, and Postmodernist Acts of the Imagination.* Ed. Arthur F. Kinney. Newark: U of Delaware P, 1996. 177–94.

———, ed. Romeo and Juliet: *Critical Essays.* New York: Garland, 1993.

Appelbaum, Robert. "'Standing to the Wall': The Pressures of Masculinity in *Romeo and Juliet.*" *Shakespeare Quarterly* 48 (1997): 251–72.

Appleby, Andrew B. *Famine in Tudor and Stuart England.* Stanford: Stanford UP, 1978.

Archer, Ian W. *The Pursuit of Stability: Social Relations in Elizabethan London.* Cambridge: Cambridge UP, 1991.

Aristotle. *Poetics.* Trans. S. H. Butcher. New York: Hill, 1961.

Armstrong, Edward A. *Shakespeare's Imagination.* 1946. Lincoln: U of Nebraska P, 1963.

Artaud, Antonin. "The Theater and the Plague." *The Theater and Its Double.* Trans. Mary Caroline Richards. New York: Grove, 1958. 15–32.

Babb, Lawrence. *The Elizabethan Malady: A Study of Melancholia in English Literature from 1580–1642.* East Lansing: Michigan State Coll. P, 1951.

Barricelli, Jean-Pierre, Joseph Gibaldi, and Estella Lauter, eds. *Teaching Literature and Other Arts.* New York: MLA, 1990.

Barthes, Roland. "From Work to Text." *Textual Strategies: Perspectives in Post-structuralist Criticism.* Ed. Josué V. Harari. Ithaca: Cornell UP, 1979. 73–81.

Battenhouse, Roy. *Shakespearean Tragedy: Its Art and Its Christian Premises.* Bloomington: Indiana UP, 1969.

"Beam." *Oxford English Dictionary.* 2nd ed. 1989.

Beckerman, Bernard. *Shakespeare at the Globe, 1599–1609.* New York: Macmillan, 1962.

Beecher, Donald, and Massimo Ciavolella. "Jacques Ferrand and the Tradition of Erotic Melancholy in Western Culture." Ferrand 1–102.

Beier, A. L. "Social Problems in Elizabethan London." *Journal of Interdisciplinary History* 9 (1978): 203–21.

Belsey, Catherine. "The Name of the Rose in *Romeo and Juliet.*" *Yearbook of English Studies* 23 (1993): 126–42. Rpt. in Porter, *Critical Essays* 64–81.

———. *The Subject of Tragedy: Identity and Difference in Renaissance Drama.* New York: Methuen, 1985.

Bergeron, David M., and Geraldo U. de Sousa. *Shakespeare: A Study and Research Guide.* Rev. ed. Lawrence: UP of Kansas, 1987.

Berry, Herbert. *Shakespeare's Playhouses.* AMS Studies in the Renaissance 19. New York: AMS, 1987.

Berry, Ralph. "*Romeo and Juliet*: The Sonnet-World of Verona." *The Shakespearean Metaphor.* Totowa: Rowman, 1978. 37–47.

Bertram, Paul, and Bernice Kliman, eds. *The Three-Text* Hamlet: *Parallel Texts of the First and Second Quartos and First Folio.* New York: AMS, 1991.

Bijvoet, Maya C. *Liebestod: The Function and Meaning of the Double Love-Death.* New York: Garland, 1988.

Blayney, Peter W. M. "The Publication of Playbooks." *A New History of Early English Drama.* Ed. John D. Cox and David Scott Kastan. New York: Columbia UP, 1997. 383–422.

Bly, Mary. "Bawdy Puns and Lustful Virgins: The Legacy of Juliet's Desire in Comedies of the Early 1600s." Wells, Romeo 97–109.

Boose, Lynda. "The Father and the Bride in Shakespeare." *PMLA* 97 (1982): 325–47.

Bray, Alan. "Homosexuality and Signs of Male Friendship in Elizabethan England." *History Workshop Journal* 29 (1990): 1–19.

———. *Homosexuality in Renaissance England.* London: Gay Men's, 1982.

Brecht, Bertolt. *Brecht on Theatre: The Development of an Aesthetic.* Ed. and trans. John Willett. New York: Hill, 1964.

Breed, Warren. "Suicide and Loss in Social Interaction." Shneidman, *Essays* 188–202.

Brenner, Gerry. "Shakespeare's Politically Ambitious Friar." *Shakespeare Studies* 13 (1980): 47–58.

Bristol, Michael. "Charivari and the Comedy of Abjection in *Othello.*" *Materialist Shakespeare: A History.* Ed. Ivo Kamps. London: Verso, 1995. 142–56.

Brodsky, Vivien. "Widows in Late Elizabethan London: Remarriage, Economic

Opportunity and Family Orientations." *The World We Have Gained: Histories of Population and Social Structure.* Ed. Lloyd Bonfield, Richard M. Smith, and Keith Wrightson. Oxford: Blackwell, 1986. 122–54.

Brooke, Arthur. *Romeus and Juliet.* Ed. P. A. Daniel. London: New Shakespeare Soc., 1875.

———. *Romeus and Juliet: Being the Original of Shakespeare's* Romeo and Juliet. Ed. J. J. Munro, 1908. New York: AMS, 1970.

———. *The Tragicall Historye of Romeus and Juliet.* Bullough 284–363.

Brooke, Nicholas. *Shakespeare's Early Tragedies.* London: Methuen, 1968.

Brown, John Russell. *Free Shakespeare.* London: Heinemann, 1974.

———. *Shakespeare's Plays in Performance.* New York: St. Martin's, 1967.

Brown, Stephen J. "The Uses of Shakespeare in America: A Study in Class Domination." *Shakespeare: Pattern of Excelling Nature.* Ed. David Bevington and Jay L. Halio. Newark: U of Delaware P, 1978. 230–38.

Bryant, James C. "The Problematic Friar in *Romeo and Juliet.*" *English Studies* 55 (1974): 340–50.

Bullough, Geoffrey, ed. *Early Comedies, Poems,* Romeo and Juliet. London: Routledge, 1957. Vol. 1 of *Narrative and Dramatic Sources of Shakespeare.*

Bulman, J. C., and H. R. Coursen, eds. *Shakespeare on Television: An Anthology of Essays and Reviews.* Hanover: UP of New England, 1988.

Burton, Robert. *Anatomy of Melancholy.* Ed. Holbrook Jackson. 1932. New York: Vintage, 1977.

Cahn, Victor L. *Shakespeare the Playwright.* New York: Greenwood, 1991.

Calderwood, James L. "*Romeo and Juliet*: A Formal Dwelling." *Shakespearean Metadrama.* Minneapolis: U of Minnesota P, 1971. 85–119.

Callaghan, Dympna. "The Ideology of Romantic Love: The Case of *Romeo and Juliet.*" *The Weyward Sisters: Shakespeare and Feminist Politics.* Ed. Callaghan, Lorraine Helms, and Jyotsna Singh. Oxford: Blackwell, 1994. 59–101.

Carew, Thomas. *The Poems of Thomas Carew.* Ed. Rhodes Dunlap. Oxford: Clarendon–Oxford UP, 1949.

Cartwright, Kent. "Theatre and Narrative in *Romeo and Juliet.*" *Shakespearean Tragedy and Its Double: The Rhythms of Audience Response.* University Park: Pennsylvania State UP, 1991. 43–87.

Chambers, E. K. *The Elizabethan Stage.* 4 vols. Oxford: Clarendon–Oxford UP, 1951.

———. *William Shakespeare: A Study of Facts and Problems.* 2 vols. Oxford: Clarendon–Oxford UP, 1930.

Chapman, George. *Bussy D'Ambois. The Plays of George Chapman: The Tragedies.* Ed. Allan Holaday. Cambridge: Brewer, 1987. 7–263.

———. *May Day. The Plays of George Chapman: The Comedies.* Ed. Allan Holaday. Urbana: U of Illinois P, 1970. 311–96.

Charlton, H. B. *Shakespearian Tragedy.* Cambridge: Cambridge UP, 1948.

Charney, Maurice. *How to Read Shakespeare.* New York: McGraw, 1971.

Churchill, Caryl. Softcops *and* Fen. London: Methuen, 1986.

Cibber, Theophilus. *Romeo and Juliet*. 1748. London: Cornmarket, 1969.

Cirillio, Albert R. "The Art of Franco Zeffirelli and Shakespeare's *Romeo and Juliet*." *TriQuarterly* 16 (Fall 1969): 68–93.

Cloud, Random. "The Marriage of Good and Bad Quartos." *Shakespeare Quarterly* 33 (1982): 421–31.

Cole, Douglas. Introduction. Cole, *Twentieth-Century Interpretations* 1–18.

———, ed. *Twentieth-Century Interpretations of* Romeo and Juliet. Englewood Cliffs: Prentice, 1970.

Colie, Rosalie L. "*Othello* and the Problematics of Love." *Shakespeare's Living Art*. Princeton: Princeton UP, 1974. 135–67.

———. *The Resources of Kind: Genre-Theory in the Renaissance*. Ed. Barbara K. Lewalski. Berkeley: U of California P, 1973.

Colman, E. A. M. *The Dramatic Use of Bawdy in Shakespeare*. London: Longman, 1974.

"Consort." *Oxford English Dictionary*. 2nd ed. 1989.

Cook, Ann Jennalie. *Making a Match: Courtship in Shakespeare and His Society*. Princeton: Princeton UP, 1991.

———. *The Privileged Playgoers of Shakespeare's London, 1576–1642*. Princeton: Princeton UP, 1981.

Corrigan, Timothy. *A Cinema without Walls: Movies and Culture after Vietnam*. New Brunswick: Rutgers UP, 1991.

Coursen, H. R. *Shakespeare in Production: Whose History?* Athens: Ohio UP, 1996.

Cox, Marjorie. "Adolescent Processes in *Romeo and Juliet*." *Psychoanalytic Review* 63 (1976): 379–92.

Cressy, David. "Foucault, Stone, Shakespeare and Social History." *English Literary Renaissance* 21 (1991): 121–33.

Cribb, T. J. "The Unity of *Romeo and Juliet*." *Shakespeare Survey* 34 (1981): 93–104.

Crowl, Samuel. "Watching the Torches Burn Bright: The Diary of a Royal Shakespeare Company Observer." *Shakespeare Observed: Studies in Performance on Stage and Screen*. Athens: Ohio UP, 1992. 102–21.

D'Aguiar, Fred. *The Longest Memory*. Dresden: Avon, 1996.

Dalsimer, Katherine. "Middle Adolescence: *Romeo and Juliet*." *Female Adolescence: Psychoanalytic Reflections on Works of Literature*. New Haven: Yale UP, 1986. 77–112.

Dash, Irene G. *Wooing, Wedding, and Power: Women in Shakespeare's Plays*. New York: Columbia UP, 1981.

Davis, Lloyd. "Desire and Presence in *Romeo and Juliet*." *Shakespeare Survey* 49 (1996): 57–68.

Dekker, Thomas. *The Wonderfull Yeare 1603*. Ed. G. B. Harrison. New York: Barnes, 1966.

Dent, R. W. *Shakespeare's Proverbial Language: An Index*. Berkeley: U of California P, 1981.

Dessen, Alan C. "Q1 *Romeo and Juliet* and Elizabethan Theatrical Vocabulary." Halio, *Texts* 107–22.

————. *"Romeo Opens the Tomb."" Recovering Shakespeare's Theatrical Vocabulary.* Cambridge: Cambridge UP, 1995. 176–95.

Dickey, Franklin M. *Not Wisely but Too Well: Shakespeare's Love Tragedies.* San Marino: Huntington, 1957.

Dillon, Janette. "Is There a Performance in This Text?" *Shakespeare Quarterly* 45 (1994): 74–86.

Donaldson, Peter S. *Shakespearean Films / Shakespearean Directors.* Media and Popular Culture Series. Boston: Unwin, 1990.

Donne, John. The Elegies *and* The Songs and Sonnets. Ed. Helen Gardner. Oxford: Oxford UP, 1965.

————. *The Poems of John Donne.* Ed. Herbert Grierson. London: Oxford UP, 1933.

————. "The Sun Rising." *Seventeenth-Century Prose and Poetry.* 2nd ed. Ed. Alexander M. Witherspoon and Frank J. Warnke. New York: Harcourt, 1982. 738–39.

Douglas, Mary. *Purity and Danger: An Analysis of Concepts of Pollution and Taboo.* New York: Praeger, 1966.

Downes, John. *Roscius Anglicanus.* 1708. Los Angeles: Augustan Reprint Soc., 1969.

Drakakis, John, ed. *Shakespearean Tragedy.* New York: Longman, 1992.

Draper, John W. "Shakespeare's 'Star-Crossed Lovers.'" *Review of English Studies* 15 (1939): 16–34.

Dreher, Diane E. *Domination and Defiance: Fathers and Daughters in Shakespeare.* Lexington: UP of Kentucky, 1985.

Dryden, John. "An Essay on the *Dramatique Poetry* of the Last Age." *The Conquest of Granada by the Spaniards.* Pt. 2. Ed. John Loftis and David Stuart Rodes. Berkeley: U of California P, 1978. 203–18. Vol. 11 of *The Works of John Dryden.*

Dubrow, Heather. *Echoes of Desire: English Petrarchanism and Its Counterdiscourses.* Ithaca: Cornell UP, 1995.

————. *Genre.* The Critical Idiom 42. London: Methuen, 1982.

————. *A Happier Eden: The Politics of Marriage in the Stuart Epithalamium.* Ithaca: Cornell UP, 1990.

Du Laurens, André. *A Discourse of the Preservation of the Sight: Of Melancholike Diseases.* London, 1599.

Ebisch, Walther, with Levin L. Schücking. *A Shakespeare Bibliography.* 1931. New York: Blom, 1968.

————. *Supplement for the Years 1930–1935 to* A Shakespeare Bibliography. 1936. New York: Blom, 1968.

Eco, Umberto. "*Casablanca:* Cult Movies and Intertextual Collage." *Modern Criticism and Theory: A Reader.* Ed. David Lodge. New York: Longman, 1988. 446–55.

Edelman, Charles. *Brawl Ridiculous: Swordfighting in Shakespeare's Plays.* Manchester: Manchester UP, 1992.

Elyot, Thomas. *The Book Named The Governor.* Ed. Stanford E. Lehmberg. London: Dent, 1962.

Evans, Bertrand. "The Brevity of Friar Laurence." *PMLA* 65 (1950): 841–65.

————. *Shakespeare's Comedies*. Oxford: Clarendon–Oxford UP, 1960.

————. *Shakespeare's Tragic Practice*. Oxford: Clarendon–Oxford UP, 1979.

Evans, Robert O. *The Osier Cage: Rhetorical Devices in* Romeo and Juliet. Lexington: U of Kentucky P, 1966.

Everett, Barbara. "*Romeo and Juliet*: The Nurse's Story." *Critical Quarterly* 14 (1972): 129–39.

Faber, M. D. "The Adolescent Suicides of *Romeo and Juliet*." *Psychoanalytic Review* 59 (1972–73): 169–81.

————. "Shakespeare's Suicides: Some Historic, Dramatic, and Psychological Reflections." Shneidman, *Essays* 30–58.

Farberow, Norman L. "Crisis, Disaster, and Suicide: Theory and Therapy." Shneidman, *Essays* 373–98.

Farberow, Norman L., and Edwin S. Shneidman, eds. *The Cry for Help*. New York: McGraw, 1961.

Farley-Hills, David. "The 'Bad' Quarto of *Romeo and Juliet*." *Shakespeare Survey* 49 (1996): 27–44.

Farrell, Kirby. "Love, Death, and Patriarchy in *Romeo and Juliet*." *Play, Death, and Heroism in Shakespeare*. Chapel Hill: U of North Carolina P, 1989. 131–47.

Ferguson, W. Craig. "Compositor Identification in *Romeo* Q1 and *Troilus*." *Studies in Bibliography* 42 (1989): 211–18.

Ferrand, Jacques. *A Treatise on Lovesickness*. Trans. of *Erotomania*. Trans. and ed. Donald A. Beecher and Massimo Ciavolella. Syracuse: Syracuse UP, 1990.

Fletcher, Anthony. *Gender, Sex, and Subordination in England, 1500–1800*. New Haven: Yale UP, 1995.

Fletcher, Anthony, and John Stevenson, eds. *Order and Disorder in Early Modern England*. Cambridge: Cambridge UP, 1985.

Fletcher, John. *The Faithful Shepherdess*. Ed. Fredson Bowers. Cambridge: Cambridge UP, 1976. Vol. 3 of *The Dramatic Works in the Beaumont and Fletcher Canon*.

————. *The Knight of Malta*. Fletcher, *Works* 7: 78–163.

————. *The Mad Lover*. Fletcher, *Works* 3: 1–75.

————. *The Works of Francis Beaumont and John Fletcher*. Ed. A. R. Waller. 10 vols. Cambridge: Cambridge UP, 1905–12.

Forse, James. "*Arden of Feversham* and *Romeo and Juliet*: Two Elizabethan Experiments in the Genre of 'Comedy-Suspense.'" *Journal of Popular Culture* 29.3 (1995): 85–102.

Foster, Donald W. "The Webbing of *Romeo and Juliet*." Porter, *Critical Essays* 131–49.

Foucault, Michel. *Madness and Civilization: A History of Insanity in the Age of Reason*. 1965. New York: Vintage, 1988.

Fowler, Alastair. *Kinds of Literature: An Introduction to the Theory of Genre and Modes*. Cambridge: Harvard UP, 1982.

Franson, J. Karl. "'Too Soon Marr'd': Juliet's Age as Symbol in *Romeo and Juliet*." *Papers on Language and Literature* 32 (1996): 244–62.

Fraser, Russell. *Shakespeare: The Later Years*. New York: Columbia UP, 1992.

———. *Young Shakespeare.* New York: Columbia UP, 1988.

Frey, Charles. "Making Sense of Shakespeare's Language: A Reader-Based Response." *Teaching Shakespeare into the Twenty-First Century.* Athens: Ohio UP, 1997. 96–104.

———. "Teaching Shakespeare in America." *Shakespeare Quarterly* 35 (1984): 541–60.

Frye, Northrop. "The Argument of Comedy." *Shakespeare: Modern Essays in Criticism.* Ed. Leonard F. Dean. New York: Oxford UP, 1967. 79–89.

———. *Fools of Time: Studies in Shakespearean Tragedy.* Toronto: Toronto UP, 1967.

———. "*Romeo and Juliet.*" *Northrop Frye on Shakespeare.* Ed. Robert Sandler. New Haven: Yale UP, 1986. 15–33.

Garber, Marjorie. *Coming of Age in Shakespeare.* London: Methuen, 1981.

———. *Dream in Shakespeare: From Metaphor to Metamorphosis.* New Haven: Yale UP, 1974.

Garner, Shirley Nelson, and Madelon Sprengnether, eds. *Shakespearean Tragedy and Gender.* Bloomington: Indiana UP, 1996.

Garofalo, Reebee. *Rockin' Out: Popular Music in the USA.* Boston: Allyn, 1997.

Genet, Jean. The Maids *and* Deathwatch. Trans. Bernard Frechtman. New York: Grove, 1954.

The Geneva Bible: A Facsimile of the 1560 Edition. Introd. Lloyd E. Berry. Madison: U of Wisconsin P, 1969.

Girard, René. *Violence and the Sacred.* Trans. Patrick Gregory. 1972. Baltimore: Johns Hopkins UP, 1977.

Goddard, Harold C. *The Meaning of Shakespeare.* Chicago: U of Chicago P, 1951.

Gohlke [Sprengnether], Madelon. "'I Wooed Thee with My Sword': Shakespeare's Tragic Paradigms." Lenz, Greene, and Neely 150–70.

Goldberg, Jonathan. "Romeo and Juliet's *Open Rs.*" *Queering the Renaissance.* Ed. Goldberg. Durham: Duke UP, 1994. 218–35.

———. "'What? In a Names That Which We Call a Rose': The Desired Texts of *Romeo and Juliet.*" *Crisis in Editing: Texts of the English Renaissance.* Ed. Randall McLeod. New York: AMS, 1994. 173–201.

Goldman, Michael. *Shakespeare and the Energies of Drama.* Princeton: Princeton UP, 1972.

Granville-Barker, Harley. "*Romeo and Juliet.*" *Prefaces to Shakespeare.* Vol. 2. Princeton: Princeton UP, 1947. 300–49.

Grazia, Margreta de. "The Essential Shakespeare and the Material Book." *Textual Practice* 2.1 (1988): 69–86.

Greenblatt, Stephen. "Culture." *Critical Terms for Literary Study.* Ed. Frank Lentricchia and Thomas McLaughlin. 2nd ed. Chicago: U of Chicago P, 1995. 225–32.

Greene, Robert. *Friar Bacon and Friar Bungay.* Ed. J. A. Lavin. London: Benn, 1969.

Greg, W. W. *The Editorial Problem in Shakespeare: A Survey of the Foundations of the Text.* 3rd ed. Oxford: Clarendon–Oxford UP, 1954.

———. *The Shakespeare First Folio: Its Bibliographical and Textual History*. Oxford: Clarendon–Oxford UP, 1955.

Griffin, Alice. Introduction. *Rebels and Lovers: Shakespeare's Young Heroes and Heroines*. Ed. Griffin. New York: New York UP, 1976. ix–xvi.

Gurr, Andrew. "The Date and Expected Venue of *Romeo and Juliet*." *Shakespeare Survey* 49 (1996): 15–25.

———. *Playgoing in Shakespeare's London*. Cambridge: Cambridge UP, 1987.

———. *The Shakespearean Stage, 1574–1642*. 2nd ed. Cambridge: Cambridge UP, 1980.

Habicht, Werner, D. J. Palmer, and Roger Pringle, eds. *Images of Shakespeare: Proceedings of the Third Congress of the International Shakespeare Association, 1986*. Newark: U of Delaware P, 1988.

Hager, Alan. *Understanding* Romeo and Juliet. Literature in Context ser. Westport: Greenwood, 1999.

Halio, Jay L., ed. *The First Quarto of* King Lear. New Cambridge Shakespeare. Cambridge: Cambridge UP, 1994.

———. "Handy-Dandy: Q1/Q2 *Romeo and Juliet*." Halio, *Texts* 125–50.

———, ed. *Shakespeare's* Romeo and Juliet: *Texts, Contexts, and Interpretation*. Newark: U of Delaware P, 1995.

Hanabusa, Chiaki. "Edward Alde's Types in Sheets E–K of *Romeo and Juliet* Q1 (1597)." *Papers of the Bibliographical Society of America* 91 (1997): 423–28.

Hanmer, Thomas. *The Works of Mr. William Shakespear*. London, 1743–44.

Hapgood, Robert. *Shakespeare the Theatre Poet*. Oxford: Oxford UP, 1988.

———. "*West Side Story* and the Modern Appeal of *Romeo and Juliet*." *Shakespeare Jahrbuch* 8 (1972): 99–112.

Haroutunian-Gordon, Sophie. *Turning the Soul: Teaching through Conversation in the High School*. Chicago: U of Chicago P, 1991.

Harrison, Thomas P. "*Romeo and Juliet, A Midsummer Night's Dream*: Companion Plays." *Texas Studies in Literature and Language* 13 (1970–71): 209–13.

Hawkins, Harriet. "Disrupting Tribal Difference: Critical and Artistic Responses to Shakespeare's Radical Romanticism." *Studies in the Literary Imagination* 26.1 (1993): 115–26.

Henderson, Katherine Usher, and Barbara F. McManus, eds. *Half-Humankind: Contexts and Texts of the Controversy about Women in England, 1540–1640*. Urbana: U of Illinois P, 1985.

Herrick, Marvin T. *Tragicomedy: Its Origin and Development in Italy, France, and England*. Urbana: U of Illinois P, 1962.

Higham, Charles. *The Art of the American Film*. New York: Anchor, 1974.

Hill, Christopher. *Reformation to Industrial Revolution: A Social and Economic History of Britain, 1530–1780*. London: Weidenfield, 1967.

Hinman, Charlton, ed. *The First Folio of Shakespeare: The Norton Facsimile*. 2nd ed. Introd. Peter W. M. Blayney. New York: Norton, 1996.

————. *The Printing and Proofreading of the First Folio of Shakespeare.* 2 vols. Oxford: Clarendon–Oxford UP, 1963.

Hirsh, James E. *The Structure of Shakespearean Scenes.* New Haven: Yale UP, 1981.

Hodgdon, Barbara. "Absent Bodies, Present Voices: Performance Work and the Close of Romeo and Juliet's Golden Story." *Theatre Journal* 41 (1989): 341–59.

————. "*William Shakespeare's Romeo + Juliet:* Everything's Nice in America?" *Shakespeare Survey* 52 (1999): 88–98.

Holding, Peter. Romeo and Juliet: *Text and Performance.* Basingstoke: Macmillan, 1992.

Holland, Norman. "Mercutio, Mine Own Son the Dentist." *Essays on Shakespeare.* Ed. Gordon Ross Smith. University Park: Pennsylvania State UP, 1965. 3–14.

Holmer, Joan Ozark. "'Draw, If You Be Men': Saviolo's Significance for *Romeo and Juliet.*" *Shakespeare Quarterly* 45 (1994): 163–89.

————. "'Myself Condemned and Myself Excus'd': Tragic Effects in *Romeo and Juliet.*" *Studies in Philology* 88 (1991): 345–62.

————. "'O, What Learning Is!' Some Pedagogical Practices for *Romeo and Juliet.*" *Shakespeare Quarterly* 41 (1990): 187–94.

Hoppe, Harry R. *The Bad Quarto of* Romeo and Juliet: *A Bibliographical and Textual Study.* Ithaca: Cornell UP, 1948.

Houghton, Norris, ed. *Romeo and Juliet / West Side Story.* New York: Dell, 1965.

Huebert, Ronald. *John Ford: Baroque English Dramatist.* Montreal: McGill-Queen's UP, 1977.

Huebner, Steven. *The Operas of Charles Gounod.* Oxford: Clarendon–Oxford UP, 1990.

Hunt, Maurice. "Use and Abuse in *Romeo and Juliet.*" *Journal of the Rocky Mountain Medieval and Renaissance Association* 5 (1984): 119–32.

Hunter, G. K. "Shakespeare's Earliest Tragedies: *Titus Andronicus* and *Romeo and Juliet.*" *Shakespeare Survey* 27 (1974): 1–9.

Ingleby, David. "The Social Construction of Mental Illness." *The Problem of Medical Knowledge: Examining the Social Construction of Medicine.* Ed. Peter Wright and Andrew Treacher. Edinburgh: Edinburgh UP, 1982. 123–43.

The Internet Shakespeare Editions. Ed. Michael Best. U of Victoria. 18 Jan. 1998 <http://web.uvic.ca/shakespeare>.

Irace, Kathleen O. *Reforming the "Bad" Quartos: Performance and Provenance of Six Shakespearean First Editions.* Newark: U of Delaware P, 1994.

Jacobs, Jerry. *Adolescent Suicide.* New York: Wiley, 1971.

Jansen, Sue. *Censorship: The Knot That Binds Power and Knowledge.* New York: Oxford UP, 1988.

Jones, John. *Shakespeare at Work.* Oxford: Clarendon–Oxford UP, 1995.

Jorgens, Jack J. *Shakespeare on Film.* Bloomington: Indiana UP, 1977.

Jorgensen, Paul. "Castellani's *Romeo and Juliet:* Intention and Response." *Film Quarterly* 10 (1955): 1–10.

Jowett, John. "Henry Chettle and the First Quarto of *Romeo and Juliet.*" *Papers of the Bibliographical Society of America* 92 (1998): 53–74.

Kahn, Coppélia. "Coming of Age in Verona." *Modern Language Studies* 8 (1977–78): 5–22. Rev. and rpt. in Lenz, Greene, and Neely 171–93; and in Kahn, *Man's Estate: Masculine Identity in Shakespeare.* Berkeley: U of California P, 1981. 83–103.

Kemble, John Philip. *Shakespeare's* Romeo and Juliet, a *Tragedy.* 1811. Vol. 8 of *The John Philip Kemble Promptbooks.* Ed. Charles H. Shattuck. Charlottesville: UP of Virginia, 1974.

Kernberg, Otto F. "Adolescent Sexuality in the Light of Group Processes." *Psychoanalytic Quarterly* 49 (1980): 27–47.

Knowles, Ronald. "Carnival and Death in *Romeo and Juliet*: A Bakhtinian Reading." *Shakespeare Survey* 49 (1996): 69–85.

Kristeva, Julia. "The Bounded Text." *Desire in Language: A Semiotic Approach to Literature and Art.* Ed. Leon S. Roudiez. Trans. Thomas Gora, Alice Jardine, and Roudiez. New York: Columbia UP, 1980. 36–63.

———. "Romeo and Juliet: Love-Hatred in the Couple." *Tales of Love.* Trans. Leon S. Roudiez. New York: Columbia UP, 1987. 209–28.

Laroque, François. "Tradition and Subversion in *Romeo and Juliet*." Halio, Romeo and Juliet: *Texts* 18–36.

Leary, William G. *Shakespeare Plain: The Making and Performing of Shakespeare's Plays.* New York: McGraw, 1977.

Leech, Clifford. "The Moral Tragedy of *Romeo and Juliet*." *English Renaissance Drama: Essays in Honor of Madeleine Doran and Mark Eccles.* Ed. Standish Henning, Robert Kimbrough, and Richard Knowles. Carbondale: Southern Illinois UP, 1976. 59–75.

———. "On Editing One's First Play." *Studies in Bibliography* 23 (1970): 61–70.

Lengeler, Rainer. "'Mongrel Tragi-comedy': Chaosdarstellung und Gattungsmischung in *The Spanish Tragedy* und *Romeo and Juliet*." *Renaissance-Poetik / Renaissance Poetics.* Ed. Heinrich F. Plett. Berlin: De Gruyter, 1994. 271–85.

Lenker, Lagretta T. Introduction. *Youth Suicide Prevention: Lessons from Literature.* Ed. Sara Munson Deats and Lenker. New York: Plenum, 1989. 1–11.

Lenz, Carolyn Ruth Swift, Gayle Greene, and Carol Thomas Neely, eds. *The Woman's Part: Feminist Criticism of Shakespeare.* Urbana: U of Illinois P, 1980.

Levenson, Jill L. "'Alla Stoccado Carries It Away': Codes of Violence in *Romeo and Juliet*." Halio, *Texts* 83–96.

———. "The Definition of Love: Shakespeare's Phrasing in *Romeo and Juliet*." *Shakespeare Studies* 15 (1982): 21–36.

———. *Shakespeare in Performance:* Romeo and Juliet. Manchester: Manchester UP, 1987.

Levin, Harry. "Core, Canon, and Curriculum." *College English* 43 (1981): 352–62.

———. "Form and Formality in *Romeo and Juliet*." *Shakespeare Quarterly* 11 (1960): 3–11.

Liebler, Naomi Conn. "Poor Sacrifices: A Note on *Romeo and Juliet*." *Shakespeare's Festive Tragedy: The Ritual Foundations of Genre.* London: Routledge, 1995. 148–55.

Logan, Maureen F. "Star-Crossed Platonic Lovers; or, Bowdler Redux." *English Journal* 74.1 (1985): 53–55.

Lower, Charles. "*Romeo and Juliet,* IV.v: A Stage Direction and Purposeful Comedy." *Shakespeare Studies* 8 (1975): 177–94.

Lucking, David. "'And All Things Change Them to the Contrary': *Romeo and Juliet* and the Metaphysics of Language." *English Studies* 78 (1997): 8–18.

———. "That Which We Call a Name: The Balcony Scene in *Romeo and Juliet.*" *English* 44 (1995): 1–16.

MacDonald, Michael. *Mystical Bedlam: Madness, Anxiety, and Healing in Seventeenth-Century England.* Cambridge: Cambridge UP, 1981.

Maclean, Ian. *The Renaissance Notion of Woman: A Study in the Fortunes of Scholasticism and Medieval Science in European Intellectual Life.* Cambridge: Cambridge UP, 1980.

Maguire, Laurie E. *Shakespearean Suspect Texts: The "Bad" Quartos and Their Contexts.* Cambridge: Cambridge, UP, 1996.

Mahood, M. M. *Shakespeare's Wordplay.* 1957. London: Methuen, 1965.

Manvell, Roger. *Shakespeare and the Film.* New York: Praeger, 1971.

Marcus, Leah S. "Renaissance / Early Modern Studies." *Redrawing the Boundaries: The Transformation of English and American Literary Studies.* Ed. Stephen Greenblatt and Giles Gunn. New York: MLA, 1992. 41–63.

Marks, Peter. "What Light? It Is the East, and Juliet Is a Son." Rev. of *Romeo and Juliet,* dir. Joe Calarco. *New York Times* 23 Jan. 1998: B3.

Marlowe, Christopher. *Complete Plays and Poems.* Ed. E. D. Pendry and J. C. Maxwell. London: Dent, 1976.

———. *Dr. Faustus.* Marlowe, *Complete Plays* 271–326.

———. *The Jew of Malta.* Marlowe, *Complete Plays* 327–91.

Marsh, Derick R. C. *Passion Lends Them Power: A Study of Shakespeare's Love Tragedies.* Manchester: Manchester UP, 1976.

McAllister, Rita. "Sergey Prokofiev." *The New Grove Dictionary of Music and Musicians.* Ed. Stanley Sadie. Vol. 15. New York: Groves Dictionaries, 1998.

McDonald, Russ. *The Bedford Companion to Shakespeare: An Introduction with Documents.* Boston: St. Martin's, 1996.

———. "The Flaw in the Flaw." O'Brien 8–12.

McGrath, Patrick. *Papists and Puritans under Elizabeth I.* London: Blandford, 1967.

McGuire, Philip C. "On the Dancing in *Romeo and Juliet.*" *Renaissance and Reformation* 5 (1981): 87–97.

———. *Speechless Dialect: Shakespeare's Open Silences.* Berkeley: U of California P, 1985.

McNeir, Waldo F., and Thelma N. Greenfield, eds. *Pacific Coast Studies in Shakespeare.* Eugene: U of Oregon P, 1966.

Meyer, Arnold Oskar. *England and the Catholic Church under Queen Elizabeth.* Trans. J. R. McKee. 1916. New York: Barnes, 1967.

Miller, Scott. *From Assassins to West Side Story: The Director's Guide to Musical Theatre.* Portsmouth: Heinemann, 1966.

Moisan, Thomas. "'O Any Thing, of Nothing First Create!': Gender and Patriarchy and the Tragedy of *Romeo and Juliet*." In *Another Country: Feminist Perspectives on Renaissance Drama*. Ed. Dorothea Kehler and Susan Baker. Metuchen: Scarecrow, 1991. 113–36.

———. "Rhetoric and the Rehearsal of Death: The 'Lamentations' Scene in *Romeo and Juliet*." *Shakespeare Quarterly* 34 (1983): 389–404.

Mommsen, Tycho. "'Hamlet,' 1603; and 'Romeo and Juliet,' 1597." *Athenaeum* 7 Feb. 1857: 182.

Mooney, Michael E. "Text and Performance: *Romeo and Juliet*, Quartos 1 and 2." *Colby Quarterly* 26 (1990): 122–32.

Morris, J. Allen. *Richard Topcliffe: "A Most Humbell Pursuivant of Her Majestie."* Citadel Monograph Ser. 4. Charleston: Citadel, 1964.

Muir, Kenneth, and S. Schoenbaum, eds. *A New Companion to Shakespeare Studies*. Cambridge: Cambridge UP, 1971.

Mulvey, Laura. "Visual Pleasure and Narrative Cinema." *Screen* 16.3 (1975): 6–18.

Muslin, Hyman L. "Romeo and Juliet: The Tragic Self in Adolescence." *Adolescent Psychiatry* 10 (1982): 106–17.

Neely, Carol Thomas. "'Documents in Madness': Reading Madness and Gender in Shakespeare's Tragedies and Early Modern Culture." *Shakespeare Quarterly* 42 (1991): 315–38.

Nevo, Ruth. "Tragic Form in *Romeo and Juliet*." *Studies in English Literature* 9 (1969): 241–58.

Norman, Marc, and Tom Stoppard. Shakespeare in Love: *A Screenplay*. New York: Hyperion, 1998.

Nosworthy, J. M. "The Two Angry Families of Verona." *Shakespeare Quarterly* 3 (1952): 219–26.

Novy, Marianne. *Love's Argument: Gender Relations in Shakespeare*. Chapel Hill: U of North Carolina P, 1984.

Nugent, S. Georgia. "Ancient Theories of Comedy: The Treatises of Evanthius and Donatus." *Shakespearean Comedy*. Ed. Maurice Charney. New York: New York Literary Forum, 1980. 259–80.

Nygren, Anders. *Agape and Eros*. Trans. Philip S. Watson. 1932. London: S.P.C.K., 1953.

O'Brien, Peggy, ed. *Shakespeare Set Free: Teaching* Romeo and Juliet, Macbeth, A Midsummer Night's Dream. New York: Washington Square, 1993.

Ong, Walter J. *Fighting for Life: Contest, Sexuality, and Consciousness*. Ithaca: Cornell UP, 1981.

Onions, C. T. *A Shakespeare Glossary*. 2nd rev. ed. Oxford: Clarendon–Oxford UP, 1953.

Outhwaite, R. B. "Death, the English Crown, and the 'Crisis of the 1590s.'" *The European Crisis of the 1590s: Essays in Comparative History*. Ed. Peter Clark. London: Allen, 1985. 23–43.

Papp, Joseph, and Elizabeth Kirkland. *Shakespeare Alive!* New York: Bantam, 1988.

Partridge, Eric. *Shakespeare's Bawdy*. New York: Dutton, 1948.

Paster, Gail Kern. "Quarreling with the Dug; or, I Am Glad You Did Not Nurse Him." *The Body Embarrassed: Drama and the Disciplines of Shame in Early Modern England.* Ithaca: Cornell UP, 1993. 33–46.

Pearlman, E. "Shakespeare at Work: *Romeo and Juliet.*" *English Literary Renaissance* 24 (1994): 315–42.

Peterson, Douglas. "*Romeo and Juliet* and the Art of Moral Navigation." McNeir and Greenfield 33–46.

Pollard, Alfred W. *Shakespeare Folios and Quartos: A Study in the Bibliography of Shakespeare's Plays, 1594–1685.* London: Methuen, 1909.

Porter, Joseph A., ed. *Critical Essays on Shakespeare's* Romeo and Juliet. New York: Hall, 1997.

———. *Shakespeare's Mercutio: His History and Drama.* Chapel Hill: U of North Carolina P, 1988.

Prujean, Thomas. *Aurorata: Love's Looking Glass Divine and Humane.* London, 1644.

Puttenham, George. *The Arte of English Poesie.* Ed. Gladys Doidge Willcock and Alice Walker. Cambridge: Cambridge UP, 1936.

Rabkin, Norman. *Shakespeare and the Common Understanding.* New York: Free, 1967.

Rees, Joan. "Juliet's Nurse: Some Branches of a Family Tree." *Review of English Studies* 34 (1983): 43–47.

Reid, S. W. "The Editing of Folio *Romeo and Juliet.*" *Studies in Bibliography* 35 (1982): 43–66.

Richards, I. A. *Practical Criticism.* London: Paul, 1929.

Richmond, Hugh M. "Peter Quince Directs *Romeo and Juliet.*" *Shakespeare and the Sense of Performance: Essays in the Tradition of Performance Criticism and in Honor of Bernard Beckerman.* Ed. Marvin Thompson and Ruth Thompson. Newark: U of Delaware P, 1989. 219–27.

Riess, Amy J., and George Walton Williams. "'Tragical Mirth': From *Romeo* to *Dream.*" *Shakespeare Quarterly* 43 (1992): 214–18.

Roberts, Jeanne Addison. "Triple-Threat Shakespeare." O'Brien 3–7.

Rose, Mark, ed. *Shakespeare's Early Tragedies: A Collection of Critical Essays.* Englewood Cliffs: Prentice, 1995.

Rosenberg, Marvin. "Sign Theory and Shakespeare." *Shakespeare Survey* 40 (1987): 33–40.

Rougemont, Denis de. *Love in the Western World.* Trans. Montgomery Belgion. New York: Pantheon, 1956.

———. *Passion and Society.* Trans. Montgomery Belgion. London: Faber, 1956.

Rozett, Martha Tuck. "The Comic Structures of Tragic Endings: The Suicide Scenes in *Romeo and Juliet* and *Antony and Cleopatra.*" *Shakespeare Quarterly* 36 (1985): 152–64.

Rubenstein, Frankie. *A Dictionary of Shakespeare's Sexual Puns and Their Significance.* London: Macmillan, 1984.

Rustin, Michael. "Thinking in *Romeo and Juliet.*" *The Good Society and the Inner World: Psychoanalysis, Politics, and Culture.* New York: Verso, 1991. 231–53.

Salkeld, Duncan. *Madness and Drama in the Age of Shakespeare.* New York: Manchester UP, 1993.

Schmidgall, Gary. "Wherefore *Romeo?*" *Shakespeare and Opera.* New York: Oxford UP, 1990. 292–97.

Schmidt, Alexander. *Shakespeare-Lexicon.* Ed. Gregor I. Sarrazin. 6th ed. 2 vols. Berlin: De Gruyter, 1971.

Schoenbaum, Samuel. *Shakespeare's Lives.* Oxford: Clarendon–Oxford UP, 1970.

———. *William Shakespeare: A Compact Documentary Life.* New York: Oxford UP, 1977.

———. *William Shakespeare: A Documentary Life.* New York: Oxford UP, 1975.

Scholes, Robert E. *Semiotics and Interpretation.* New Haven: Yale UP, 1982.

Scragg, Leah. *Discovering Shakespeare's Meaning.* Totowa: Barnes, 1988.

Sedgwick, Eve Kosofsky. *Between Men: English Literature and Male Homosocial Desire.* New York: Columbia UP, 1985.

Shakespeare, William. *The Complete Works of Shakespeare.* Ed. David Bevington. Updated 4th ed. New York: Longman, 1997.

———. *A Midsummer Night's Dream.* Ed. Harold F. Brooks. Arden Shakespeare. London: Routledge, 1983.

———. The Most Excellent and Lamentable Tragedie of Romeo and Juliet: *A Critical Edition.* Ed. George Walton Williams. Durham: Duke UP, 1964.

———. *The Norton Shakespeare.* Ed. Stephen Greenblatt et al. New York: Norton, 1997.

———. *Othello.* Ed. E. A. J. Honigmann. Arden Shakespeare, 3rd ser. London: Nelson, 1997.

———. *The Parallel* King Lear, *1608–23.* Prepared by Michael Warren. Berkeley: U of California P, 1989.

———. *The Riverside Shakespeare.* Ed. G. Blakemore Evans et al. 1st ed. Boston: Houghton, 1974.

———. *The Riverside Shakespeare.* Ed. G. Blakemore Evans et al. 2nd ed. Boston: Houghton, 1997.

———. *Romeo and Juliet.* Ed. John F. Andrews. Everyman Shakespeare. London: Dent, 1993.

———. *Romeo and Juliet.* Ed. David Bevington. Bantam Shakespeare. New York: Bantam, 1988.

———. *Romeo and Juliet.* Ed. J. A. Bryant, Jr. Signet Classic Shakespeare. New York: Dutton-NAL, 1998.

———. *Romeo and Juliet.* Ed. Dympna Callaghan. Bedford Shakespeare. Boston: Bedford–St. Martin's, forthcoming.

———. *Romeo and Juliet.* Ed. G. Blakemore Evans. New Cambridge Shakespeare. Cambridge: Cambridge UP, 1984.

———. *Romeo and Juliet.* Ed. Brian Gibbons. Arden Shakespeare, 2nd ser. London: Methuen, 1980.

———. *Romeo and Juliet.* Ed. John E. Hankins. Pelican Shakespeare. New York: Penguin, 1970.

———. *Romeo and Juliet.* Ed. Lynette Hunter and Peter Lichtenfels. Arden Shakespeare, 3rd ser. London: Methuen, forthcoming.

———. *Romeo and Juliet.* Ed. Barbara A. Mowat and Paul Werstine. New Folger Library Shakespeare. New York: Washington Square, 1992.

———. *Shakespeare: The Complete Works.* Ed. G. B. Harrison. New York: Harcourt, 1948.

———. *The Tragedy of King Lear.* Ed. Jay L. Halio. New Cambridge Shakespeare. Cambridge: Cambridge UP, 1992.

———. *Troilus and Cressida.* Ed. David Bevington. Arden Shakespeare, 3rd ser. London: Nelson, 1998.

Shakespearean Criticism: Volume 11. Ed. Sandra K. Williamson and James E. Person, Jr. Detroit: Gale, 1990.

Shakespearean Criticism: Volume 33. Ed. Dana R. Barnes and Marie Lazzari. Detroit: Gale, 1997.

Sharpe, J. A. *Crime in Early Modern England, 1550–1750.* London: Longman, 1984.

Shneidman, Edwin S. *Definition of Suicide.* New York: Wiley, 1985.

———, ed. *Essays in Self-Destruction.* New York: Science House, 1967.

———, ed. *On the Nature of Suicide.* San Francisco: Jossey-Bass, 1969.

Sidney, Philip. *An Apology for Poetry.* Ed. Forrest G. Robinson. Indianapolis: Bobbs-Merrill, 1970.

———. *The Poems of Sir Philip Sidney.* Ed. W. A. Ringler. Oxford: Oxford UP, 1962.

Siegel, Paul N. "Christianity and the Religion of Love in *Romeo and Juliet.*" *Shakespeare Quarterly* 12 (1961): 371–92.

Sinfield, Alan. *Faultlines: Cultural Materialism and the Politics of Dissident Reading.* Berkeley: U of California P, 1992.

Slack, Paul. *The Impact of Plague in Tudor and Stuart England.* London: Routledge, 1985.

Slater, Ann Pasternak. "Petrarchanism Come True in *Romeo and Juliet.*" Habicht, Palmer, and Pringle 129–50.

Smallwood, R. L. "*'Tis Pity She's a Whore* and *Romeo and Juliet.*" *Cahiers Elisabéthians* 20 (1981): 49–70.

Smidt, Kristian. "Star-Crossed and Stumbling." *Unconformities in Shakespeare's Tragedies.* New York: St. Martin's, 1990. 27–44.

Smith, Gordon Ross. *A Classified Shakespeare Bibliography, 1936–1958.* University Park: Pennsylvania State UP, 1963.

Smith, James C. "Ptolemy and Shakespeare: The Astrological Influences on *Romeo and Juliet.*" *Selected Papers from the West Virginia Shakespeare and Renaissance Association* 7.2 (1982): 66–70.

Snow, Edward. "Language and Sexual Difference in *Romeo and Juliet.*" *Shakespeare's "Rough Magic": Renaissance Essays in Honor of C. L. Barber.* Ed. Peter Erickson and Coppélia Kahn. Newark: U of Delaware P, 1985. 168–92.

Snyder, Susan. *The Comic Matrix of Shakespeare's Tragedies.* Princeton: Princeton UP, 1979.

———. "Ideology and the Feud in *Romeo and Juliet.*" *Shakespeare Survey* 49 (1996): 87–96.

———. "*Romeo and Juliet*: Comedy into Tragedy." *Essays in Criticism* 20 (1970): 391–402. Rpt. in Andrews, Romeo and Juliet: *Critical Essays* 73–83.

Sophocles. *Antigone. Plays: One.* Trans. Don Taylor. London: Methuen, 1986. 129–88.

Spevack, Marvin. *The Harvard Concordance to Shakespeare.* Cambridge: Belknap-Harvard UP, 1973.

Stauffer, Donald A. "The School of Love: *Romeo and Juliet.*" *Shakespeare: The Tragedies.* Ed. Alfred Harbage. Englewood Cliffs: Prentice, 1986. 28–33.

Stavig, Mark. *The Forms of Things Unknown: Renaissance Metaphor in* Romeo and Juliet *and* A Midsummer Night's Dream. Pittsburgh: Duquesne UP, 1995.

Stewart, Stanley. "Romeo and Necessity." McNeir and Greenfield 47–67.

Stilling, Roger. *Love and Death in Renaissance Tragedy.* Baton Rouge: Louisiana State UP, 1976.

Stirling, Brents. *Unity in Shakespearian Tragedy.* New York: Columbia UP, 1957.

Stone, Lawrence. *The Crisis of the Aristocracy, 1558–1641.* Oxford: Clarendon–Oxford UP, 1965.

———. *The Family, Sex, and Marriage in England, 1500–1800.* New York: Harper, 1977.

Strindberg, August. *Miss Julie. Six Plays of Strindberg.* Trans. Elizabeth Sprigge. Garden City: Doubleday, 1955. 59–114.

Stuckey, Elspeth J. *The Violence of Literacy.* Portsmouth: Boynton, 1991.

Styan, J. L. *The Shakespeare Revolution: Criticism and Performance in the Twentieth Century.* Cambridge: Cambridge UP, 1977.

———. *Shakespeare's Stagecraft.* Cambridge: Cambridge UP, 1967.

Tanselle, G. Thomas. "Time in *Romeo and Juliet.*" *Shakespeare Quarterly* 15 (1964): 349–61.

Taylor, Gary, text ed. *Romeo and Juliet.* By William Shakespeare. CD-ROM. New York: Columbia UP, 1997.

Thompson, Ann, and John O. Thompson, eds. *Shakespeare: Meaning and Metaphor.* Brighton: Harvester, 1987.

Thomson, Leslie. "'With Patient Ears Attend': *Romeo and Juliet* on the Elizabethan Stage." *Studies in Philology* 92 (1995): 230–47.

Tilley, Morris P. *A Dictionary of the Proverbs in England in the Sixteenth and Seventeenth Centuries.* Ann Arbor: U of Michigan P, 1950.

Tillyard, E. M. W. *The Elizabethan World Picture.* London: Chatto, 1943.

Tourneur, Cyril. *The Atheist's Tragedy.* Ed. Brian Morris and Roma Gill. London: Benn, 1976.

Traub, Valerie. *Desire and Anxiety: Circulations of Sexuality in Shakespearean Drama.* New York: Routledge, 1992.

Turner, Victor W. *The Ritual Process: Structure and Anti-structure.* Chicago: Aldine, 1969.

Tuve, Rosemond. *Elizabethan and Metaphysical Imagery.* Chicago: U of Chicago P, 1947.

Underdown, D. E. "The Taming of the Scold: The Enforcement of Patriarchal Authority in Early Modern England." Fletcher and Stevenson 116–36.

Urkowitz, Steven. "Five Women Eleven Ways: Changing Images of Shakespearean Characters in the Earliest Texts." Habicht, Palmer, and Pringle 292–304.

———. "'I Am Not Made of Stone': Theatrical Revision of Gesture in Shakespeare's Plays." *Renaissance and Reformation* ns 10 (1986): 79–93.

———. "Two Versions of *Romeo and Juliet* 2.6 and *Merry Wives of Windsor* 5.5.215–45: An Invitation to the Pleasures of Textual/Sexual Di(Per)versity." *Elizabethan Theater: Essays in Honor of S. Schoenbaum.* Ed. R. B. Parker and S. P. Zitner. Newark: U of Delaware P, 1996. 222–38.

Vendler, Helen. "Sonnets 33, 60, *Romeo and Juliet* 1.5.93–106, Sonnets 94, 105, 116, 129." *Teaching with Shakespeare: Critics in the Classroom.* Ed. Bruce McIver and Ruth Stevenson. Newark: U of Delaware P, 1994. 23–59.

Voss, Paul J. "The Antifraternal Tradition in English Renaissance Drama." *Cithara* 33 (1993): 3–16.

Walton, James Kirkwood. *The Quarto Copy for the First Folio of Shakespeare.* Dublin: Dublin UP, 1971.

Warren, Michael. *The Parallel* King Lear, *1608–1623.* Berkeley: U of California P, 1989.

Waters, D. Douglas. "*Romeo and Juliet* as Tragedy." *Christian Settings in Shakespeare's Tragedies.* Rutherford: Fairleigh Dickinson UP, 1994. 121–40.

Wells, Stanley. "Juliet's Nurse: The Uses of Inconsequentiality." *Shakespeare's Styles: Essays in Honour of Kenneth Muir.* Ed. Philip Edwards, Inga-Stina Ewbank, and G. K. Hunter. Cambridge: Cambridge UP, 1980. 51–66.

———, ed. Romeo and Juliet *and Its Afterlife.* Cambridge: Cambridge UP, 1996. Vol. 49 of *Shakespeare Survey.*

———, ed. *Shakespeare: A Bibliographical Guide.* Oxford: Clarendon–Oxford UP, 1990.

Wells, Stanley, and Gary Taylor, with John Jowett and William Montgomery. *William Shakespeare: A Textual Companion.* Oxford: Clarendon–Oxford UP, 1987.

Werstine, Paul. "Narratives about Printed Shakespeare Texts: 'Foul Papers' and 'Bad' Quartos." *Shakespeare Quarterly* 41 (1990): 65–86.

———. "Touring and the Construction of Shakespeare Textual Criticism." *Textual Formations and Reformations.* Ed. Laurie E. Maguire and Thomas L. Berger. Newark: U of Delaware P; London: Assoc. UP, 1998. 45–66.

Whittier, Gayle. "The Sonnet's Body and the Body Sonnetized in *Romeo and Juliet.*" *Shakespeare Quarterly* 40 (1989): 27–41.

Williams, George Walton. "The Printer and the Date of *Romeo and Juliet* Q4." *Studies in Bibliography* 18 (1965): 253–54.

Woodbridge, Linda. *Women and the English Renaissance: Literature and the Nature of Womankind, 1540–1620.* Urbana: U of Illinois P, 1984.

Wrightson, Keith. *English Society, 1580–1680.* New Brunswick: Rutgers UP, 1982.

Wymer, Rowland. *Suicide and Despair in the Jacobean Drama.* New York: St. Martin's, 1986.

Audiovisual Materials

Branagh, Kenneth, and Glyn Dearman, dirs. *Romeo and Juliet.* Recording. With Branagh and Samantha Bond. 3 sound discs. BBD Audio, ISBN 0553455370, 1993.

Campbell, Norman, dir. *Romeo and Juliet.* Film. With Megan Porter Follows and Antonio Cimolino. CBC, 1993. Col. videocassette. 162 min. Available for rental or purchase on 1/2" videocassette or for purchase on CD-ROM from Films for the Humanities and Sciences, PO Box 2053, Princeton, NJ 08543-2053.

Castellani, Renato, dir. *Romeo and Juliet.* Film. With Laurence Harvey, Susan Shentall, and Flora Robson. Rank Organisation, 1954. Col. 135 min. Available for purchase only on 1/2" videocassette from Filmic Archives, The Cinema Center, Botsford, CT 06404-0386 and for rental on 1/2" videocassette from Films for the Humanities and Sciences, PO Box 2053, Princeton, NJ 08543-2053.

Cukor, George, dir. *Romeo and Juliet.* Film. With Leslie Howard, Norma Shearer, and John Barrymore. MGM, 1936. Videocassette. 126 min. Available for purchase only on 1/2" videocasette from Filmic Archives, The Cinema Center, Botsford, CT 06404-0386.

Hunt, Hugh, prod. *Romeo and Juliet.* 1953 recording. With Claire Bloom and Alan Bodel. 2 cassettes. EMI Records Ltd., LFP 7296, 1987.

Luhrmann, Baz, dir. *William Shakespeare's Romeo and Juliet.* Film. With Leonardo DiCaprio, Claire Danes, and Brian Dennehy. Twentieth-Century Fox, 1996. Col. 120 min. Available for rental and purchase on 1/2" videocassette from local video-rental stores.

Madden, John, dir. *Shakespeare in Love.* Film. With Gwyneth Paltrow, Joseph Fiennes, Geoffrey Rush, Ben Afleck, and Judi Dench. Miramax Films / Universal Pictures, 1998. Col. 120 min. Available for rental and purchase on 1/2" videocassette from local video-rental stores.

Messina, Cedric, dir. *Romeo and Juliet.* Video production. With Rebecca Saire and Patrick Ryecart. BBC-TV/ Time-Life, Inc., 1978. Col. videocassette. 167 min. Available for purchase only on 1/2" videocassette from Insight Media, 2162 Broadway, New York, NY 10024 and from Filmic Archives, The Cinema Center, Botsford, CT 06404-0386.

Ozawa, Seiji, cond. Boston Symphony Orchestra. *Romeo and Juliet.* 1986. Deutsche Grammophon, 423 268-1/2/4, 1987.

Prokofiev, Sergei. *Romeo and Juliet: Ballet in Three Acts.* Film. Dir. Paul Czinner. With Margot Fonteyn and Rudolph Nureyev. Embassy Pictures/Poetic Films, 1966. Col. videocassette. 124 min. Available for purchase only on 1/2" videocassette from Novacom Video, Inc., PO Box 2068, Manorhaven, NY 11050 and from Facets Multimedia, Inc., 1517 West Fullerton Ave., Chicago, IL 60614.

Rylands, George, dir. *Romeo and Juliet.* 1960 recording. The Marlowe Society and Professional Players. 4 cassettes. Argo, KZ PC 208–211, 1973.

Sackler, Howard, dir. *Romeo and Juliet.* 1961 recording. With Claire Bloom and Albert Finney. 2 cassettes. Caedmon, CPN 228, 1995.

Wise, Robert, and Jerome Robbins, dirs. *West Side Story.* Film. With Natalie Wood, Rita Moreno, and George Chakiris. United Artists, 1961. Col. 151 min. Available for purchase only on 1/2" videocassette from Filmic Archives, The Cinema Center, Botsford, CT 06404-0386. Possibly available for rental on 1/2" videocassette from local video-rental stores.

Zeffirelli, Franco, dir. *Romeo and Juliet.* Film. With Leonard Whiting, Olivia Hussey, and Laurence Olivier. BHE Verona Productions/Paramount Pictures, 1968. Col. 139 min. Available for purchase only on 1/2" videocassette from Filmic Archives, The Cinema Center, Botsford, CT 06404-0386. Possibly available for rental on 1/2" videocassette from local video-rental stores.

INDEX

Modern Language Association of America
Approaches to Teaching World Literature
Joseph Gibaldi, series editor

Achebe's Things Fall Apart. Ed. Bernth Lindfors. 1991.

Arthurian Tradition. Ed. Maureen Fries and Jeanie Watson. 1992.

Atwood's The Handmaid's Tale *and Other Works.* Ed. Sharon R. Wilson, Thomas B. Friedman, and Shannon Hengen. 1996.

Austen's Pride and Prejudice. Ed. Marcia McClintock Folsom. 1993.

Baudelaire's Flowers of Evil. Ed. Laurence M. Porter. 2000.

Beckett's Waiting for Godot. Ed. June Schlueter and Enoch Brater. 1991.

Beowulf. Ed. Jess B. Bessinger, Jr., and Robert F. Yeager. 1984.

Blake's Songs of Innocence and of Experience. Ed. Robert F. Gleckner and Mark L. Greenberg. 1989.

British Women Poets of the Romantic Period. Ed. Stephen C. Behrendt and Harriet Kramer Linkin. 1997.

Brontë's Jane Eyre. Ed. Diane Long Hoeveler and Beth Lau. 1993.

Byron's Poetry. Ed. Frederick W. Shilstone. 1991.

Camus's The Plague. Ed. Steven G. Kellman. 1985.

Cather's My Ántonia. Ed. Susan J. Rosowski. 1989.

Cervantes' Don Quixote. Ed. Richard Bjornson. 1984.

Chaucer's Canterbury Tales. Ed. Joseph Gibaldi. 1980.

Chopin's The Awakening. Ed. Bernard Koloski. 1988.

Coleridge's Poetry and Prose. Ed. Richard E. Matlak. 1991.

Dante's Divine Comedy. Ed. Carole Slade. 1982.

Dickens' David Copperfield. Ed. Richard J. Dunn. 1984.

Dickinson's Poetry. Ed. Robin Riley Fast and Christine Mack Gordon. 1989.

Narrative of the Life of Frederick Douglass. Ed. James C. Hall. 1999.

Eliot's Middlemarch. Ed. Kathleen Blake. 1990.

Eliot's Poetry and Plays. Ed. Jewel Spears Brooker. 1988.

Ellison's Invisible Man. Ed. Susan Resneck Parr and Pancho Savery. 1989.

Faulkner's The Sound and the Fury. Ed. Stephen Hahn and Arthur F. Kinney. 1996.

Flaubert's Madame Bovary. Ed. Laurence M. Porter and Eugene F. Gray. 1995.

García Márquez's One Hundred Years of Solitude. Ed. María Elena de Valdés and Mario J. Valdés. 1990.

Goethe's Faust. Ed. Douglas J. McMillan. 1987.

Hebrew Bible as Literature in Translation. Ed. Barry N. Olshen and Yael S. Feldman. 1989.

Homer's Iliad *and* Odyssey. Ed. Kostas Myrsiades. 1987.

Ibsen's A Doll House. Ed. Yvonne Shafer. 1985.

Works of Samuel Johnson. Ed. David R. Anderson and Gwin J. Kolb. 1993.

Joyce's Ulysses. Ed. Kathleen McCormick and Erwin R. Steinberg. 1993.

Kafka's Short Fiction. Ed. Richard T. Gray. 1995.

Keats's Poetry. Ed. Walter H. Evert and Jack W. Rhodes. 1991.

Kingston's The Woman Warrior. Ed. Shirley Geok-lin Lim. 1991.

Lafayette's The Princess of Clèves. Ed. Faith E. Beasley and Katharine Ann
    Jensen. 1998.
Lessing's The Golden Notebook. Ed. Carey Kaplan and Ellen Cronan Rose. 1989.
Mann's Death in Venice *and Other Short Fiction*. Ed. Jeffrey B. Berlin. 1992.
Medieval English Drama. Ed. Richard K. Emmerson. 1990.
Melville's Moby-Dick. Ed. Martin Bickman. 1985.
Metaphysical Poets. Ed. Sidney Gottlieb. 1990.
Miller's Death of a Salesman. Ed. Matthew C. Roudané. 1995.
Milton's Paradise Lost. Ed. Galbraith M. Crump. 1986.
Molière's Tartuffe *and Other Plays*. Ed. James F. Gaines and
    Michael S. Koppisch. 1995.
Momaday's The Way to Rainy Mountain. Ed. Kenneth M. Roemer. 1988.
Montaigne's Essays. Ed. Patrick Henry. 1994.
Novels of Toni Morrison. Ed. Nellie Y. McKay and Kathryn Earle. 1997.
Murasaki Shikibu's The Tale of Genji. Ed. Edward Kamens. 1993.
Pope's Poetry. Ed. Wallace Jackson and R. Paul Yoder. 1993.
Shakespeare's King Lear. Ed. Robert H. Ray. 1986.
Shakespeare's Romeo and Juliet. Ed. Maurice Hunt. 2000.
Shakespeare's The Tempest *and Other Late Romances*. Ed. Maurice Hunt. 1992.
Shelley's Frankenstein. Ed. Stephen C. Behrendt. 1990.
Shelley's Poetry. Ed. Spencer Hall. 1990.
Shorter Elizabethan Poetry. Ed. Patrick Cheney and Anne Lake Prescott. 2000.
Sir Gawain and the Green Knight. Ed. Miriam Youngerman Miller and
    Jane Chance. 1986.
Spenser's Faerie Queene. Ed. David Lee Miller and Alexander Dunlop. 1994.
Stendhal's The Red and the Black. Ed. Dean de la Motte and Stirling Haig. 1999.
Sterne's Tristram Shandy. Ed. Melvyn New. 1989.
Stowe's Uncle Tom's Cabin. Ed. Elizabeth Ammons and Susan Belasco. 2000.
Swift's Gulliver's Travels. Ed. Edward J. Rielly. 1988.
Thoreau's Walden *and Other Works*. Ed. Richard J. Schneider. 1996.
Voltaire's Candide. Ed. Renée Waldinger. 1987.
Whitman's Leaves of Grass. Ed. Donald D. Kummings. 1990.
Wordsworth's Poetry. Ed. Spencer Hall, with Jonathan Ramsey. 1986.
Wright's Native Son. Ed. James A. Miller. 1997.